Sing ular Per form anc es

Reinscribing the
Subject in
Francophone
African
Writing

Michael Syrotinski

University of Virginia Press
CHARLOTTESVILLE AND LONDON

University of Virginia Press
© 2002 by the Rector and Visitors of
the University of Virginia
All rights reserved
Printed in the United States of
America on acid-free paper
First published 2002

1 3 5 7 9 8 6 4 2

LIBRARY OF CONGRESS CATALOGING-IN-PUBLICATION DATA

Syrotinski, Michael, 1957–
    Singular performances : reinscribing the subject in Francophone African
writing / Michael Syrotinski.
        p.   cm.
Includes bibliographical references and index.
    ISBN 0-8139-2144-9 (hard : alk. paper) — ISBN 0-8139-2145-7 (pbk. : alk. paper)
    1. African literature (French)—History and criticism.
    2. Subjectivity in literature. I. Title.
    PQ3980.5 .S97 2002
    840.9′96—dc21
                                                                    2002006068

To Isabel, for her many singular performances, and for being herself.
To Calum, so he knows that love can take many forms.
To Christine, who has shared the excitement of this project, and who makes everything worthwhile.

Contents

Acknowledgments

This book has accrued many debts of gratitude in the course of its composition. Research Leave Awards from the Arts and Divinity Faculty of the University of Aberdeen, and from the Arts and Humanities Research Board, provided me with valuable time off from my teaching duties and enabled me to complete my book. Parts of several chapters were presented initially as papers at the Universities of Aberdeen, Leeds, Cardiff, Keele, Nottingham, Glasgow, Edinburgh, and at the Life/Writing Seminar at Royal Holloway, London, the French Institute in London, and the Francophone Division panel of an MLA conference in San Francisco. I would like to thank the organizers of these occasions for having given me the opportunity to test out my ideas, and also those who engaged and challenged me after the presentations in ways that helped me to focus my thinking more clearly. I am very appreciative to Celia Britton, Patrick Erouart-Siad, Charles Forsdick, Christine Laennec, David Murphy, Kevin Newmark, Eliza Nichols, and Michael Sheringham, as well as the three anonymous readers for the University of Virginia Press, who all read parts or the whole of earlier drafts. Their attentive readings and insightful advice helped me to make the manuscript stronger than it would have been otherwise. My undergraduate and postgraduate students of Francophone African literature at the University of Aberdeen have given me much pleasure over the years, and much pause for thought. Their input into this book's coming into being, even if less discernible, is certainly far from negligible. The manuscript would almost certainly not have met its deadline were it not for Shona Potts, also my first doctoral dissertation student, who agreed to take over several of my classes during the crucial final stages. For that I am immensely grateful.

Sections of the manuscript have been previously published: part of chapter 3 appeared in the *Journal of African Travel Writing* 7 (1999), 66–79, as an essay "When in Rome . . . : Irony and Subversion in Bernard Dadié's Travel Writing"; a portion of chapter 4 was first published in the *ASCALF Yearbook* 4 (2000) as "Creative Bigamy in Tierno Monénembo's *Cinéma*"; and a shorter version of chapter 7 originally appeared in a different guise as an article for a special issue of *Paragraph* (24 [Nov. 2001]), "Francophone Texts and Postcolonial Theory," edited by Celia Britton and myself. Permission to reproduce the relevant sections of these earlier versions is gratefully acknowledged. The collaboration with Celia on the issue of *Paragraph* is a small mark of a far greater intellectual and pedagogical debt. Her unfailing support in all matters, inspirational partnership in teaching our Francophone literature course, and real friendship have meant more to me than I can express.

The staff at the University of Virginia Press have been extremely professional and supportive throughout, in particular Cathie Brettschneider, who guided the manuscript through the review process with considerable skill, and whose precise editorial interventions were always thoughtful and right to the point. Ruth Melville did a wonderful job of copyediting the manuscript with a rare combination of sensitivity and rigor. The staff at both the Interlibrary Loans and Acquisitions sections of the Queen Mother Library at Aberdeen, especially William Donald and Lesley Hendry, got to know me well, and I want to thank them warmly for their prompt and cheerful granting of everything on my wish list, no matter how obscure and apparently unobtainable.

Various other people, too numerous to mention, stepped in to help out on the domestic front in the inevitable squeeze between work and home life, but I do want to give particularly heartfelt thanks to Elaine Fyfe and to all the staff at Harmeny School. My greatest debts, though, are to my family, and to them I dedicate this book.

Singular Performances

Introduction

This book has its point of departure in the observation that writing in Francophone Africa is often concerned—explicitly or implicitly, in diverse forms and in varying degrees of complexity—with questions of subjectivity and narrative agency. This emphasis on the writing subject should hardly be surprising for a literary tradition that is still in the process of establishing and defining itself, and yet within the critical literature on Francophone African writing there has been no sustained theoretical discussion of this central concern. My own approach is an extended and fairly open-ended dialogue between Francophone African literature, African philosophy, and literary theory, and takes as its focal point a radical and irreducible ambivalence that is at the heart of the notion of the subject.

A succinct and precise formulation by the Congolese author Sony Labou Tansi in the preface to his novel *L'état honteux* [The shameful state] will help to illustrate what I mean by this. Sony writes: "J'écris, ou je crie, un peu pour forcer le monde à venir au monde" [I write, or I cry out, in a sense to force the world to come into the world].[1] His expression captures perfectly the tensions and contradictions inherent in a projected affirmation of an African writing subject that can neither take the form of a preexisting given, reemerging out of a buried past, whether colonial or precolonial, nor claim to break free from this past, in a gesture of absolute liberation. In Sony's writing, the world doubles up as something other than what it is. This doubleness can be read in Sony's phrase as a subject split between writing ("j'écris") and voice ("je crie"), or between the enduring cultural aftereffects of the colonial era and a deeper sense of an African identity that finds its expression in local idiom. The range of opposed terms suggested by this split subject (false consciousness vs. authenticity, intellectual vs. emotional, rational vs. sensual, and so on) is not one that is structured as an opposition in Sony's phrase; rather, the conjunction "or" describes a complementary or supplementary relationship, and it is the subject, the "I," that holds these together. This ambivalent subject of contemporary Francophone Africa perhaps does not (yet) exist, but this is precisely what makes it such a crucial placeholder, as it were, and why it both precedes and supersedes other related concepts to which it is nonetheless inextricably bound (such as the self, the individual, identity, or agency) and therefore to my mind occupies a more significant theoretical position.

As will be clear from my opening chapter, and from subsequent references in later chapters, the work of V. Y. Mudimbe is in this context fundamental. As Christopher Miller puts it in the introduction to his *Theories of Africans,* Mudimbe's work "makes manifest a sea change in African discourse." What is the precise nature of this "sea change"? Miller continues, quoting Mudimbe, "The African 'subject-object' now has 'the absolute freedom of thinking of himself or herself as the starting point of an absolute discourse.'"[2] However, this subjective freedom is not, Mudimbe continually reminds us, as simple and as "absolute" as it appears, and in his work he articulates very clearly the paradoxes and contradictions of the subject's claim to rise up anew out of the ruins of colonialism. It is nonetheless a necessary "starting point," and what I do in this study is to show how the texts of a diverse selection of writers from Francophone Africa provide possible solutions to the question of how one can, as Mudimbe puts it, "reconcile the demands of an identity and the credibility of a claim to knowledge with the process of refounding and reassuming an interrupted historicity within representations."[3] Mudimbe's own project is on the one hand an impressively vast *descriptive* survey of the ways in which Africa has been represented, or misrepresented, by a succession of Western discourses over the centuries, and on the other a *prescriptive* manifesto of sorts (though not in any dogmatic sense), indicating the different future paths African thinking and writing might follow if it is to institute paradigms that are not simply derived from Western precedents. For him it is essential that this should involve an element of risk, challenging apparently stable and unquestioned models of subjectivity, and he advocates choosing the "adventure of uncertainty" over the "intellectual safety" of established forms of scientific or philosophical knowledge.[4] For the specific concerns of my own study, risking the subject in this way requires redefining the place and function of Francophone African literature. My book is thus allied to projects such as Jonathan Ngate's,[5] which attempt in effect to rewrite the literary history of Francophone African writing, although my principle of organization is not essentially historical or thematic. Instead, I consider the subject as a means of looking more closely at the texture and rhetoric of the writings I have chosen, attending to their literary qualities rather than their status as cultural or sociological documents. At the same time, I situate them within broader theoretical or philosophical contexts.

For Mudimbe, the origins of a great deal of contemporary Africanist discourses can best be located by traveling "upstream," as it were, and back to a Cartesian source. In a philosophical commentary in the preface to his book *Parables and Fables,* which at first appears to have little bearing on the problem of an African subject, Mudimbe reflects upon the Cartesian *cogito* in its relation to two contrasting twentieth-century French theories of subjectivity, that of Jean-Paul Sartre and of Claude Lévi-Strauss, emphasizing the latter's avowed debt to Rousseau.[6] Mudimbe sets up a broad homology linking the basic premises of the *cogito* to Sartrean existentialism, and Rousseau's theory of the subject to Lévi-Strauss's structuralist anthropology. He does this in order to show how the history of the philosophical concept of the subject is essentially characterized by the competing claims of, on the one hand, theories of intentionality or agency, from Descartes's *cogito* to the dialectics of Sartre's existentialism; and on the other, theories of cultural or structural determination, starting with Rousseau's "I am not 'me' but the most humble of 'others,'" an anti-Cartesianism which for Lévi-Strauss was, as Mudimbe puts it, "the philosophical basis and the founding motto of ethnology."[7] In other words, structuralist anthropology's "I as an other" is a fundamental rejection of the self-sufficiency or self-reflexivity of the *cogito,* but for Mudimbe this opens up a new dialectic in which self and other come to be engaged in a subtle play of identity and alterity, of self-recognition and self-difference: Lévi-Strauss's journeys are equally those of his own subjectivity, just as Sartre's philosophy of the subject is at the same time a necessary integration of the other in an existential determination of the self. This is described by Maurice Merleau-Ponty in a phrase Mudimbe quotes: "Myself and the other are like two nearly concentric circles which can be distinguished only by a slight and mysterious slippage."[8] What Mudimbe terms the (im)possible dialogue between Sartre and Lévi-Strauss thus reveals a fundamental philosophical incompatibility but also a mutual interdependence, and the "subject" is at the very core of this paradox. Mudimbe's ploy now comes into clearer focus, since his strategy in pitting these apparently incompatible thinkers against each other is to seek some way of bridging and moving beyond the opposition between agency and structure. It is not by chance that he should take as one of his major points of reference Lévi-Strauss's enactment and expression of his own subjective freedom, since Mudimbe uses a similar strategy himself, as we shall see, in his ongoing project of "decolonizing" the African mind.

If the subject is a relatively recent philosophical invention, the African subject also has a history, in the sense in which Michel Foucault uses the term, a history that is predetermined by the paradigms of Cartesian philosophy and their successive transformations. This is not an abstract extrapolation or adaptation of Foucault on Mudimbe's part, since Africa has, ever since the commercial exploitation by European traders of its land and peoples beginning in the fifteenth century, figured as the other of modern European philosophical discourse. As Emmanuel Chukwudi Eze puts it, "Such formulations of philosophical prejudices against Africa and Africans (and other non-European peoples generally) were easily circulated and recycled among modern European philosophers—with little originality."[9] In detailing the explicit language of "savagery" and "subhumanity" one finds in the philosophical and political writings of Hume, Kant, Hegel, and Marx, Eze shows how this in effect paved the way for the colonialist expansion that was to follow: "Colonial and capitalist expansions are therefore a logical necessity for the realization of the obviously universal European Idea, and by labelling the non-European territories and peoples as 'backward' in 'industry,' they become legitimate prey for colonial and colonialist activities."[10] So the unitary individual self-reflexive subject of Descartes, the transcendental interpretations of this subject by German idealist philosophy, the phenomenological subject of Husserl and Heidegger, and so on, have all operated as exclusionary discourses, inaccessible to the African subject. A great deal of the labor of contemporary African philosophy, as will become clearer from my first chapter, has been concerned with bringing to light this discursive exclusion, and with opening up avenues that would allow Africans to recover agency and occupy subject positions, in spite of the pitfalls of this fundamentally ambivalent undertaking.

There has nevertheless been an important shift in contemporary French philosophy and theory which seems to hold out the promise of a closer convergence, and more productive alliances, between European and African discourses. I am thinking of theories of subjectivity that have put the concept of a unified, fully intentional subject into question. In very broad terms, the revolution in the human sciences ushered in by structuralist accounts of language displaced the subject from its position as primary source and producer of meaning, and in many subsequent formulations it is seen as a systemic effect, as constructed or produced within discourse. The subject is thus no longer viewed as a free agent, but as *subject to* another power. So we have, for example, Jacques Lacan's psychoanalytical theory of the formation of the subject and of the unconscious as functions of linguistic or tropological processes; Louis Althusser's notion of "interpellation," in which subject formation takes place when the subject recognizes itself as it is "hailed" by the voice speaking from the place of discursive authority, and thus comes into being as an effect of ideological subjection; Foucault's theses on the subject as produced by a whole range of regulatory and disciplinary regimes (institutional, social, sexual, and so on); or, as we have just seen, the anti-Cartesianism of Lévi-Strauss's structuralist anthropology. As different accounts of subject production, these could, to varying degrees, be mapped onto the scene of the philosophically sanctioned colonialist subjugation of the African other (as Mudimbe indeed does with both Foucault and Lévi-Strauss), and would thus appear to offer greater theoretical support or be more open to an African subjectivity, since the subject's exclusion would be determined as a random effect of power. Merely to recast the question of the subject in oppositional terms—as *either* an agent of power *or* a subject that is predetermined and formed in a process of discursive subordination or subjection—does not offer a way out of the impasse that debates on subjectivity and agency all too often fail to move beyond (that is, how can the subject be both the condition of agency and the effect of the power that subordinates it?).

Judith Butler has argued, in *The Psychic Life of Power: Theories of*

Subjection, that the subject is the locus of a radical and *irreducible* ambivalence. As she says, "Part of the difficulty, I suggest, is that the subject is itself the site of this ambivalence in which the subject emerges both as the *effect* of a prior power and as the *condition of possibility* for a radically conditioned form of agency. A theory of the subject should take into account the full ambivalence of the conditions of its operation."[11] This paradox describes very well the dilemma that the Francophone African subject is caught within, and many of the writers I will look at, starting most importantly with Mudimbe, do not resist this ambivalence but rather work with it, in diverse and intriguing ways. As Butler rightfully says, the subject in its particular cultural place and moment has everything to gain by taking this ambivalence as a point of departure rather than a dead end: "In this sense, the subject cannot quell the ambivalence by which it is constituted. Painful, dynamic, and promising, this vacillation between the already-there and the yet-to-come is a crossroads that rejoins every step by which it is traversed, a reiterated ambivalence at the heart of agency."[12]

While Butler's concern in her study is ultimately with the figure of the psyche "turning against itself," and the subsequent effects of this on social power, I take the model of an irreducible ambivalence of the subject as the key to understanding the Francophone African texts I will be reading. I argue that the question of subjectivity can best be approached by looking at the performative dimension of the texts, their constant questioning and reassertion of their own narrative agency, over and above their more directly referential meaning. In this respect, I consider the work of a number of African and non-African theorists to be extremely helpful, and in particular I turn to postcolonial theory as well as, perhaps surprisingly, deconstruction. Indeed, I suggest at a number of points that postcolonial theory is at its most insightful and incisive when it makes explicit its debt to certain deconstructive maneuvers. In tandem with postcolonial theory, deconstruction can offer, to my mind, rigorous procedures of reading or the necessary critical tools and analytical subtlety to engage with the terms and rhetorical operations provided by the texts themselves. Literary criticism of Francophone African writing—unlike the corresponding Anglophone tradition—has remained peculiarly resistant to much recent postcolonial theory, and I see my study as an attempt to redress this imbalance, or to open up and encourage new dialogues.

The book is organized, then, as a series of readings of a range of mostly contemporary, mostly West African Francophone writers, each of whom is contextualized within a specific debate relating to African subjectivity. The opening chapter, on the concept of a reaffirmed philosophical subject, is principally a survey and critical introduction to Mudimbe's work, which is situated within the context of contemporary Francophone African philosophy. I shift the focus of my analysis of Mudimbe's work to a consideration of his writing as subjective narrative performance, through reading his novel *L'écart* [*The Rift*]. This is the fictionalized diary of the main character and first-person narrator, Nara, whose life is consumed by the struggle to affirm an African subjectivity in the face of the apparently overwhelming forces of history, anthropology, and psychoanalysis.

Where would one look to find the most explicit examples of a reaffirmation of the Francophone African subject? The obvious place, which has its precedent in African American slave narratives, is autobiography, and this is the focus of the second chapter, "The Autobiographical Subject as History-Teller." The autobiographical "I" and the subject are not, of course, identical, and Francophone African autobiography is seen as a problematic, irreducibly ambivalent enterprise (divided between, for example, French and African, writing and orality, collectivity and individuality). I explore the relationship between autobiography and history in two writers, Bernard Dadié and Aoua Kéita. For Bernard Dadié the autobiographical genre ends up being a significant political and historical act, and this same dynamic can be found in Aoua Kéita's *Femme d'Afrique* [African woman], but to very different ends.

In Dadié's texts this ambivalence or doubleness is richly exploited for its *ironic* qualities, in marked contrast to the tragic mode it assumes with Camara Laye, for example. The third chapter addresses this notion of an ironic subject more directly by reading Dadié's travel narratives, which mimic ironically the Western tradition of travel writing. Irony puts into question the transparency both of objective description and of self-expression, and thus has important ramifications for the question of subjectivity (that is, how can ironic mimicry avoid falling back into a dependency on the Western object it ironizes?). Irony also reveals, as Dadié is keenly aware, a dilemma at the heart of language itself, and with this in mind I trace in some detail the itineraries of his own rhetorical and linguistic strategies.

In chapter 4 I consider the question of the "cinematic" in its relation both to historical memory and to the process of subject formation, through a comparative reading of Ousmane Sembene's 1996 novel based on his film of the same name, *Guelwaar,* and the 1997 novel *Cinéma,* by the exiled Guinean writer Tierno Monénembo. Both of these novels illustrate Homi Bhabha's insight, which I elaborate upon in the course of my readings, that "looking/hearing/reading as sites of subjectification in colonial discourse are evidence of the importance of the visual and auditory imaginary for the *histories* of societies."[13]

One of the important themes for Sembene in *Guelwaar* is the under-valued role, but also the unexpected strength, of women in contemporary African society. I spend the next two chapters exploring questions of gender and female African subjectivity from two rather different angles. In chapter 5 I think through the relationship between gender and essentialism in an African context. After reviewing some recent theoretical contextualizations of this question, I look at two of Mudimbe's novels which are attempts to write from the perspective of a female African subject, *Le bel immonde* [*Before the Birth of the Moon*] and *Shaba deux.* I argue that in these texts the two women characters and first-person narrators represent a radical subversion of male-centered historical discourse. But although Mudimbe makes a powerful and persuasive case for the central role of African women in any genuine political and social transformation, it is women themselves who have to be the agents of this change, which can only occur through a performative self-transformation. Chapter 6 is thus devoted to the works of two innovative women writers, Véronique Tadjo and Werewere Liking, who dramatize in exemplary fashion this reinscription of a female African subjectivity. It is important to consider in this respect what a subjective female political commitment unmoored from the "national allegories" of the early Francophone male authors would consist of.

The final chapter speculates on the fate, or the future, of the African subject. I explore Sony Labou Tansi's rewriting of African history and time, in relation to Marxist political solutions to post-Independence Africa. I consider the future, paradoxically, as a question of "ghostwriting." The chapter is principally a reading of Sony's *La vie et demie* [Life and a half], and I come back to Sony as the writer who to my mind best articulates the African subject that is both already and not yet a subject. I develop my reading with the help of Derrida's *Specters of Marx,* and also take the term "ghostwriter" in its editorial sense as a way of exploring questions of originality and plagiarism which have dogged Francophone African writing over the years.

I am only too conscious of the potential risks involved in turning to the sophistication and abstraction of contemporary theory to read Francophone African writing, and a few prefatory remarks might be in order here. Since my approach is less historical or literary historical than thematic, I have tended to be rather free-ranging in my selection of texts, choosing those that work best to dramatize, in different ways, my main thesis about the "reinscription" of subjectivity. One of the intended effects of this approach is to unsettle the notion of a kind of Francophone African "canon," and the standard history within which it is often uncritically contextualized. For this reason I tend to steer clear of the colonial/postcolonial schema, which I find quite problematic, especially when it is reduced to a set of critical stereotypes, such as "hybridity," "the Other," "the postcolonial subject," and so on.[14] Indeed, the notion of an all-purpose postcolonial subject is a naive starting point I continuously critique. If theory, including postcolonial theory, is integral to my readings, my approach is to take the African texts very much on their own terms, introducing theory in a strategic manner in order to let the texts themselves resonate more fully.

This is not to say that I wish to be in any sense dismissive of the primacy of African history and culture generally. I acknowledge the importance of what James Clifford terms "thick" cultural and historical contextualization, and by no means neglect historicization or cultural references where necessary. In fact, history is at the heart of four of the chapters of the book (chapters 1, 2, 4, and 6). One of the emphases of my book is how complex the question of African history becomes when one reads these texts more closely. I certainly would not dispute that culturally or anthropologically oriented analyses of literature, such as performed (supremely well) by critics such as Christopher Miller or James Clifford, are of vital importance in the field of African studies. I see my own work as operating alongside and in dialogue with them, and thus at points necessarily in disagreement with them (notably around the question of the place of deconstruction in reading African literature).

In one sense, my own argument about a reaffirmed African subjectivity as a means of cultural and political transformation might seem to render my study superfluous (that is, these texts are in no need of a further theoretical "recolonization"). However, I would concur with Gayatri Spivak that this kind of disavowal can hide a dangerous (because unconscious) complicity with the very discursive power and oppositional logic that objectified Africans as a homogenized mute Other in the first place.[15] So what ultimately emerges from this mutually respectful and collaborative dialogue between contemporary theory and the literary texts I read is not the African subject as a single, "homogenized" entity but the infinitely complex and irreducibly plural celebration of singular Francophone African *subjectivities*.

1

V. Y. Mudimbe,
African Philosophy,
and the
Return of the
Subject

V. Y. Mudimbe is one of most important figures of contemporary African studies, but also one of the most eclectic and difficult to read. As will become apparent in the course of this chapter, and in subsequent references to his work in later chapters, I find the conclusions he reaches in his critical writings, as well as the ways in which he comes to these conclusions, an extremely useful starting point for a more wide-ranging, and perhaps equally eclectic, study of Francophone African philosophical and literary writing. I would like to begin my own engagement with Mudimbe's texts by offering a snapshot biographical portrait of Mudimbe and his many achievements, since I believe it will be helpful, not only because I want to provide "background" to the writings I will be discussing, but because he himself makes reference to certain crucial events and influences, in a gesture whose strategic importance I will return to later on.

Mudimbe at the Margin of Margins

Valentin Yves (or Vumbi Yoka) Mudimbe was born in 1941 in what was the Belgian Congo, subsequently Zaire (now the Democratic Republic of Congo). He attended school in the Belgian Congo and then at the age of nine went to live in a Benedictine monastery in Rwanda, training for eight years to become a monk before deciding to leave the seminary because of his growing discomfort in Rwanda, both with political developments and with the Catholic Church. As his intellectual autobiography testifies, this experience marked him profoundly and accounts for his extraordinary familiarity with Latin and Greek culture and theological history.[1] In 1966 he went to Besançon in France to specialize in applied linguistics (studying with, among others, Henri Meschonnic), and then to Belgium in 1968, where he studied with the great Belgian philologist Willy Bal, completing two doctoral theses, on the concept of "air" and on Ber Borochov's language, respectively. He spent the late 1960s and early 1970s commuting between Louvain and Paris, and working at various times in the Linguistics and Romance Studies departments at Lovanium University and the University of Paris–Nanterre, becoming increasingly interested in the history of ideas. It was during this time that his "French" intellectual influences were formed—principally Foucault, Lévi-Strauss, Sartre, de Certeau, Lacan, Althusser, Derrida—but he was also part of a group of important anthropologists working at Nanterre at the time, and befriended many of the African writers and intellectuals who moved between Africa and Paris (Senghor, Jacques Rabemananjara, Alioune Diop, Aké Loba, J. B. Tati-Loutard, Abiola Irele, Paulin Hountondji, and Kwasi Wiredu, to name but a few of the best known).

By the early 1970s Mudimbe's rather unconventional itinerary had left him, as he puts it in the preface to *Parables and Fables,* on "the margin of margins." He goes on to explain: "black, Catholic, African, yet agnostic; intellectually Marxist, disposed towards psychoanalysis, yet a specialist in Indo-European philology and philosophy."[2] Around this time he was diagnosed with bone cancer, which prompted, "in a surge of defiance" (*Parables,* x), a prolific output, including his first collection of poems, *Entretailles* (1973); a novel, *Le bel immonde* (translated into English as *Before the Birth of the Moon*); and his first collection of "philosophical" essays, *L'autre face du royaume* (1973). He returned to Zaire in 1973 to continue teaching, setting up a number of institutes and playing leading roles in the International Congress of African Studies and the International African Institute in London. He left Africa for the United States in 1982, eager to escape Mobutu's ever more despotic hold on Zaire, and took up a post at Haverford College. Even though *L'odeur du père* appeared only in 1982, according to Mudimbe it "belongs to my African period" (*Parables,* xi). He subsequently moved to Duke University, where he became Ruth F. DeVarney Professor of Romance Studies and Comparative Literature, and he now divides his time between Duke University and Stanford University, where he teaches in the Department of French and Italian.

My own rather modest ambition in this chapter is not to try to give a comprehensive overview of his thought, which would go very much against the grain of the sheer multiplicity of his writing and its profoundly unsettling quality. Rather, I would like to attempt a more sustained theorization of a particular question, and to see how it is constantly recontextualized within his work: that is, the problem of subjectivity. While my focus in this chapter is the work of V. Y. Mudimbe and the particular emphasis he places on the dilemmas facing the African subject, his texts will be read as a point of convergence of several trends or key theoretical issues within African, and specifically Francophone African, philosophy. This has been an important recent development in African writing, and Mudimbe is a pivotal figure in this intellectual history. I will show—by reading one of his novels, *L'écart,* in the light of his theories—how his fictional texts dramatize most effectively what I will term a "performative reinscription of subjectivity," a concept I hope will become clear in the course of my discussion.

An African *Cogito*

The labor of much of Mudimbe's critical writings, as they develop between the publication of *L'autre face du royaume* and *The Idea of Africa,* takes the form of a patient and extremely thorough excavation of the various discourses that have historically informed Western conceptions of Africa. As he says, for example, reviewing twentieth-century ethnology:

> Durkheim's prescriptions on the pathology of civilizations, Lévy-Bruhl's theses on prelogical systems of thought, as well as Frazer's hypothesis on primitive societies, bear witness, from a functional viewpoint, to the same epistemological space in which stories about Others, as well as commentaries on their difference, are but elements in the history of the Same and its knowledge.[3]

Two of his most constant allies in this vast enterprise are Claude Lévi-Strauss and Michel Foucault, both of whom, in different ways, invoke archaeological metaphors for rethinking the ways in which Western civilization has conceived of Others and Otherness. For Lévi-Strauss, archaeology reveals to us historical depths under the immediately perceptible evidence of the earth's surface, just as structuralist anthropology claims to reveal the hidden complexity of social organizations beneath the visible data of traditional ethnographic observation (which according to Lévi-Strauss is misread because read ethnocentrically). Foucault's probing analyses of the "archaeology of knowledge" likewise explore the complicity between formations of power and epistemological orders in Western civilization. To quote D. A. Masolo:

> While Foucault's essential concern is with the culture of the West, Mudimbe's pain is with modern African cultural dependence on the West. While Foucault does not accept the categories which are customarily used to describe Western culture, Mudimbe's major theme is that the various Western discourses on Africa and Africans have conditioned the establishment of the conceptual categories in which Africans today conceive and express their own identity.[4]

Both Foucault and Lévi-Strauss radically put into question a humanist tradition by tracing the emergence of the concept, or construct, of "Man" as a rational, thinking subject that is the center of a world ordered by his own epistemological frames of reference.

Mudimbe, in turn, recognizes and exploits the methodological usefulness of Lévi-Strauss's and Foucault's theories for a reevaluation of discourses of Africanism by showing how Western ethnology and other human and social sciences are in fact all part of the same discursive order, what he calls the "colonializing structure" of Western discourse about other cultures. The *cogito* is thus read as the source and theoretical foundation of the discursive *Weltanschauung* that legitimized the entire colonial period and its related ventures. In *The Invention of Africa* Mudimbe refers to this ideologically overdetermined appropriation of Cartesianism as a "socialization of the *cogito*" (190), and he later refines this theoretical paradigm, in *Parables and Fables* and elsewhere, by describing it in terms of three closely interlocking systems of power/knowledge: colonial politics, the anthropological sciences, and Christianity's "civilizing mission." This is articulated in *L'odeur du père,* again following Foucault, as the operation of a Western *ratio* that predetermines the conditions and possibilities of the values or codes it employs in relation to the non-Western object of its gaze (he says, for example, that it is the *episteme* of the nineteenth and early twentieth centuries that *invented* the concept of a static, prehistoric, primitive tradition). This leads Mudimbe to critique *synchronically* conceived projects such as those of the early "primitivists," but also more recent *diachronic,* dialectical accounts of the evolution of African history and social organization, such as Peter Rigby's Marxist-informed analyses. I would like to look a little more closely at his discussions of these two principal theoretical axes, paying particular attention to the nuanced quality that is an often overlooked aspect of his writing.

Mudimbe has no difficulty exposing the ideological and epistemological subtexts behind the "primitivist" discourses of Froebenius, Delafosse, Lévy-Bruhl, and others that dominated anthropology and ethnology at the end of the nineteenth century and in the first half of the twentieth.[5] He spends rather longer, however, reflecting upon a defining text of early anticolonialist writing, Placide Tempels's 1945 *La philosophie bantoue* [*Bantu Philosophy*]. This is the attempt by the Belgian missionary turned self-styled philosopher to describe Bantu belief systems among the Luba in what was the Belgian Congo by considering them as a fully developed ontology. This was a remarkable text for its time, since it seemed to go against the grain of the predominant anthropological objectification of "primitive" peoples, and to recognize in their thinking a system as complex and as valid as Western philosophy. Tempels does not accord these belief systems the status of an explicit philosophy, but derives what he terms an ontology from his understanding of the importance for the Luba of a primordial natural "force." According to Tempels, "Force is the nature of being, force is being, being is force."[6] On closer inspection, however, it is clear not only how much Tempels owes to Henri Bergson's *élan vital,* and the whole antirationalist trend in Western philosophy and literature that Bergson's ideas are often said to have inspired, but also how compromised Tempels's "anticolonialism" is as a consequence. The terms in which he describes Bantu ontology, as well as his methodological procedures, are essentially derived from Western philosophy, and his project can in fact be read, as Mudimbe states, as consistent with the ultimate goal of civilizing and evangelizing the Bantu people (*Invention,* 138).

To this extent, Mudimbe's analysis of Tempels essentially echoes that voiced by African critics since Fabien Eboussi-Boulaga's 1968 essay in *Présence africaine,* "La bantoue problématique." According to Eboussi-

Boulaga, Tempels's ontological system was incoherent, inadequate, and unconscious, and it reduced Bantu temporality to a fixed, atemporal, mythified past. Mudimbe develops this point in his introduction to *The Idea of Africa,* in an important insight about the flawed epistemology of Tempels's thesis, and of the latter's "ethnophilosophical" disciples, by showing how his *subjective* vision of Bantu belief systems masqueraded as a new form of *objectivity:* "Negating its subjective foundation, ethnophilosophy claimed to be a perfect 'scientific' translation of a 'philosophical' implicit system which is out there in the quotidian experience, and it qualified itself as an objectivist discourse."[7] As Mudimbe points out, only the most self-deluded of "scientific" theories or practices would today make any absolutist claims to objectivity. This does not, however, mean one ought simply to dismiss Tempels's work as fanciful, irrelevant, or outmoded, since it is precisely its status as a kind of mythical discourse in itself which then casts it in a new light for Mudimbe and accounts to a large extent both for its ahistoricism and for its enduring influence on African thinkers. In attempting to define its theoretical makeup more precisely, and to place it within the author's own personal history and spiritual evolution, Mudimbe describes Tempels's thesis as "the fuzziness of a thought born of cross-breeding between ethnological curiosity, evangelical ambiguities, and colonial purpose" (*Invention,* 141).

If this "fuzziness" is what characterizes synchronic, mythified representations of African culture, Marxist theories of dialectical materialism and socioeconomic relations of production and exchange appear to offer a means of demystifying and rehistoricizing such accounts. Mudimbe uses the occasion of an extended reading of Peter Rigby's book on Ilparakuyo Maasai pastoralists in Tanzania, *Persistent Pastoralists: Nomadic Societies in Transition,* to think through the possibilities of a constructive dialogue between Marxism and African anthropology. Rigby's methodological premises are in many ways congruent with Mudimbe's own theses on the subjectivism and ahistoricism of traditional anthropology, and they also reveal the critical potential for a Marxist reinterpretation of time and history in an African context. As Mudimbe says, "Rigby's critique of idealist models that have so far dominated Africanist discourses underscores the productivity of a Marxist evaluation of the history of African anthropology," given that the diverse approaches that Rigby discusses—Lévy-Bruhl's abstract mentalism, Malinowski's functionalism, Leach's structuralist models, and the philosophical-theological orientation of Mbiti and other African writers—"seem all to represent anti-Marxist stances and very subtly contribute to the controversial thesis of the ahistoricity of African experience of time."[8] Rigby's own invocation and application of Marxist theory is an attempt to transform current social relations into what would effectively be "socialist" economic relations (encouraging semi-sedentarization of herds, redefining traditional divisions of labor, and so on).

Mudimbe does not disagree with the main thrust of Rigby's book and indeed sees it as a significant, perhaps necessary, politicization of anthropology as a social science. Where he does feel that Rigby's project is on uncertain ground is the manner in which he translates the experiences of his position as an "insider" (despite his position as a Western-educated anthropologist, Rigby's indigenous family connection gives him what Mudimbe terms an "existential authority") into the theoretical space of his book itself, and its subsequent retranslation back into material social transformations. For Mudimbe, the "transition from interpretation to action" (Rigby's own expression) is by no means as straightforward as it seems from an epistemological perspective, since it involves the exercise of a "dubious power" which, according to Mudimbe, Rigby does not acknowledge, this being "the power of the anthropologist": "In reality, his interpretive practice witnesses to a metapower: a capacity of transforming a place into a conceptual space and of moving from this space to the original place" ("Marxist Discourse," 171). In theoretical terms, Rigby's project, linking the subjectivism of phenomenology (his own lived experiences) to the objectivism of Marxism and structuralism, although contradictory, is in Mudimbe's eyes well founded. Rigby's failure to attend to the epistemological consequences of his own unacknowledged "metapower," however, leads Mudimbe to question more generally "the observable limitations of the Marxist method" ("Marxist Discourse," 183). These limitations are recast in terms of the existential dialectic of self and other, subject and object, *en-soi* and *pour-soi,* that frames Mudimbe's own account of the construction of the African other as an object of knowledge.

The impossibility of seeing the other ontologically, what Mudimbe calls a "logical madness," is the paradox that structures colonialist discourse generally and produces in the essay a succinct summary of Mudimbe's own theoretical position:

All colonialisms and imperialisms are predicated on a similar rational madness. They have been justifying themselves as means of bringing to life and to light the nonexistent other, or the incipient other who was still at the phase of an in-itself. Their normative policies used to expound ways and techniques of "inventing" a for-itself for the in-itself. What I am suggesting here is an immense paradox: there is a relation of congruence between the philosophical solipsism born from the Cartesian cogito and the expansion of the European space which actualized the conditions of possibility for arranging reasons and processes of converting non-Western peoples, reducing them to a European historicity, and promoting a universal will to truth. ("Marxist Discourse," 177–78)

The danger of adapting Marxist theory is that, if applied uncritically, it simplifies the "complexity of the dynamics of the lived in the real place" and thus constitutes a "questionable translation" ("Marxist Discourse," 192). This was in fact borne out in most African countries that adopted socialist programs following Independence. As Mudimbe states quite bluntly: "African socialisms were a mystification and everyone knows it" ("Marxist Discourse," 183). Unreflective transposition also ignores the continuing power of the paradox (what one might also term the paradox of the "metapower") that Mudimbe highlights and that is the constant focus of his own work. As if to underline this, his essay on Rigby is punctuated by autobiographical references to his own very paradoxical relationship to Marxism in the 1960s, summed up in the rather cryptic confession that "I am not a 'professional' anti-Marxist" ("Marxist Discourse," 184). That the most eloquent demonstration of the essay's argument should take the form of a turn to the autobiographical, to a subjective reimplication, has further consequences which I would like to explore later in this chapter.

If the various discourses of Africanism produced by "outsiders," however sympathetic in intention, merely end up "inventing" an African *pour-soi,* what does Mudimbe have to say about those written by Africans themselves? While one might expect this to be the very space within which an African subjectivity, liberated from its colonial or anthropological objectification, is at last able to express itself, such uncritical optimism is for Mudimbe the most dangerous of all, and is a kind of willful blindness to the very discursive "metapower" to which Africans are in fact subjected. Mudimbe thus devotes a considerable amount of his analytical labor to demonstrating how African writers and thinkers, in several very different fields, are caught in this epistemological trap. *Négritude,* certainly, on now familiar grounds. It appeared as a radical, emancipatory movement that allowed for a subjective affirmation, yet it was in fact consistent with the ideologies underpinning the colonial literature of exoticism and was, as Mudimbe notes, "the product of a singular moment in the history of Europe, and more particularly of French thought, whose marks it bears."9 This is not a particularly original insight, but while there has been a great deal of critical commentary on the French literary sources of *négritude,* Mudimbe's perspective is broader. For him *négritude,* particularly Senghor's more essentialist version proclaiming a distinctively African mode of apprehension of the world, emerged from within the parameters of the Western philosophical tradition, which saw the West as embodying the values of rationality, civilization, cultural maturity, and so on, and Africa as emotional, sensual, uncivilized, and closer to nature. In this sense it was openly indebted to early ethnologists. To quote Mudimbe in *L'odeur du père,*

> L. S. Senghor emphasizes strongly the contributions of anthropology, and more precisely the kind of attention that anthropologists brought to bear. At that time Froebenius, Delafosse and others, who were sensitive to cultural difference, offered young Blacks, who because of colonization had forgotten what it meant truly to be African, reasons to stand up to the prevailing ideology.10

Mudimbe's assessment of *négritude* later on in *The Invention of Africa* is much more nuanced in approach, and he examines in particular the significance of the philosophical orientation given to it by Sartre in his famous essay in praise of the *négritude* poets, "Orphée noir." Sartre frames *négritude* in existentialist terms, as a question of "l'être-dans-le-monde du Nègre" [the Negro's being-in-the-world] and then goes on to place it in a broader Marxist perspective that certainly contributed to its efficacy as a political movement.11 As Mudimbe says, "It is Sartre who [. . .] transformed *négritude* into a major political event and a philosophical criticism of colonialism" (*Invention,* 83). Sartre's contention that its racial affirmation should be seen as a stage to be surpassed or overcome within the dialectical process that would theoretically result in a raceless and classless world society was of course a double-edged endorsement. Mudimbe sums this up in a compelling image when he says that Senghor had asked for a cloak to celebrate *négritude* but was instead given a shroud. Sartre's text is seen, however, as more than just part of the literary history of the movement; it is, rather, "a major ideological moment, perhaps one of the most important" (*Invention,* 85), one that in fact defines the political stakes of the future of African studies if it is not to fall back into the "ideological manipulation" (*Invention,* 87) of anthropology and its related discourses: "Sartre established a cardinal synthesis. By rejecting both the colonial rationale and the set of culturally eternal values as bases for society, his brief treatise posited philosophically a relativist perspective for African social studies [. . .] his insights illuminated the trends and preoccupations of African scholarship" (*Invention,* 86).

Sartre's insight into the importance of a negative, self-reflexive moment in the affirmations of *négritude,* and by extension African studies generally (summed up in his paradoxical definition of *négritude* as an "antiracist racism"), was thus according to Mudimbe not simply an example of a globalist Marxism canceling out the specificity of the African situation but an idea far-reaching in its implications. It enables Mudimbe to posit more clearly a broad theoretical axis and the two poles or perspectives between which Africanist discourses by Africans can be located: that is, on the one hand an ideological, usually ahistorical trend that consistently invokes an African past, and on the other a trend that adopts a more or less philosophically self-critical approach. In his essay "Philosophy and Theology as Political Practices," in *Parables and Fables,* Mudimbe identifies four very broad, overlapping "sets" into which one could place recent African thinking and writing, depending on where it situates itself along this axis or spectrum. Toward the traditional, ahistorical end, one would find in the first set the generation of philosophers who were avowed disciples of Placide Tempels, who were also theologians and who accepted uncritically the philosophical assumptions on which his ideas were based: Alexis Kagamé (who refined Tempels's study by grounding it in an analysis of his native Rwandan language), François-Marie Lufuluabo, Vincent Mulago, and John Mbiti.[12] Members of this broad category are referred to by Paulin Hountondji as "ethnophilosophers." Peter Rigby's grouping of Mbiti with primitivist anthropologists, mentioned earlier, now becomes clearer, since what his project does essentially is, as Mudimbe puts it, to "postulate a subjunctive mood (Que je sois! Que l'Afrique soit! [Let me be! Let Africa be!]) accounted for by an uncritical leap out of history into a Christian eschatology" (*Parables*, 191).

A second set also turns to the past in order to revalidate the present, but to explicitly political ends. This group Mudimbe terms "ideologico-philosophical," and it includes pan-Africanism (Lumumba, Senghor, Nyerere, and so on), theories of "African personality" such as *négritude*, Cheikh Anta Diop's histories of precolonial Africa, and the more militant, faithfully Marxist nationalism of post-Independence leaders such as Nkrumah or Sékou Touré. Mudimbe's reasons for including them at this end of the spectrum might not be immediately obvious, but the point is that they are all indebted to an essentially mythified version of African culture, and this helps to explain in part the failures of regimes such as Sékou Touré's in Guinea.[13] Mudimbe of course acknowledges that his schematic simplification glosses over the complexity of the links between the various members of this group and between this subgroup and, for example, the "ethnophilosophers." But he critiques along similar lines African historians such as Cheikh Anta Diop, Théophile Obenga, and Joseph Ki-Zerbo, who appear to depart radically from Westernized conceptions of African culture. According to Mudimbe, however, their work takes the form of an inversion of categories and values predetermined by a Western epistemology, leading to an "aestheticization"—or politically driven "hypostasis," as Mudimbe puts it—of African culture (*Invention*, 169).

When we move to the opposite end of the axis, the remaining two groups are split between, on the one hand, critical reflections by Africans who engage explicitly with Western science, such as Stanislav Adotévi's epistemological inquiries or Ibrahim Sow's work on African psychiatry, and on the other, African philosophy whose aim is to be "fully" philosophical. The latter would include critical responses of writers to earlier Africanist discourses, such as Eboussi-Boulaga's critique of Tempels mentioned earlier and Marcien Towa's forceful attacks on *négritude*, although its best-known and most charismatic representative is probably Paulin Hountondji. It was Hountondji who, in referring to Tempels and his legacy, popularized the term *ethnophilosophy*, and who articulated in his *African Philosophy* perhaps the most vigorous denunciation of its ethnocentric bias. His most controversial statement is doubtless the one with which he begins this book: "By 'African Philosophy' I mean a set of texts, specifically the set of texts written by Africans and described as philosophical by their authors themselves."[14] Hountondji has been reproached by Africans for his dismissal of the importance of traditional culture and for his elitism and his dependency on Western criteria in determining the specificity of African philosophy. In responding to these criticisms, he has qualified his initial, controversially absolutist position by revalorizing oral culture and stating that his point of departure was determined by the need to begin *somewhere* on the path to philosophical autonomy, which Hountondji sees as a prerequisite for a more pragmatic political autonomy.[15]

Mudimbe treads this path more carefully and since his earliest texts has been wary of the kinds of criticisms to which Hountondji leaves himself open. In the chapter entitled "Quel ordre du discours africain?" [What order of African discourse?] in *L'odeur du père,* a running commentary on Foucault's 1971 inaugural lecture at the Collège de France, *L'ordre du discours,* Mudimbe states the dilemma of the African subject's projected discursive decolonization as "the distance [*l'écart*] we have to take with respect to the West, and the cost to us of truly assuming this distance," and spells out the hidden dangers of any claim to break free from the West. He takes the passage in which Foucault expresses doubts about the possibility of Western philosophy escaping from its Hegelian legacy and rewrites it, substituting "the West" for "Hegel":

> [E]chapper réellement à l'Occident suppose d'apprécier exactement ce qu'il en coûte de se détacher de lui; cela suppose de savoir jusqu'où l'Occident, insidieusement peut-être, s'est approché de nous; cela suppose de savoir dans ce qui nous permet de penser contre l'Occident ce qui est encore occidental; et de mesurer en quoi notre recours contre lui est encore peut-être une ruse qu'il nous oppose et au terme de laquelle il nous attend, immobile et ailleurs.

> [But to make a real escape from the West presupposes an exact appreciation of what it costs to detach ourselves from it. It presupposes a knowledge of how close the West has come to us, perhaps insidiously. It presupposes a knowledge of what is still Western in that which allows us to think against the West; and an ability to gauge how much our resources against it are perhaps still a ruse which it is using against us, and at the end of which it is waiting for us, immobile and elsewhere.] (*Odeur du père,* 44)[16]

How, then, does Mudimbe himself propose that Africans negotiate the epistemological paradoxes and pitfalls of this path toward autonomy? We need to return at this point to his intellectual debt to Foucault and Lévi-Strauss, since this seems to provide at least a provisional way out. Both Foucault and Lévi-Strauss, in different ways, offer critiques of the rational subject of Western history and the manner in which its absorptive power, through its multifarious manifestations, reduces the Other to the Same. A structuralist approach to Africanist discourse enables an understanding of the systematic nature of the forms this Western rationality takes, and is for Mudimbe the methodological basis from which he reconstructs an "archaeology" of African knowledge, a history of its discursive forms. As we saw in the introduction, particularly with Lévi-Strauss's putting into question of the objectivity of his own position as anthropologist and the acknowledgment of his own subjective investment in the tales he was telling, the focus shifts back to the function of the subject. In this context, Mudimbe endorses Eboussi-Boulaga's project of a new, critical "récit pour soi," one founded on one's own particular social experience: "[T]he *récit* is a reconstruction of history. By necessity a negation of the present, and also a negation of the self, it is, at the same time, the only critical way to self [. . .] The notion of a critical reading, as well as that of a *récit pour soi* that might produce a regional historical account of the global history of humankind, brings us back to Lévi-Strauss's and Foucault's annihilation of the mythologies of the Same" (*Invention,* 42).

This African *via negativa* represents a refusal of the reduction of the Other to the Same and as such is a version of the Sartrean existentialist dynamic that Mudimbe often evokes. Mudimbe argues, therefore, in what at first appears as an overly simplistic counterpoint to the celebrated "disappearance of the subject" of poststructuralism and psychoanalysis or the fragmented subject of postmodernism, for the *restoration* of a fully conscious, intentional subject. This concrete, very deliberately existential and *phenomenologically* determined subject is also seen as an assertion of the singularity of its place and its time, a kind of "X marks the spot," with its particular voice being "le cri et le témoin de ce lieu singulier" [the cry of and witness to this singular place]. As he says a little later on, "our discourses justify us as singular existences engaged in a history which is itself also singular" (*Odeur du père,* 14, 33). Far from being a naive return to a certain precritical conception of human subjectivity (and its potential association with the "ethnophilosophical" resurrection of a precolonial African identity), what Mudimbe proposes is a reaffirmation of the African subject as a strategic means of contesting the supposed objectivity, or universalism, of the discursive orders that still dominate African science, philosophy, political thinking, and aesthetic theory. What is required, according to Mudimbe, in order to "rid ourselves of the 'smell' of an abusive father" [*l'odeur' d'un père abusif*] is to "fulfill ourselves, engage in a major act of excommunication, speak out and produce *differently*" (*Odeur du père*, 33).

In *L'autre face du royaume* Mudimbe uses the analogy of an African researcher riding up and down in an elevator, content in his or her freedom to determine where he or she is going but unaware that it is Western technicians who control and delimit its movement, who are the ones possessing the knowledge of its operation. The researcher is, in other words, in a discursive prison impeding true freedom of choice and action. The option of pressing the button to open the door and "escape" to his or her own space is simply not available, and he or she is left with the dilemma that Kenneth Harrow, commenting on this passage in Mudimbe, describes as follows:

> What is striking is the dilemma with which he is confronted: either emulate Western researchers or retreat into a narcissistic reverie [. . .] But this narcissistic antithesis to Western scholarship is not conceived of as a counter-discourse, or as a solution. The revolt, to be a genuine one, must transcend the limits imposed on the situation by the refusal of its givens altogether. Thus it is not the quality of the discourse provided by the technicians that is questioned, but the very dependency inherent within the circumstances in which their knowledge is supplied as a basis for the Africans.[17]

At several points Mudimbe also turns to Frantz Fanon, who is for him an important thinker of subjectivity, and whose work contains a powerful critique of *négritude*'s lack of political militantism, quoting his famous phrase in this regard: "The density of history does not determine any of my acts. I am my own foundation" (*Odeur du père*, 43).

This rather exalted, revolutionary language is, it should be noted, far more characteristic of the texts from Mudimbe's "French" period, particularly *L'odeur du père*, and it seems to be somewhat muted or qualified in the writings from *The Invention of Africa* onward. I would argue, however, that his reaffirmation of subjectivity has in fact become more deep-rooted and has developed in a way that responds to the intense debates about African philosophy in the 1990s and allows us to better understand the overall coherence of his writing, both theoretical and literary. It is precisely this shift to a self-critical, enunciative mode which prompts, indeed obliges, Mudimbe to take up a critical position with respect both to Lévi-Strauss and to Foucault, who are, as he says, ultimately part of the very heritage from which an African discourse would wish to free itself: "[D]espite their violence against the rules of the Same and the history of its conquests over all regionalisms, specificities, and differences, Lévi-Strauss and Foucault, as well as a number of African thinkers, belong to the signs of the same power." In other words, whatever the intellectual benefits to African philosophy of theories which articulate the relationship between a subject and the hidden cultural structures that circumscribe it and preempt the limitations of its experience, such theories are ultimately, as Mudimbe puts it, "engulfed in the history of the Same and its contradictions" (*Invention,* 43). This point is made by Bernard Mouralis in his book on Mudimbe, and by Manthia Diawara in an article on Mudimbe. Diawara describes the paradox as follows:

> Foucault's call for the removal of the subject and the return of pure discourse criticism posits the condition of possibility for the deployment of a new Western *ratio* and the repression of other subjectivities. The pure discourse criticism, which is part of a particular culture, enables non-Westerners to denounce the domineering presence of the West in their texts, but paradoxically does not allow them to move forward and create a discourse outside the Foucauldian system.[18]

Despite his determination to distance himself ultimately from both Foucault and Lévi-Strauss, Mudimbe does nonetheless suggest that the latter's combination of an objective, scientific method and an essentially subjective *bricolage* provides the prototype for the resolution of the epistemological aporia that the African subject is caught in. D. A. Masolo considers this continued reliance on Lévi-Strauss an unresolved ambiguity in Mudimbe's project and describes as symptomatic his apparent inability to ground his "elegant deconstructionist method" in the "idioms of everyday life." This is an important criticism of Mudimbe by one of his best readers, since the question it raises is that of the status of Mudimbe's own writings and the extent to which they can provide Africans with concrete tools for self-transformation, or as Masolo puts it, "There is a way in which it is legitimate to regard Mudimbe's project as directed beyond its mere subversive (postmodern) role. At least many of Mudimbe's African readers will, and many already do, look up to him with this expectation: that his work is not only diagnostic of a (gnostic) malady, but also prognostic of its cure." Masolo's criticism centers on the contention that Mudimbe ultimately falls back into the very epistemological "prison" from which he is attempting to free the African subject, that is, "he lamentably fails to emancipate himself from the vicious circle inherent in the deconstructionist stance." Or as he puts it later toward the end of his discussion, a genuine discourse on African ideas is possible only "if there is a realization that even Mudimbe's idea of an invented Africa is itself also a construct, an ideology which in turn requires deconstruction."[19]

In what sense could one think of Mudimbe's project as (insufficiently) "deconstructionist," and what would it mean to align his critique of the various modalities of an "invented" Africa with the "idioms of everyday life"? I will come back to the first of these two questions after a detour through the second, which relates to the political implications of Mudimbe's project and raises again the specter of Marxism in Africa.[20] We have already noted Mudimbe's paradoxical relationship to Marxist theory and praxis in his reading of Peter Rigby's *Persistent Pastoralists.* Rigby's Marxist anthropology revealed the difficulty of moving between a concrete place and a corresponding conceptual space, of translating the one into the other. Mudimbe does not reject Marxism, but condemns its uncritical adaptation and application. It seems that Mudimbe is closest, in his wide-ranging critique of discourses of Africanism, to those African writers he describes as most self-critically philosophical, such as Paulin Hountondji or Kwasi Wiredu. Despite taking the same critical distance as Hountondji does from ethnophilosophy, in all its forms and derivations, Mudimbe does not endorse the former's radical departure from traditional African cosmologies or mythologies. His detailed and very careful analyses of Luba systems of thought in *Parables and Fables,* for example, bear witness to an enduring passion for "local" knowledge, and a recognition of the power of traditional narratives generally. Can intensely scholarly, structuralist-inspired studies such as these enable him to bridge the gap between his theory and its possible relevance for ordinary Africans while at the same time avoiding the pitfalls of ethno-philosophy?

A better point of comparison might be the work of Kwasi Wiredu, the Ghanaian philosopher, who like Mudimbe argues for a "conceptual decolonization," and who along with Hountondji stresses the need to professionalize and modernize African philosophy. Wiredu argues for the need to reverse the process of the assimilation of conceptual frameworks inherited from colonialism by exploiting more systematically the resources of indigenous systems of thought (and to this extent his work overlaps with, but differs significantly from, that of Alexis Kagamé). Wiredu contrasts his activity as a professional philosopher with that of the rather superficial "philosopher-kings" of Independence, as he calls them (Nkrumah, Senghor, Nyerere, Sekou Touré, and so on), whose writings might at first appear to represent the perfect correspondence between philosophical theory and political action. He easily exposes the illusions of "popularity" around which such ideologies were constructed, stating that their "authoritarian mode of propagation, of course, ensured that the philosophies in question would affect the lives of millions of our people. But that did not necessarily imply widespread acceptance or even comprehension."[21] Wiredu considers that in order to gain credence and contemporary relevance for those it should stand to benefit, African philosophy must come from "within," as it were, and that this is best achieved by making the essential point of reference African languages and their corresponding conceptual systems or worldviews.[22] Taking the case of the Akan language and people in Ghana—"the only African language about which I am somewhat competent"[23]—his project thus seems to be a true vernacularization of philosophy, and one that has relevance both for its object of study, the Akan people, and for the academic community at large.[24] It would thus be the most exemplary instance of a specifically African conjunction, to adapt the title of his book, of cultural particulars and human universals.

Mudimbe professes tremendous intellectual admiration and professional respect for Wiredu, but not surprisingly his own reading of Wiredu's project, echoing his critique of Rigby, focuses on a certain failure to account for his subjective position, and its effects, that is "Wiredu's subjective reading of his own *Weltanschauung*" (*Idea,* 199). Returning to the Sartrean existential dilemma, which he sees as irreducible and which seems to be at the heart of most of his critiques, Mudimbe summarizes his position vis-à-vis Wiredu as follows:

> Concretely, we may say, using an apparently ambivalent expression, Akan cosmology is what it is not. In effect, I personally think of it as a discourse produced by a multiplicity of beings for themselves. And strictly speaking, to use Sartre's vocabulary, these beings cannot be only what they are. There is no way of reducing them to the status of a vague in-itself as do ordinary ethnophilosophers. In other words, I wish very much Wiredu could speak more explicitly from his own existential locality as subject. (*Idea,* 200)

Mudimbe suggests some possible factors a philosopher such as Wiredu writing "for" the Akan people might need to take into account. These would be, for example, the fact that his analyses borrow their conceptual terminology from the British analytical tradition (not to mention the English language), or the potentially infinite contextual meanings of a given expression or gesture (what Clifford Geertz characterizes as "thick description"). In fact, Mudimbe ends up describing their respective projects—although diverging precisely on the question of their "subjective choices for thinking the philosophical practice in Africa"—as procedurally very much the same, both bearing witness to "philosophy as a critical thinking [that . . .] cannot but be antidogmatic [. . .] it is always an ongoing struggle for meaning, necessarily insecure, tentative, and thus resistant to all results and axioms, even its own" (*Idea,* 200).

It is clear here that this critical self-awareness directly contradicts Masolo's contention earlier that Mudimbe fails to leave his own discursive "inventions" open to a deconstructive critique. In fact, Masolo appears to base his entire reading of Mudimbe on a fundamental misconception about deconstruction. He describes Mudimbe's project as "a historical deconstruction of the bits and pieces of the power/knowledge that have determined the representation of Africa and Africans,"[25] whereas the latter's analytical, or archaeological, work revealing how discourses of Africanism are dependent on a Western *ratio* is in fact his adaptation of a Foucauldian theoretical model. This confusion leads to the claim of a radical antiessentialism, which for Masolo is at the core of Mudimbe's alleged "deconstructive" methodology. According to Masolo: "The rejection of the essentialist position allows Mudimbe to apply Foucault to his (Mudimbe's) own project of subverting, not only the Western discursive canon through which the negative images of Africa have been invented, but also Foucault himself as part of that canon. It is only through this double subversion that it is possible to erect the African subject."[26]

The equation of "deconstruction" with a simple "antiessentialism," and by extension its popular depiction as a kind of generalized rejection of all stable concepts and values, is of course entirely antithetical to its actual operations. Rather than being the caricaturally groundless, apolitical free play of signifiers that takes apart categories such as the subject, presence, reference, speech, and so on, deconstruction (both de Man's and Derrida's versions) fundamentally asserts the unavoidable *necessity* of such concepts, attempting to trace the ways in which they are constituted within the terms of their own textual inscription and their operative limitations. Derrida himself says as much in his early work, such as *Of Grammatology* and *Writing and Difference,* and has tirelessly reiterated this position over the years. In "Deconstruction in America" in 1985, for example, he says in an interview:

> To say for example, "deconstruction suspends reference," that deconstruction is a way of enclosing oneself in the sign, in the "signifier," is an enormous naiveté stated in that form [. . .] Not only is there reference for a text, but never was it proposed that we erase effects of reference or of referents. Merely that we re-think these effects of reference. I would indeed say that the referent is textual. The referent is in the text. Yet that does not exempt us from having to describe very rigorously the necessity of these referents.[27]

Gayatri Spivak repeatedly invokes both de Man and Derrida in her postcolonial theoretical work, emphasizing in particular the latter's very early identification, in *Of Grammatology,* of the ethnocentric basis of European thought, and his understanding of how difficult it is to escape this ethnocentrism. Derrida's description of this difficulty can be seen as analogous to Mudimbe's warnings about the pitfalls of Africanist discourses: "Each time that ethnocentrism is precipitately and ostentatiously reversed, some effort silently hides behind all the spectacular effects to *consolidate an inside* and to draw from it some domestic benefit."[28]

Another early context, Derrida's critique in *Writing and Difference* of Foucault's *History of Madness,* is more directly relevant to Masolo's reading of Mudimbe.[29] In this essay, Derrida agrees with Foucault's thesis that the discursive exclusion of madness can be seen to occur as a necessary complement of the Cartesian *cogito,* taken as emblematic of the institution of a Western *ratio,* but Derrida goes on to read this archaeological analysis against the text of Descartes itself. Descartes's foundational separation of reason and madness is shown to be more problematic than Foucault allows for, and Derrida's deconstruction of the latter's argument is structurally similar to his famous critique, in *Of Grammatology,* of Lévi-Strauss's phonocentric analysis of writing as cultural violence (that is, Derrida's insistence on writing, in the larger sense, as the originary violence, which is then overlaid by the "secondary" violence of the logocentric establishment of speech as prior to writing). Foucault's project likewise attempts to locate the exclusion of madness as a historically determinate event in Descartes, whereas a more attentive reading of the text itself finds a logically anterior moment (prior to the possibility of a determination, historically or ontologically, or of the distinction itself between reason and nonreason) in which madness *has* to be seen as interior to reason, reason *has* to be able to accommodate it in order to be able to institute itself. Marian Hobson, tracing the links between these two critiques, draws the readings of Lévi-Strauss and Foucault together very concisely as follows: "Foucault historicizes the Cogito by assimilating it to a localized historical reason [. . .] The forcing of the hyperbole to re-enter the world—'la réduction à l'intramondanité,' its reduction to historical determination—is violent, just as, in the account of Lévi-Strauss, reduction to linguistic determination was the originary violence."[30]

Mudimbe's ultimate "rejection" of Lévi-Strauss and Foucault is to be read most productively, I would argue, in the light of Derrida's critique of their respective projects. This is not an antiessentialist (or "mad") rejection of essentialism (or historically determinate reason), nor a simple stepping outside of the canon to which both writers in the final analysis belong. Rather, we might take Mudimbe's adaptation of Foucault and Lévi-Strauss as a gesture that unmoors the *cogito* from its strict historical determination, but that also, in reaffirming the subject, is in Derrida's terms closer to the *cogito.* It is perhaps clearer now why Mudimbe accords the *cogito* such important privileges at the end of *The Idea of Africa.* The African *cogito* he argues for would *in its very affirmation* involve both a disarticulation of Western discursive objectification and a claim to a new form of subjective agency, encouraging inventiveness and creativity and a certain form of arationalism (which would not be an irrationalism). This is neither a claim to a self-sufficient, self-present subject nor simply the illusory project of "stepping outside" of Western logocentrism, since it involves both an inventive enunciation and the strategic dismantling of the discourses through which it is objectified. We might also better understand Mudimbe's constant invocation of Sartre, whom many critics of African literature simply stop reading once they have noted his universalizing Marxism in "Orphée noir."

Mudimbe is not alone in this strategic reaffirmation of concepts that seem as if they ought simply to be jettisoned. Kwame Anthony Appiah argues similarly, in his essay "The Postcolonial and the Postmodern," for a return to a certain humanism: "For what I am calling humanism can be provisional, historically contingent, antiessentialist (in other words, postmodern), and still be demanding [. . .] Maybe, then, we can recover within postmodernism the postcolonial writer's humanism [. . .] while still rejecting the master narratives of modernism."[31] Appiah provides a tighter theoretical articulation of this dynamic in another essay, "Tolerable Falsehoods: Agency and the Interests of Theory," in which he uses a strategic maneuver similar to Mudimbe's in seeking a way out of the double bind of structure and agency. He claims that the terms in which this opposition have been posed are inadequate, and that rather than see them as competing for the same causal space, we should radically disconnect them from each other. In reviewing how philosophical and theoretical determinations of the subject have shifted from a humanism that has "overplayed the self-reflexive actor, the autonomous individual" to a structuralist and poststructuralist emphasis on system and discourse, Appiah argues that it is wrong to set these two accounts of subjectivity in opposition to each other: "What I want to suggest, by contrast, is that we should see the relations between structural explanations and the logic of the subject as a competition not for causal space but for narrative space: as different levels of theory, with different constitutive assumptions, whose relations make them neither competitive nor mutually constitutive, but quite contingently complementary."[32] Different levels of theory would thus be determined not by considerations of "truth," agonistically opposed to the falsity of other positions, but by "interests" and "tolerable falsehoods." The language of structural determinism would thus need to acknowledge "that what this discourse stigmatizes as bourgeois humanism *remains inescapable also*" (emphasis added).[33] His position is close to how I would read Mudimbe, and significantly it is in the assertion of a new kind of narrative agency that Appiah finds a way of overcoming the opposition between agency and structure, subject and subjection.

Appiah himself, in his essay "The Postcolonial and the Postmodern," takes Mudimbe's novels as exemplary articulations of the critique of the kind of oppositional logic he is contesting. He sees Mudimbe's 1973 novel *Entre les eaux,* the story of an African priest, Pierre Landu, caught between the competing interests and demands of Marxism and Christianity, as particularly insightful in this regard. He describes the fate of Pierre Landu as a "powerful postcolonial critique of this binarism." Appiah contrasts Landu's disruption of this binary model with what he sees as the more pessimistic example of Nara, the main character of Mudimbe's 1979 novel *L'écart* [*The Rift*]. According to him, the position adopted by Nara as an African intellectual traps him within "the sort of Manicheanism that makes Africa '*a body*' (nature) against Europe's juridical reality (culture)."[34] I would argue, though, that as a novel that dramatizes the question of the African subject, it in fact probes far more deeply into the relationship between subjectivity and narrative agency in a postcolonial African context.

L'écart: Mad Writing?

L'écart is recounted in the first person in the form of Ahmed Nara's personal diary of the weeks leading up to his death, which is presented to the fictional "editor" of the book by Nara's archivist friend, Salim. Nara is an African student who, after spending time in Paris, has returned to Africa in order to complete his history dissertation on the Kuba people. The narrative present of the journal covers the last weeks of Nara's life and consists of fragmented, at times rather impressionistic notes telling of his research at the national library, time spent with his friends, the developing relationship with Aminata, an African woman, and his visits to Dr. Sano, a psychiatrist. There are also constant references back to his time in Paris, dominated by the love affair with a French woman, Isabelle, and also to his early childhood, with several reconstructed scenes of life among the Kuba in precolonial Africa.

Nara's project had aimed to "décoloniser les connaissances établies sur eux" [decolonize the knowledge already gathered about them],[35] and the critique this implies of Western anthropological accounts of the Kuba involves precisely the kind of subjective investment in his research that Mudimbe argues in favor of. As Nara says, it is "pour instaurer, en symbole bavard, les échos du moi" (116) [to establish the echoes of the Me through garrulous symbols] (88). In order to illustrate the crudeness of ethnographic description and classification, at one point he reads out a typical historical account of the relationship between the Lélé and the Kuba peoples, replacing them with Spanish and Portuguese.[36] Nara wants, of course, to take this conceptual decolonization much further than simple satire, and he says that one important consequence of studying the Kuba as a civilization equal to any European social order is that it destabilizes the operative distinctions upon which ethnology is founded, such as oral and written cultures: "Comme si le concept d'archive, de tout temps, devait coïncider avec les expressions particulières actualisées par la brève histoire de l'Europe" (67) [As if the concept of archives had, since time immemorial, to coincide necessarily with the specific expressions it was given by the short history of Europe] (46, trans. slightly modified).

The effect of the fragmentary and notational nature of his text (in particular the use of ellipses rather than exact punctuation or more precise temporal conjunctions) is to blur the distinctions between his past and present, between his own life and the world of the precolonial Kuba, between Isabelle and Aminata, and so on, thereby drawing attention to the fabric of the text itself, emphasizing *discours* at the expense of *histoire,* to use Emile Benvéniste's classic narrative opposition.[37] This is a key point, since the novel can at this level be read, referring back to Appiah's argument in "Tolerable Falsehoods," as a struggle for narrative agency. The historical rewriting of the Kuba past and the narration of Nara's present life in his journal are in fact interdependent, a co-implication that is reflected in the narrative form of his text, which resembles the preorganized state of dissertation research notes. On the one hand, it is only possible to write what might be called literature once Nara has broken free of the discursive constraints of ethnographic discourse generally, and on the other, literary narrative becomes the privileged, indeed necessary, arena of this discursive liberation. This is a paradoxical, somewhat aporetic situation (indeed, one of the senses of the "écart" of the title might be a kind of "impossible dialogue," similar to the one I discussed earlier), and this very tension is at the heart of the apparent "theme" of the novel, that is, an African intellectual driven to insanity and possible suicide by the unbearable conditions of his life and research.

The psychiatric frame of reference represented by the sessions Nara has with Dr. Sano is at the same time, however, one of several different forms of discursive subjugation or subjection that Nara contests in the novel. Dr. Sano diagnoses his profound disconnectedness from the world as schizophrenia, and there are a number of elements that seems to suggest an unresolved Oedipal complex or to point to determining factors in his childhood, such as his father's death when he was age six, his obsession with rats, which seems to date from this time, and his tendency to see both Isabelle and Aminata as mother substitutes. But these clues (along with others, such as the name "Sano" itself) also hint at something of a false trail deliberately laid by Mudimbe, an interpretive dead end designed to reflect back to us our own desire for narrative and psychological coherence in the text, and the ultimate inadequacy of this desire. It also suggests a wider significance by developing the common metaphor of Europe and Africa as doctor and patient, respectively. Denis Ekpo correctly shows how Bernard Mouralis falls into this trap in his reading of the novel. Mouralis does point out that this is a lure, but he then goes on to read Nara's unconscious desire as represented by a precolonial, pre-Oedipal identification with the Kuba, thereby displacing the psychoanalytical interpretation onto Nara's anthropological interests.[38] The problem is that in locating a kind of psychoanalytical authenticity in a "primordial" African past, Mouralis falls back into the ethnophilosophical position, whereas what the novel in fact does is to suspend the category of authenticity, or to leave it an open-ended question by making a principle of indeterminability the condition of possibility of a reinscribed subject.

We can see the same indeterminacy in the competing historical discourses of Nara and of Soum, his Marxist friend. Soum sees Nara's research into the Kuba as an escape from Africa's present-day political realities into a "mythical past." As he says at one point in response to Nara's attempts to explain to him the virtues of the symbolism of Kuba scarifications:

Des mots, des mots, mon pauvre vieux. Des mots généreux . . . Chez les Dogons, ce savoir est enfoui dans des mythes savants. Ça les avance, tu parles . . . Connaître les profondeurs des cieux et s'enfoncer dans le sous-développement . . . (43)

[Words, words, words, my boy. Beautiful words . . . Among the Dogon this knowledge is buried deep inside learned myths. And that really advances them, doesn't it . . . To know the depths of the heavens and to remain stuck in underdevelopment . . .] (27)

Soum's dialectical materialist approach to the African present is shown to have its own limitations, and Nara's doubts about its universalist claims echo those critics of Sartre's universalizing Marxism in "Orphée noir." Soum answers these doubts by quoting Marx back to Nara, and his discourse is generally characterized by an uncritical dogmatism. Yet Nara's own approach to history runs the risk of totalization and of ethnophilosophical ahistoricism: "J'aimerais repartir de zéro, reconstruire du tout au tout l'univers de ces peuples" (26) [I would like to start from scratch, reconstruct the universe of these peoples from start to finish] (13). As we saw earlier in discussing Mudimbe's critique of African experiments with scientific socialism, he is careful not to fall into the trap of dismissing either Marxism or ethnophilosophy outright, but he repositions himself with respect to both by a performative reinscription of his own existential subject-position. It would likewise be easy to qualify Nara as an ethnophilosopher, but as we have seen, his version of ethnophilosophy is indissociable from the rewriting of his present life in his journal, with its indeterminable subjectivity.

More complex than Nara's ambivalence with respect to the discourses of psychiatry and history are his relationships with Isabelle and Aminata. It seems as if the opposition that the two women represent fits into the divisions we find elsewhere in the novel. Isabelle contrasts her own European "rationalism" to Nara's African animal sensuality, which is precisely the identification that for Appiah imprisons Nara (that is, Africa as a "body"). For her, Nara writes, "J'étais un phallus . . . Ne pouvais être que cela" (34) [I was a phallus . . . Could be nothing else] (19). And later on she calls him her "totem," to which Nara replies: "Je ne suis pas un animal, Isabelle . . . Tu as voulu un nègre pour tes aridités . . . Je me complais en tes ivresses" (107) [I'm not an animal, Isabelle . . . You wanted a Negro as a cure for the barrenness of your life . . . I'm delighted to participate in your follies] (81). Although his relationship with Aminata once he is back in Africa initially stands in stark contrast to his European experiences, his memories of Isabelle become more and more pervasive, and the two women are gradually confused in his mind; indeed, with the final words of his journal they are significantly conjoined: "If only Isabelle and Aminata . . . " (126). His objectification as a sexualized body introduces an existentialist dimension to the journal: "J'ai honte d'être là avec Isabelle . . . 'Isa, être africain, c'est d'abord prendre conscience qu'on est une chose . . . pour les autres'" (117) [I am ashamed to be here with Isabelle . . . "Isa, to be African is to be first of all conscious that one is a thing . . . to others"] (89). Aminata, rather than offering Nara a means of escaping this reification, leads him into a similar feeling of existential entrapment ("I am her object," 39). The existential crisis thus "overrides" its specific cultural or geographical forms, and the discursive binarisms they generate, and it becomes apparent that the novel is more fundamentally concerned with the very Sartrean dilemma that Mudimbe places at the crux of his thinking.

L'écart has in fact often been said to belong to the tradition of the French existentialist novel, and we might see this in comparing its themes, moods, and narrative styles to those of a novel such as Sartre's *La nausée*. Nara experiences an existential anguish similar to Roquentin's in Sartre's novel, and Mudimbe's novel is also written in the form of a diary, narrating what appears to be a similar trajectory, going from a gradual demystification of the discursive orders that seemed previously to have given life its meaning to an awareness of the irreducibility of an existential subject as a basis for human freedom. The language suggesting Nara's attentiveness to the viscous, cloying physicality of the world, particularly the claustrophobic feelings aroused by Aminata's sexuality, echoes that of *La nausée*. He describes it early on as "the real test" (15) [*l'épreuve de la résine*, lit. the resin test]. He then is increasingly aware of his inability to resist Aminata's advances: "Je n'avais jamais regardé aussi intensément le cloaque dans lequel se coulait ma vie [. . .] des odeurs d'huiles montant des cuisines de plein air, flottant entre des courants de miasmes. Et, à chaque pas, le danger de plonger le pied en des étrons royaux" (54) [Never had I looked so intently at the cesspool into which my life was disappearing [. . .] smells of cooking oil coming from open-air kitchens, drifting among the air currents of sewer gas. And, with every step, the danger of plunging one's foot into this royal shit] (36). Later on: "The bottom of the slime rapidly reaches my spirit" (63). And toward the end: "Marshland. Once again, I'm adrift in [lit. flowing into] lethargy" (101); "I was stuck in mire. Inexorably . . . " (102).

By locating Nara's existentialist angst beyond the oppositions that

Isabelle and Aminata at first appear to emblematize, Mudimbe engages very deftly with Sartre's ambiguous celebration of *négritude* in "Orphée noir." Soum might be said to be applying Sartre's universalist Marxism to what he sees as Nara's ethnophilosophical resurrection of Kuba history and mythology, and to this extent Mudimbe goes along with what Diawara describes as "the manner in which universalist Marxism debunks the freedom of Africans by assimilating their struggle to that of the proletariat."[39] But while Nara, as Diawara puts it, "slips out of Soum's deterministic construct of history, Isabelle's image of the African as a totem, and the use of the Oedipus universalis to explain his desires,"[40] he is nonetheless trapped within the existential paradox that acts as a kind of theoretical ballast to Mudimbe's work more generally. This is not to say that *L'écart* is simply an existential novel in an African setting, since it poses the question of freedom not at an ontological but at a discursive level. The question of the subject as a free agent, able to determine his or her own destiny (what Nara terms "my freedom as a Negro" [28]), has to be posed within the very terms that make this freedom an illusion, or at the very least discursively predetermined. The idea of choice, although central to the novel's anxious narrative, is consequently a false choice. As Nara says, in an early flashback to his time with Isabelle: "L'imparfait de mes horreurs rend compte d'un passé: c'est, certes, encore une manière de reproche, mais au moins de pouvoir le lire me protégerait, je l'espère, des illusions de mon esprit. Je n'aurai eu ni la liberté de choisir cet enfer, ni la grâce de pouvoir tracer la route d'un paradis possible" (34) [The incompleteness of my dread accounts for a past: it is, surely, another form of self-reproach, but at least being able to interpret it would protect me, I hope, against the illusions of my mind. I would have had neither the freedom to choose this hell nor the grace to be able to track the road to a possible paradise] (20, trans. slightly modified). Although these categories are essentially false (false *insofar as* they are posited as essential or universal), they are nonetheless "tolerable falsehoods," to borrow Appiah's expression.

The various binary oppositions that structure the narrative thus function in much the same way as the "Freudian" interpretation of Nara's psychological disturbance. Nara is not free, cannot be free, within the terms in which he articulates the possibility of a discursive liberation (whether the frame of reference is psychological, historical, or anthropological), just as any reading that remains within the orbit of the text's

thematic tensions and conflicts can find no way out of an endlessly recuperative mechanism and is destined to see the African subject's claims to
autonomous agency continually thwarted by the absorptive power of the
different forms of discursive subjection. But as Nara says, "at least being
able to interpret it would protect me, I hope, against the illusions of my
mind," and it is at this metanarrative level that we find the novel's truly
disruptive force, the all-important difference, or *écart.* It is only by attending to the act or fact of the writing of the text itself that we are able
to move beyond its operative distinctions. By reaffirming the subject as
a "tolerable falsehood," by bringing existentialist Marxism back despite
its theoretical "expulsion," and by making a certain form of arationalism
essential to the very possibility of a new African discursive rationality,
Mudimbe engages in what I would call a kind of performative reinscription (which he nicely terms "reprendre" in talking elsewhere about
contemporary African art), that is, an activity that is both singular and
reduplicative, that both takes up again an interrupted tradition and also
reworks it within a contemporary sociopolitical context (*Idea,* 154). This
metanarrative level opens up the space for a subjectivity that would begin
to move beyond the dichotomies anchored down by the opposition
between structure and agency.

One has to be careful about what this implies for a reading of Mudimbe's texts themselves. Denis Ekpo, in an article quoted earlier on
L'écart as a text that can be read as a phenomenological reduction of
space and time, both at a thematic level and at the level of narrative
structure and form, argues that Mudimbe's stylistic innovations mark
him as an important "anti-novelist," or a kind of African *nouveau ro-
mancier* (new novelist).[41] This claim is based on his understanding of
Mudimbe's writing, that is, the fragmented text is read as a product of a
schizophrenic self, so that Nara's schizophrenia underwrites, as it were,
the journal's essentially nonrepresentational mode, its narrative self-
sufficiency, as if this gap were the *écart* of the title. Ekpo refers at several
points to Mudimbe's writing as "deconstructed" or "in deconstruction,"
but he takes this to mean "impersonality" or "self-referentiality." Mudimbe is for him important because he has taken African literature "out"
from the unglamorous lower regions of simple ethnological or sociological document, or political commentary, and elevated it to a degree
of (postmodern) literary respectability. Yet this is still to remain within

the very operative distinctions (literary vs. sociological, "deconstructive" writing vs. historical, linear, referential writing, and so on) that Mudimbe's text undoes.

On the other side of this divide, Mudimbe's novels have attracted criticism precisely because they are too literary, abstract, and abstruse, are not more sociologically oriented, or do not deal with more pressing problems of underdevelopment or political violence. Ekpo seems to be working under the same misconceptions about deconstruction as Masolo, that is, Mudimbe's deconstructive project and the possibility of attending to the "idioms of everyday life" are for him mutually exclusive activities, when this repeats the very binarism that Mudimbe is in fact deconstructing. The *écart* of the title of his novel thus not only points to the divisions that seem to tear Nara apart (the past and the present, Europe and Africa, Isabelle and Aminata, his alleged schizophrenia, and so on—these are the interpretive lures, so to speak) but also *names the distance itself* between these dichotomies and the performative reinscription of his narrative. The *écart* marks the gap that opens up within his subjectivity, the madness upon which his African *cogito* is founded, and the novel is less a description of a descent into madness and death than the inscription of this gap, its continuous reinscription. It is the condition of possibility, founded upon a "tolerable" impossibility, of any adequate self-determination or self-representation (in other words, to read Nara's death as necessarily determined or precipitated by his existential crisis would be to misread the text's foundational indeterminability).

The relationship between Mudimbe's novels and his theoretical works now comes back into focus. According to some critics, such as Bernadette Cailler, the two should be separated out and considered entirely independently of each other.[42] Mouralis and Diawara claim there is a necessary link but take the novels as illustrations or dramatizations of the themes of his essays, something akin to Sartre's novels and plays in relation to his philosophy. Ekpo states that there is undoubtedly a connection (particularly between *L'écart* and *L'autre face du royaume*, whose subtitle is "Introduction à une critique des langages en folie" [Introduction to a critique of languages in madness]), but that the novels do not require the theoretical texts for their elucidation, since, consistent with his reading of their avant-garde textuality, they contain all the necessary elements to say the same thing without recourse to extratextual referents.[43] Few commentators, however, have looked at the relationship the other way round and considered the extent to which his fictional texts offer us important clues about how to read his collections of essays.

As we saw earlier in his discussion of Rigby's *Persistent Pastoralists,* at a rather crucial juncture in the essay Mudimbe invoked his own involvement with Marxism, turning to his subjective experiences as a means of authorizing his argument about the problematic nature of a dogmatic application of Marxist theory to an African context. In her recent book *A Critique of Postcolonial Reason,* Gayatri Spivak has lauded Mudimbe's *The Invention of Africa* as a model of the broad, profound, and serious scholarship that needs to subtend theoretical discussions of the representation of others, or the Other (including Europe as an Other).[44] Mudimbe's subjective intervention might appear to be at odds with his exhaustively researched histories of writings on Africa in Greek and Roman texts, his studies of myths of fables, his engagement with African philosophers, and so on, which bear witness to his formidable philological training, his epistemological rigor, and his academic seriousness. But this "subjectivism" is much more than the simple addition of a personal accent to his work and is in fact a strategic move common to Mudimbe's essays, or to the way in which he often frames a cluster of them. As we saw at the beginning of this chapter, he begins his preface to *Parables and Fables* in an autobiographical mode and makes it clear that this gesture has to be taken as a willing submission to his own thesis about the crucial importance of a reinscribed subjectivity in decolonizing discursive inventions of "Africa." He says that in his early collection of poems *Entretailles* (1973) he wished to "express the tension of a communion in which the very project of its expression would supersede the warring elements," and then reviewing his studies from his "African" period he writes, "I wished to invoke the rights of the subject and focus on the still-compelling soundness of a philosophy of subjectivity" (*Parables,* x, xi). Mudimbe acknowledges in a coda to the book the strategic significance of his subjectivist intervention in his discussion of Rigby, and says of this particular set of essays, "In this collection of subjective essays, instead of substituting positive images for the negative ones of yesterday that are still actual in today's media, I chose to expound my own reading and situate it at a very specific level"; and a little further on, "What comes out of this choice, now that I can look at it as a definite object, is an obsessive theme on otherness and a statement about the reader, that is, myself" (192, 193). Finally, he stresses that this autobiographical turn is not for his own personal fulfillment, but that he is saying something more universal, about emancipatory possibilities for Africans generally: "What my text indicates and designates is *our common and subjective freedom:* we can read and comment about the passions present in transcribed oral traditions, written texts, and performances in African and European languages and, indeed, reconstruct and/or deconstruct the history, arguments, and paradigms of the anthropological and colonial libraries" (193, emphasis added).

He develops this idea of the collective dimension of his project in the coda to *The Idea of Africa,* putting a greater emphasis on narrative agency. As he says, "These are thus my stories to my children," his own children, but also "those of their generation that might read me" (210). So although it is, as he confesses, "a subjective monologue about memories and interpretations" (212), it is precisely through this very act of subjective reinscription that he gives "storytelling," as a fundamental reclaiming and reorganization of knowledge, a truly political force. Mudimbe's "theoretical" essays thus come to assume their full power once they are taken to be, like his novels, subjective theoretical fictions. In effect, his collections of poetry, his account of his trip to the United States in the 1970s, and his novels, as well as his theoretical texts, are always firmly grounded in the autobiographical, and their status as "écrits de circonstance" is clearly marked. It should have come as no surprise that he chose to celebrate his fiftieth birthday by writing his intellectual autobiography, published as *Le corps glorieux des mots et des êtres* [The glorious body of words and beings]. We might ask, along with Mudimbe himself, whether this focus on agency as a problem of literary narrative does justice to the range and complexity of questions he reflects upon. As he puts it: "Telling stories is a way of disarticulating an author's pretensions, as well as of reformulating the supposed logical derivations of even a mathematical demonstration. In effect, the story organizes its own basis, operations, objectives and anticipations" (*Idea,* 213). And given that, as we have seen, the relationship between his theory and fiction is more than a simple literary "application" of his ideas, Mudimbe's reaffirmed subjectivity has the effect, ultimately, of putting into question the organization of Western disciplinary boundaries and hierarchies, that is, what we might term the West's "stories," particularly about Africa.

2

The
Autobiographical
Subject as
History-Teller

Despite its central role in the emergence of a literary tradition, there have been few attempts to circumscribe or contextualize Francophone African autobiography as a specific genre, with its own set of problems and ramifications, although several recent volumes of essays have begun to redress this critical lacuna.[1] One thing we can assert at the outset is that autobiography—to a far greater extent than in European literature—is for African writers an act of profound *political* significance, since the hitherto unexperienced form of self-affirmation it represents is a far more momentous act than it is for most Western autobiographers, many of whom are already established writers before they turn their hand to autobiography.[2] This in itself is not unusual, as it is often the case with minority, marginal, oppressed, or colonized groups that autobiography is the first step in a process of revalidation, or of reclaiming an identity.

In thinking about African narratives from this perspective one might make comparisons with the African American tradition and the period during and after the abolition era, when there was a proliferation of slave narratives. Indeed, many of the major African American writers of the nineteenth and early twentieth centuries began their writing careers essentially as autobiographers; one thinks, for example, of Frederick Douglass's *Narrative of the Life of Frederick Douglass, an American Slave,* Harriet Jacobs's *Incidents in the Life of a Slave Girl,* or Booker T. Washington's *Up from Slavery.* On the face of it, the same can be said for many

Francophone African writers, such as Camara Laye, Ousmane Sembene, Cheikh Hamidou Kane, or Aké Loba.[3] While in both cases the writing of autobiography confers importance and dignity on an individual life and at the same time serves as a historical document, a personal testimony that "sets the record straight," we should be attentive to the specificity of each emergent literature, and the entirely different set of historical and political circumstances involved. Thus, while many African American writers were self-educated, and their story was usually one of a long, continual struggle against the violently oppressive racism of the South, told once the author had fought his or her way out of this situation, for (primarily colonized) Francophone African writers, the very fact of their being able to write at all was in most cases an indication of a fairly "privileged" formal French educational training.

If all African writing has to confront, directly or indirectly, the ambiguities it inherits as a consequence of its colonial history, one should be concerned to chart the particular dimension and nuances of each set of double binds or hybrid conditions. The questions posed of sub-Saharan Francophone African autobiography thus have to do most obviously with *language* (can the African writer in French represent a personal or cultural identity through a language that is almost certainly not his or her own native tongue?), *history* (should the writer reject the present tragedies of the African world and look to the past for a sense of identity, or should he or she accept the cultural hybridity that has come with colonialism and look to the future?), and *cultural forms* (how does a writer coming from an oral tradition of collective artistic expression reconcile this legacy with the individualism that is a mainstay of Western literature, and all the more so of Western autobiography?). Within the recent literary history of Francophone Africa, autobiography tends to be devalued *as literature* when set against more innovative pre-Independence or postcolonial fiction writing, and to be read essentially as testimony, thereby taking on the status of a kind of nonliterary or preliterary genre, even among Africans. Within the Western literary tradition, this same devaluation has marked much women's writing, which was usually considered unimportant because it was so often in the form of personal narrative (diaries, letters, memoirs, and so on).

A classic early autobiographical text, Camara Laye's *L'enfant noir,* is especially interesting in terms of the traditionally held view that autobiography should function primarily as authentic testimony, since it was initially strongly criticized by African writers, in particular Mongo Beti, for being precisely *inaccurate* as a social document, and for deliberately avoiding any explicit stand with respect to the colonialist context of the time when the novel was published, 1953. The elegiac tone of the book is due in large part to the poignant nostalgia the narrator expresses for these childhood years, and his regret that he has not followed in his father's footsteps, that he has cut himself off from the community to which he belonged, and that he has, as he puts it, "left my father too soon." This sense of loss is more than a matter of tone or sentiment, however, since it goes to the very heart of the book. Christopher Miller has argued that the book's conscious enactment of its own hybrid condition is less a "repression of politics" than a "subtle subversion of colonial domination from within." This hybridity he describes as follows: "*L'Enfant noir* wants to describe the coherence of the traditional Mande world but keeps tripping over the conditions of its own creation: the break with the total system that motivates the nostalgic return."[4] The young Camara Laye is singled out in his community, and is already set apart, *because* he is destined to go on to receive a French education. Miller reads the division as the separation between "Camara" (the patronym or "jamu" which ties him to his father, and by genealogical extension to his entire, glorious family history) and "Laye" (the given name which individuates him, takes him away from Africa toward France and Francophone authorship). The book's doubleness, its sense of irretrievable loss within the very act of narrative retrieval, is the condition of its writing.

What interests me in particular in this interplay between autobiography, testimony, and the rewriting of history is that it is often relayed through a structure of exemplarity, which the African context seems readily to provide. In other words, the value and importance of collective participation in community—through, for example, the oral tradition, customs and rituals, ethnic identification—and the importance of ancestral or genealogical filiation mean that the singularity of a life to which the autobiography bears witness is seen at the same time as representative of the community. This is clearly reflected in the titles of these early autobiographies: *L'enfant noir, Femme d'Afrique, Koucoumba, l'étudiant noir*, and so on. Autobiography thus testifies not only to an individual life but also to the life of a community, and beyond that to a critical moment in African history, namely, the process of decolonization, which occurs against the backdrop of a sometimes traumatic shift from orality to literacy. Autobiography is significant in what it can tell us about the relationship between the subject and this particular historical narrative. The narratives that are produced are thus distinct from the various "autobiographical" modes that have long been part of the African tradition (*récits de vie,* autobiographical poems, the griot's or praise singer's self-presentation before narrating the family history, and so on) and one might venture the hypothesis that Francophone African autobiography is both a symptom of colonial alienation and at the same time potentially the means by which that alienation is overcome. I would like to explore this dynamic by rereading two other well-known texts of early Francophone African autobiography: Bernard Dadié's *Climbié* and Aoua Kéita's *Femme d'Afrique: La vie d'Aoua Kéita racontée par elle-même* [African woman: The life of Aoua Kéita narrated by herself].

Dadié's Grammaphonic Narrator

Climbié was completed in 1952 and published in 1956. It covers the first thirty-five years of Dadié's life, from 1916 to 1951. Although it appears to be an autobiographical novel, Dadié deliberately avoids classifying any of his works according to the categories of the European literary tradition. In talking of his works in general, he has nonetheless underlined the autobiographical impulse behind his writing:

> En tout cas ce ne sont pas des romans. C'est pourquoi je ne me considère pas comme romancier. Dans toutes ces oeuvres, il n'y a pas un personnage imaginé que nous puissions suivre . . . Au contraire, c'est un personnage réel, toujours moi, qui regarde [. . .] les différences et les points communs dans la perspective de l'humanisme universel. Nulle fiction si ce n'est dans le personnage de Climbié, et cela dans une certaine mesure seulement.

> [In any case they are not novels. This is why I do not consider myself a novelist. In all of these works, there is not some imaginary character whom we can follow . . . On the contrary, there is a real character, myself, who is looking at [. . .] the differences and points in common within the perspective of universal humanism. There is no fiction except in the case of Climbié, and there only to a certain extent.]5

Climbié is of particular interest, it seems to me, in its relation to Dadié's revival of the oral tradition. Dadié's first work, published in 1954, was a collection of African folklore legends, *Légendes africaines,* and he wrote a number of *contes* (folktales), entitled *Le pagne noir,* in 1955. Along with Birago Diop, he was one of the first writers to return to the oral tradition, and to make this return a significant step in reclaiming a literary, historical, and cultural heritage. Dadié himself has written of the importance of oral tales in an essay entitled "Le rôle de la légende dans la culture populaire des Noirs d'Afrique" [The role of legends in the popular culture of Black Africans], in which he says, "Tales and legends are our museums, our monuments, our commemorative street plaques, in short, our only books."[6] *Climbié* owes a lot of its style and narrative technique to the oral tradition, but I would argue that this "debt" does not just take the form of elements that are simply "borrowed" or adapted from orality. I would suggest that the text itself participates in the shift from orality to literacy, and as a result *Climbié* ends up being something other than a new genre or simply a hybrid, multiple genre. In the process it enables us to circumscribe more precisely the space that Francophone African autobiography, in many ways a pioneering literary movement, was instrumental in staking out.

The book tells the story, in the third person (although Climbié is clearly intended to be Dadié himself), of the passage from childhood to adolescence and young adulthood of Climbié as he grows up in the Côte d'Ivoire, leaves to go to the then prestigious Ecole William Ponty in Senegal, works in Dakar for ten years, and returns to the Côte d'Ivoire to become involved in the growing anticolonialist movement. It traces Climbié's path from innocence or ignorance of the historical and social conditions determining his life to a gradual political awakening: Dadié was, like Climbié in the book, imprisoned in 1949 for his political activism with the Rassemblement Démocratique Africain. Perhaps more significantly, the book recounts the education, the coming into being, of a writer. As Climbié gradually moves from being an innocent by-stander or spectator to a politically aware activist or actor helping to shape his country's destiny, we get increasingly longer glimpses into his inner thoughts, and to this end Dadié makes effective use throughout of free indirect discourse. Climbé also goes from being a child-listener to an adult-narrator by the end of the book, when he tells the story, ironically, of his inability to make a living selling books, since no one will buy them. The merging of the narrator and the main character is thus achieved by the end of the book. The text is characterized by elements derived from the oral tradition: for example, several tales are woven into the narrative; there are scenes describing griots imparting proverbial wisdom; the narrator has persistent recourse to the present tense in order to convey the immediacy of an oral narrative and to bring reader and narrator closer together; there is a good deal of repetition of certain phrases, and so on. Climbié himself becomes a storyteller by the end ("It's a long story, but it's worth telling . . . ," 148) and completes the circular process of the main character catching up with the narrator. While this is a common enough structure in the European autobiographical or *Bildungsroman* tradition, Climbié's transformation is quite distinctive in that he has undergone a major shift from a predominantly oral mode to a very self-conscious literary style. Yet this shift, and its far-reaching consequences, are prefigured quite early on in the text.

In the opening scene, Climbié is chased by the headmaster after being caught trying to write with charcoal on the wall of the school. However, far from wishing to deface the school building, he was simply engrossed in the sheer pleasure of learning to write and fails to understand his crime:

> Climbié était dégoûté de cette école où l'on ne permettait pas aux enfants d'écrire sur les grands tableaux que sont les murs. Péniblement on calligraphie une lettre, deux lettres que, tête penchée, on admire ensuite, satisfait du progrès réalisé. Puis on efface, on recommence afin de se faire la main. Avoir dix-huit en écriture, ce n'est pas facile et moins facile encore d'obtenir un de ces bons points que tout élève exhibe orgueuilleusement. On efface. Ça salit un peu le mur. C'est tout. Est-ce une faute bien grave qu'écrire sur le mur de l'école? La joie d'apprendre pour l'enfant, l'enthousiasme qui l'emporte, dirigent ses mains: sa fringale de savoir, son désir ardent de lire rapidement tous les livres de classe, lui mettent le charbon entre les doigts, lui font tirer la langue, pencher la tête, tout cela, hélas, n'est pas compris des grandes personnes. Si l'on ne peut écrire sur les murs de l'école, sur quels autres murs pourrait-on écrire? Vraiment, les grandes personnes, d'habitude si réfléchies, ne le sont plus lorsqu'elles ont affaire à des gosses . . . (98)

[Climbié was sick and tired of a school which forbade children to write on the walls, which were like big slates. Laboriously each child would draw one letter, two letters, which, keeping his head down, he would then admire, satisfied with the progress he had made. Then he would erase, and start over again, to train his hand. To get a score of eighteen in handwriting was not easy, and it was even harder to get one of those high marks that any student likes to show off. So one erased. It would dirty the wall a little, that's all. Is it so bad to write on the walls of a school? A child's joy in learning, the enthusiasm that sweeps him up, directs his hands. The keen appetite to learn, the passionate desire to read through the textbooks rapidly, all of them, compels him to take the charcoal between his fingers, makes him stick out his tongue and lower his head. All that, alas, is not understood by grown-ups. If you cannot write on the walls of a school, then what walls can you write on? Really now, grown-ups, usually so thoughtful, are no longer so when they have to deal with youngsters.] (2)

Climbié is transgressive from the beginning, stepping outside the limits imposed on him by the French colonial system. In a sense, the symbolic escape and dash for freedom continues until the end of the book. A number of interesting reversals are at work in this opening scene; in using charcoal to write on a white wall, Climbié is writing in black (as a black) on white, as opposed to the standard white on black of chalk on the slate. Thus Climbié is already writing in French (differently, as a black voice overlaying a white language), and he is doing so before he has even learned to write. Climbié also seems in this passage to be far more reasonable, as a child, than the adult colonials who would punish him for his transgression. So the colonial view of Africans as children needing the benefits of an "adult" civilization is also inverted here. Although Climbié is at his "degree zero" of critical insight at this point, the double register that is opened up by the play of reversals endows him with as much "grown-up" wisdom as he will have by the end of the book. Indeed, this reversal can be seen at a further remove to affect the very direction of the entire narrative (oral to written), since Climbié is at the start a writer and at the end a storyteller. As we shall see in the following chapter, this same principle of reversal is at work in Dadié's witty travel writings, where European culture is reevaluated through the eyes of an African traveler.

In the course of the book, the narrator intervenes at several points to make lucid political comments on the situation he is describing. The critical distance is not just ironic in its tone but ironic *inasmuch as* it is doubled up. Irony implies two different, contradictory frames of reference, and Dadié makes ample use of this potential to humorous ends. The irony is often directed against the pretensions of ethnography, the "science" used to legitimate colonialist ideology. In one scene at school, for example, the pupils invent the nickname *Cabou* for their headmaster. When the headmaster overhears them using it one day, the game seems to be up. However, Assé, "the most mischievous of the students," is quick to reply, "Dans notre langue, c'est ainsi que nous appelons la loupe" (114) [In our language, that's what we call a magnifying glass] (21), and the headmaster duly notes it down. The narrator comments: "Ah! que de chercheurs ont dû un jour être induits en erreur de la même façon que le Directeur; et, un jour, il soutiendra mordicus, que les Nègres de Côte-d'Ivoire appellent la loupe *Cabou*" (114) [How many scholars must have been misled in the same way as the Headmaster! Then one day, somewhere, he would defend to his death the proposition that the Negroes in the Côte d'Ivoire call the magnifying glass a *Cabou*] (21). Later on, following the suicide of the police commissioner, the narrator laments: "Ah! ces Blancs! . . . N'aurons-nous jamais fini de raconter l'histoire des Blancs désabusés qui se tuent en Afrique? Parce qu'une fiancée n'a pas répondu à une lettre, pan! on se tue, parce que l'argent a manqué dans la caisse, pan! on se tue" (133) [Ah, these Whites! . . . Will we never stop telling stories about disillusioned Whites who kill themselves in Africa? Because a fiancée hasn't answered a letter, bang! someone kills himself. Because money is missing from the cashbox, bang! someone kills himself] (43).[7]

However, irony is not used primarily to satirize colonialism or to expose the absurdities of the European way of life, although this is one of its most telling effects. The ironic position that the narrator assumes with respect to the whites allows him to create a gap (that narrows as the story progresses) between himself and his character Climbié. One feature that is thus highlighted is the shift from a world in which orality is the predominant form of cultural expression to a world opened up by literature. Dadié uses the device of having a narrator who already knows telling the story of Climbié, who gradually gains insight into what is going on around him and learns to articulate it. As an adolescent, for example, his uncle Assouan Koffi shows him a book illustrating antiblack racial violence in Harlem, and Climbié is still too young to understand: "Climbié ne comprenait pas tout cela. Ce qui l'avait frappé, c'était ce nègre bien habillé enchaîné et escorté par des policiers blancs dans une grande rue où les gens marchaient sans même regarder ce qui se passait autour d'eux" (136) [Climbié did not understand all this. What struck him was that this well-dressed Negro was in handcuffs and being escorted down a main street, where the people passing by did not even notice what was going on around them] (47). His uncle acts as a spokesman for the adult narrator and begins to explain racial prejudice to Climbié, urging him to read and learn the history of his people.

One of the most symptomatic moments in the book in terms of the space that Dadié is staking out in *Climbié* comes when Climbié is at school in Grand-Bassam in the Côte d'Ivoire. The scene is a description of the common and notorious practice in French schools in Franco-phone African colonies of undermining the children's use of native languages. The best student was given a little wooden cube called a *symbole,* which had to be passed on to any pupil unfortunate enough to be caught speaking his or her native language, who in turn got rid of it in the same way. The *symbole* thus functioned as a kind of stigma and was obviously used as a very effective means of dividing the students against themselves and imposing mandatory use of "correct" French. As the narrator explains:

> Vraiment le sabotage collectif de la langue française est quelque chose de terrible. Partout l'on entend "baragouiner" une langue aussi subtile, aérienne, féminine, une langue qui ressemble à du vent allant au gré de la brise, lorsqu'une amie vous la chuchote à l'oreille, une langue qui semble le suave murmure d'une madone, une langue qui laisse après elle une traînée persistante de notes joyeuses! [. . .] Il fallait d'urgence trouver un remède à cette endémie, car à force d'entendre "ma commandant, lui y a dit que son femme il a gagné petit," "moi, y a pas moyen miré Pernod," pour "mon commandant, il dit que sa femme a accouché," "je ne vois pas le Pernod," nombreux étaient les Européens qui avaient fini par avoir les nerfs à fleur de peau [. . .] Le Nègre parlait mal un français que l'Européen ne comprenait pas. L'Européen essayait donc de baragouiner, la mort dans l'âme, à sa façon, son doux français, que le Nègre encore ne comprenait pas.

Alors, énervé, exaspéré, s'en voulant presque à lui-même d'avoir descendu sa langue du socle où l'ont mise les autres nations, ne sachant quel saint linguiste ou polyglotte évoquer, il hurlait: "Alors, vous ne comprendrez jamais le français?" (107–8)

[The collective sabotage of the French language was indeed a terrible thing. Everywhere one heard pidgin versions of a language which is so very refined, airy, and feminine, a language which is like down floating in the breeze or the words a sweetheart whispers in your ear, a language resembling the soft murmur of a madonna, a language which leaves behind it a memory of melody! [. . .] It was absolutely imperative to find a cure for this epidemic, so that one might hear *Mon commandant, il dit que sa femme a accouché* instead of *Ma commandant, lui y a dit que son femme il a gagné petit,* or *Je ne vois pas le Pernod* instead of *Moi, y a pas moyen miré Pernod.* After hearing such language for a while, many Europeans became so thin-skinned, so nervously on edge, that their hands and feet, already fidgety, would fly out of control [. . .] the black man spoke French so poor that no European understood it. Then the Europeans, to the death of his soul, would try to pidgin-talk his beautiful language, which still the black man did not understand. Finally, nervous and exasperated, angry with himself for having brought down his language from the pedestal where other nations had put it, and not knowing which saint, linguistic or polyglot, to invoke, he would shout: "So then, will you never learn to understand French?] (13–14)

The passage again illustrates the way in which the French language functioned metonymically as one of the main vehicles for the imposition of cultural values. But, what is the relationship of the narrator to the French language here? Given Dadié's elegant classical style, one would think he was siding with the French authorities. However, his sympathy is obviously with Climbié, and from that perspective the passage on the French language reads quite ironically. The children here are clearly innocent of any crime and are in fact able to make the shift from their native language to a kind of creolized French that is perfectly understandable even if it is grammatically transgressive. The problem arises—and the *symbole* is introduced—precisely because the French are unable to go halfway. Where the children have been able to circumscribe a creolized space for themselves, the French colonials come up with a kind of blank, *bara-*

gouiner, which is used for both the children's successful "corruption" of classical French and the French officials' frustrated attempts to meet the children on their own linguistic ground. The verb *baragouiner* is well chosen here, since its etymology—it was applied to Bretons, and comes from the Breton words *bara* (bread) and *gwen* (wine)—clearly evokes the origin of the *symbole,* which was first used with Breton schoolchildren. Faced with linguistic strangeness, the French language falls back on its own myth of being the language of philosophical clarity, of rationality, and of civilized thought. The linguistic and ideological stakes in defending this space are high, and while the child Climbié seems unaware of the disruption caused in occupying it, the adult narrator clearly revels in its subtle power. Although the immediate and apparent victory of the *symbole* belongs to the French, the linguistic territory it cedes is precisely the space within which Dadié is able to write a book such as *Climbié.*[8]

In the second half of the story, while Climbié is in prison, he goes through periods of increasing introspection, as illustrated here by one short passage:

> Certains mots dans la bouche de l'Africain auraient-ils un autre sens? Climbié voudrait ne pas réfléchir. Mais peut-on s'empêcher de réfléchir?
>
> Lui, Climbié, il est un "objet," parce qu'il n'est pas un citoyen-métro. Il n'a même pas, juridiquement, la même valeur que tous ses amis naturalisés Français qui sont là autour de lui. A quoi a-t-il droit? (216)
>
> [Is it that certain words, on the lips of an African, have a different meaning? Climbié did not want to think about it. But can anybody stop thinking?
>
> He, Climbié, was an "object," because he was not a natural-born French citizen. He did not even have the same value, juridically, as all the naturalized friends who were there with him. What did he have a right to?] (143)

The language here is alive with intellectual questioning and indicates both a personal soul-searching and a final political awakening. Indeed, it is difficult to discern who is talking at certain points. Is it free indirect discourse, or is it the narrator addressing us directly? It is as if the narrator has now almost caught up with himself at this stage, a process that is in one sense completed when Climbié narrates his story at the end in the first person.[9] It also brings into clearer focus why Dadié would choose to write an autobiography in the third person, since the story it tells is one of acquiring historical and narrative agency, of moving from being an object to a subject of history.

It is through irony that Dadié expresses this hybrid quality of *Climbié,* and in this respect irony functions as a structural device that foregrounds the unique historical circumstances of the book's composition. It is neither a nostalgic yearning for an idyllic precolonial world, nor a detached, "objective" account of this period in the history of the Côte d'Ivoire, but the story of a transition from a world in which orality is the dominant mode of self-representation to one in which literature takes on an increasing importance. Orality is not only *represented* but inextricably bound up with the narrative development. However, is there by the end a sense of a loss of the oral tradition? Is it also the story of the irretrievable passing away not only of a way of life but also of the immediacy associated with orality? Several passages in *Climbié* do seem to suggest this. At one point, for example, the narrator comments: "Climbié, chaque jour un peu plus, oublie ses sources . . . " (106) [Every day, slowly but surely, Climbié forgot his origins . . .] (11). If we are to look to Dadié's own renderings of folktales, which are doubtless indissociable from his ardent remembering of his own childhood experiences, we may find something of an answer. In one of the legends, "L'aveu" [The confession], we find a regret very similar to the one expressed in *Climbié.* The narrator of this tale, in lamenting the way young Africans are abandoning their language and culture, talks of "the old syntax being abandoned today by a generation which, captivated by the mirages of the West, is punctuating its language with ninety percent foreign words."[10] It takes a while to realize that this kind of "contemporary" observation should have no place in a traditional legend. Dadié's "intervention" is extremely significant, since it is nothing less than an act of subjective reinscription into the entire oral narrative tradition, which requires that a legend be told anew each time, with the individual variations and rhetorical embellishments as important as the "main story line." In fact the "oral tradition" is anything but the pure logocentrism one wistfully imagines it to be, and critics such as Henry Louis Gates Jr.

have shown the oral language inherited by Americans of African descent to be extremely rich in pure fabrication, inventive wordplay, and random troping.[11]

The question remains whether this focus on the text's doubleness, on its own rhetorical status, has the effect of defusing its political potential. I would argue that it does not, but rather it is precisely because of its unique historical context that it is an act (or a performance) of extreme political effectiveness. The assertion of this "difference within" resituates the book and firmly anchors it within its time (or rather, *Climbié* is a rewritten history and the history of that rewriting; the telling itself in effect opens up a new historical space and time). In other words, if *Climbié* tells the story of its own coming into being, then this becoming doubles as an act of reappropriation of a history, and performs the dual function of enlightening a European audience (who think they know this history) and, for an African audience, of narrating their people's own struggle (through the representative of Climbié) to understand, to form a political consciousness, and to recover the right to become their own "history-tellers." We will see in Aoua Kéita's *Femme d'Afrique* another version of this process, and an equally important testimony to the central role of autobiography in the reaffirmation of subjectivity and historical agency.

Attending to the Birth of Na(rra)tion

Published in 1975, *Femme d'Afrique*—along with Nafissatou Diallo's account of her childhood and quasi-ethnographic record of life in pre-Independence Senegal, *De Tilène au Plateau: Une enfance dakaroise,* which appeared in the same year—marks the entrance of women into Francophone African autobiographical writing. Both Kéita and Diallo were, coincidentally, midwives, although this should not be surprising, given that midwifery and teaching were the only two professions available to educated African women of their generation, although their very different origins and experiences produced markedly distinct narratives. Kéita was a bold and outspoken militant activist, both for the USRDA (Union Soudanaise du Rassemblement Démocratique Africain) as well as for the nascent women's organizations associated with this anticolonial political movement, and then subsequently a leading political figure in Mali in the early years following Independence. Until very recently both Kéita's and Diallo's texts have been taken simply as sociohistorical records of the times and have thus suffered from the tendency to view such texts as nonliterary or preliterary, as memoirs rather than literary autobiography.[12] Yet their very existence should alert any reader, however dismissive, to the fact that simply as the first explicitly autobiographical texts by African women, they are quite exceptional. Kéita's account of her life, from her early childhood in the 1930s to the eve of Mali's Independence in 1960 (even though it was written in 1975 and makes occasional reference to the subsequent course of events following Independence), is in fact a remarkable historical and cultural overview of the period in what was the French Sudan, especially of the growing women's movement, in which she played such a central role, and of the turbulent years of jockeying for political power among the various parties in the 1950s.

Her exceptional status, though, has left critics unable to agree upon the quality or significance of her text itself. As a highly articulate and well-read *évoluée,* and as someone very conscious of her privileged social position and noble lineage within the Malinké community in the French Sudan, Kéita has been accused of various forms of elitism or condescension toward her less privileged compatriots. Madeleine Borgomano, for instance, makes the rather questionable assertion that Kéita, along with all African women autobiographers, writes principally for a Western audience: "The addressee of the discourse of these texts seems to be essentially the other, the white man, the foreigner."[13] Jane Turrittin, in writing on *Femme d'Afrique* as an important sociohistorical document, compares Kéita's quite narrowly circumscribed political role, rather unfavorably, to the more radical feminist program set out by Sékou Touré in Guinea.[14] And Nicki Hitchcott expresses disappointment at Kéita's resistance to the "intimate confessional" mode, seeing in her adoption of the more "masculine" style of objective testimonial something of a betrayal both of a "feminist" solidarity and of the expectation of personal, emotional revelations (or what she terms the private space of Kéita's "herstory"), which are said to distinguish women's from men's autobiographical practices. As Hitchcott puts it, "Frequent slippages between the first and third persons suggest an objectification of herself as functional unit: whenever 'je' becomes 'la sage-femme' [midwife], then the autobiographical pact is broken and the empathetic reader disengages from the text."[15]

I would like to take up this last point, since it draws attention to the narrative form of Kéita's autobiography, but only to again disqualify it as autobiography on the basis of the assumption that male and female autobiography are two distinct genres, a binarism that brings with it a whole range of associated oppositions: memoirs vs. autobiography, public vs. private, history vs. herstory, literate vs. oral, Western vs. African, constructed self vs. "natural" self, and so on. But I would like to argue, to the contrary, that it is precisely an attention to the narrative modality of Kéita's text that makes many of these distinctions inoperative and moreover allows us to gain a better grasp of the truly radical implications of this text. I would like to contextualize my own reading in terms of the relationship between the formation, or birth, of a nation and the coming into being of a very self-consciously female African autobiographical subject. In the case of Kéita's autobiography, subject-formation and nation-formation are closely intertwined, and this allegorical relationship seems to be confirmed by her decision to end her story at the dawn of Independence, and the birth of the nation of Mali, which then becomes the teleological justification for the preceding historical narrative.

The word *nation* is linked etymologically to *native* and *nature*, both derived from the Latin root *natus* (born), and although the whole question of nationalism and nations is one of considerable complexity, this etymology nonetheless points to the enduring view that nations are essentially defined by a natural bond between the indigenous inhabitants of a country and that country as the place of one's birth, a kind of atavistic connection that is apparently as deep-rooted as the etymology suggests.[16] More recent theories of nationalism have questioned this assumption of a natural, given order and have traced the history of the concept of nation, seeing it as a relatively recent invention or political myth. Ernest Gellner, in his *Nations and Nationalism,* describes this myth as follows: "But nationalism is *not* the awakening of an old, latent, dormant force, though that is how it does indeed present itself. It is in reality the consequence of a new form of social organization, based on deeply internalized, education-dependent high cultures, each protected by its own state."[17] This analysis leads Gellner to critique nationalism as an ideology that produces the myth of its own naturalization, and that depends on the perpetuation of this myth. The "people" as a kind of preindustrial homogenous collectivity is thus seen as an invention of nationalism. As Gellner puts it: "Generally speaking, nationalist ideology suffers from pervasive false consciousness. Its myths invert reality: it claims to defend folk culture while it is in fact forging high culture; it claims to protect an old folk society while in fact helping to build up an anonymous mass society."[18] This analysis would appear to apply to much early Francophone African writing, which is indeed the product of a small privileged educated class who, like Kéita, speak about, and also claim to speak for, the many, often in the name of "traditional" culture.

Benedict Anderson, in his *Imagined Communities,* redefines Gellner's model, providing a corrective to the negative implications of the latter's notion of invented nationalism as "false consciousness," and instead draws out the creativity of this narrative process of inventions of community, that is, "the style in which they are imagined."[19] Anderson translates Gellner's concept of nationalism as "high culture" inventing its own atavistic roots into a process of gradual transformation of the relationship between nation, narration, and time, aided largely by the spread in the eighteenth and nineteenth centuries of what he terms "national print-languages." He adapts Walter Benjamin's opposition in "Theses on the Philosophy of History" between the "Messianic" time of the past, when all time was fused into *simultaneity,* and the discrete, relativized, "homogenous, empty time" of the modern era, what he calls the time of the "meanwhile," in which the cosmic-universal simultaneity of sacred ontology is transformed into "transverse, cross-time, marked not by prefiguring and fulfilment, but by temporal coincidence, and measured by clock and calendar."[20] In other words, time as differential seriality replaces time as synchronicity. Anderson sees this fundamental shift as a necessary prelude to the horizontal, homogenous worlds of modern nations, and thus as the condition of possibility of narratives of imagined communities. While certainly offering a more sophisticated model than Gellner of the development of nationalism as a problem of narrative, he does not challenge the basic premise of Gellner's argument, namely, that we move from the origin of a supposedly natural order of existence within a community to one that is mediated by narrative, whether conceived of as "false consciousness" or as a necessary modality of "invention." For both theorists of nationalism, this historical process itself is conceived in terms of a sequence or linear progression that is in essence *naturalized.* The trouble with both models for our concerns is that they cannot account for the many ambivalent, ironic, or rebellious positions that the Francophone African subject takes up *within* apparently "homogenized" national narratives, and Kéita's autobiography is one such example.

If one were to read *Femme d'Afrique* simply as political memoirs, as a "homogenous narrative" of the nationalist movement in the French Sudan—and thus classed among the memoirs of lives of notable Africans, such as Birago Diop's five-volume *Mémoires* or Amadou Hampaté Bâ's *Amkoullel, l'enfant Peul: Mémoires*—it would seem to exemplify Gellner's thesis of "high" cultural appropriation of a "low" indigenous community, and in its concern for realism and chronometric precision to conform also to Anderson's model of the "horizontal time" of modern narratives of the nation. However, it is also possible to read it as rooted in, and indebted to, the "griot" tradition of praise singing, as a story of the heroine's glorious triumph over adversity, a heroine who is also the praise singer herself. Although she is narrating the process of decolonization in the French Sudan and the emergence of the African nation of Mali, the story she tells is indissociable from the emergence of her own autobiographical self, the coming into being of her subjectivity. Her text plays out the analogy between autobiography as a moment or movement of self-determination and self-narration, and the political and historical self-determination that comes with Independence. The text's ambivalence makes it impossible to locate it either as an example of "folk culture" or as a narrative participating in the construction of the "imagined community" of Mali, since its "nationalism," as well as its subjectivity, is formed in the process of negotiating between these two positions. In consequence, it provides important insights into the relationship between autobiography, gender, and history in an African context.

Kéita's gender is of course central to her story, and not only in terms of the symbolism of the link between her professional role as a midwife and the ways in which she attends with equal devotion to the birth of her nation. Although this metaphor might appear to naturalize and reinscribe her political role in terms of what was culturally acceptable for women of her time, her life was in fact one of constant transgression of social rules and expectations (she struggles against the French, against the intransigence and patriarchy of local chiefs, against Islamic beliefs and practices such as polygamy, against dress codes, and so on). Her relationship with her mother exemplifies the ambivalence that characterizes the contradictory nature of her text. While her mother represents the very forces of tradition that Kéita challenges, both culturally and politically, she is at the same time a crucial point of reference for her daughter throughout her narrative, and the sign of her continuing attachment to tradition through (maternal) genealogical filiation. Kéita explains to the reader at one point: "Portant le nom de ma grand'mère maternelle, ma mère m'appelait toujours «mah», ce qui signifie «maman». Elle ne prononçait le nom «Aoua» que lorsque, mécontente, elle me faisait des observations" [Since I had the same name as my maternal grandmother, my mother would always call me "mah," which means "mama." She only used the name "Aoua" when she was unhappy and telling me off for something].[21] A little later she says, "Ma mère me disait souvent qu'elle regrettait d'avoir donné le nom de sa mère à une fille qui parle beaucoup, qui parle comme une griotte" [My mother would often tell me that she was sorry she had given her mother's name to a daughter who talks a lot, who talks like a *griotte*] (154).

There is an interesting contrast here to Camara Laye's divided identity. While his sense of loss derives from his premature separation from his community ("I left my father too soon"), Kéita's relationship to her mother is one of constant departure and *return,* despite the latter's disapproval of her daughter's political activities and nontraditional lifestyle. Her given name is a source of conflict between mother and daughter because the mother wants her daughter to be as quiet and unassuming as her own mother was, to be worthy of the name "mah."[22] However, it is precisely by talking "comme une griotte" that she takes on the mantle of her family name, the illustrious Kéita. Although she never becomes a mother (she is forced by her mother-in-law into divorcing her husband because of her infertility, and her mother is in fact the only one able to console her during the period of this devastating loss), it is through Aoua's narrative that her mother lives on and that the latter's stories, which so captivated Aoua in her childhood, are preserved.

Kéita gives several examples of her traditional storytelling talents early on in her autobiography, but it is the manner in which she tells her *own* story that is most significant. She is always very conscious of her status as an exceptional woman: she is, for example, "the only emancipated young woman in Gao at the time" (32), "the only woman in the group who could read" (110), and is in her professional capacity celebrated as one of the greatest midwives of her age. On returning to Gao after thirteen years away, she is greeted as a returning heroine: "Clear the way, Aoua Kéita has arrived, our chief has arrived, the mother of our children has come, our mother has come!" (84). She receives equal recognition for her political activities, is often applauded at party meetings, and in fact generally charts her rise to stardom in the party ranks. As such she presents herself as something of a legendary figure, and this may appear as the height of self-glorification and immodesty, but it conforms entirely to the excessive praise-giving role of the "griot" or "griotte." The art of speaking is in fact traditionally reserved for women and griots in many African oral traditions, although female griots are often constrained in ways that male griots are not.[23] They are, to quote Sonia Lee, "not allowed to sing the genealogies or transmit the public speeches of the notable men in society."[24] Kéita does this quite freely, and thus reinscribes herself into a traditional genealogy while at the same time subverting it.

What is unusual about this text, though, is that because she is an autobiographer, Kéita is both the subject and the object of her tale of glorious rise to prominence, so that the subtitle of her text—"la vie d'Aoua Kéita racontée par elle-même"—is not superfluous but expresses perfectly the fusion of first and third person, subject and object. Rather than indicating an unfortunate "objectification" of herself as "la sage-femme," or a "slippage" from first to third person, this ambivalence is the very essence of her narrative. Although the subtitle, in its emphatic use of the third person, is reminiscent of the subtitles of African American slave narratives, this fusion of first and third persons has a very different function in Kéita's text. As a narrative form the text is without precedent, it is sui generis, and as such can be seen as a founding text, or more precisely a text about founding a genre, about instituting (the self and the nation), and is in this respect analogous to the Malinké epic of Soundiata, the founder of the great Mali empire in the thirteenth century. Although a unique text, it is not intended for all that to be incomparable or inimitable but to serve as a model or stimulus for future generations of writers; indeed, at one point in the narrative, she recommends to her literate fellow countrymen to put their experiences down in writing, thereby contributing to the constitution of "a historical treasure-trove for future generations" (239).

Kéita's text is not, of course, a retelling of the Soundiata epic and cannot be directly compared to the many written versions that now exist; it relates to that epic very differently.[25] On the one hand, its almost obsessive concern for precise historical detail is incompatible with the fluidity and variation one might expect from an oral epic, while on the other, this rewritten history is itself authorized only by Kéita's reclaiming of her heritage as a "griotte" through a matrilineal genealogical descendance. It is thus situated in a very equivocal position between orality and historical testimony. One of the most telling moments of return to her childhood that interrupts the historical linearity of the narrative, and once more underlines the influence of her mother in her life, comes late in her story when she relates as a girl seeing her mother give birth to her younger brother (265–67). She learns subsequently that her mother would always refuse the intervention of a midwife, preferring to deliver all her children unassisted. One could thus pursue the analogy between writing and giving birth further: if Kéita is both subject and object of her own narrative, her mother is also both subject and object of the birthing process, both midwife and mother. Given Kéita's inability to become a mother herself, does she, as some have suggested, sublimate her infertility into the symbolic role, as a famous midwife, of "mother of the people"?

This would seem to be the perfect metaphor for her "exemplarity," the connection between her individual life and that of her nation. In fact, both *mother* and *people* are terms that are considerably complicated in the course of the narrative. The qualities Kéita most associates with "motherhood" are pride and a defiant self-sufficiency, which are characteristics of both mother and daughter. The aloof, iconic status that critics often accord to Kéita's "symbolic" motherhood (seen, for example, in her camaraderie with the other "elite" women activists, mainly the wives of the male political leaders) goes hand in hand, however, with her grassroots activism as a tireless campaigner for the USRDA, her attention to the minutiae of daily life and the material conditions of rural women, and her determination to educate women about voting rights, money management skills, basic hygiene, childbirth methods, postnatal care, and so on. She actively takes advantage of the many contacts she makes through her midwifery, of course, but also uses a more deliberate strategy of getting to meet women through such activities as knitting, embroidery, and sewing. She travels a great deal, spends time with a vast number of people, especially rural women of many different ethnic groups, and despite her role as a political representative, never reifies them or sees them as a collective group, and indeed often admits to her inability to "reach" many of them. "The people" thus becomes an unstable, shifting referent in the text. The "progress" she makes with her own educational efforts is paralleled by an increased self-questioning and humility with respect to rural women and traditional beliefs, an awareness of the limitations of what she is able to achieve for women in her country.

So there is in the text a double, bidirectional, or counterdirectional movement: self and nation are at once constantly being formed, but also *un*formed or deconstituted. We can see this in the title itself, *Femme d'Afrique,* which is caught between the modesty of her contingent existence as just another African woman, one of the many she celebrates in the course of her narrative, and the very self-consciously literary awareness of her iconic and legendary status as "mother of the people," representing all African woman. Kéita is thus *neither* just the "representative" female subject, *nor* the isolated objective (possibly masculinized) witness to this important moment in Mali's history, but is somewhere in between the two, in a third, "performative," space, which is other than a kind of autobiographical androgyny.[26] What this writing performs, in a sense, is the breakdown of the allegory of exemplarity, which we might see as feminist to the extent that it renders inoperable the rather static conflation of individual masculine destiny and national destiny which we find in much early African writing. This irruptive movement undoes the text's homogeneity, its autonomy or "autotelic" structure, but is at the same time the process that enables the subject and nation to come into being.

It is perhaps Homi Bhabha who has most forcefully articulated the performative thrust of this ambivalent inscription in national narratives. In "DissemiNation," one of the key chapters in *The Location of Culture,* Bhabha describes this ambivalence as a split between "signifying the people as an a priori historical presence, a pedagogical object," and "the people constructed in the performance of narrative, its enunciatory 'present' marked in the repetition and pulsation of the national sign."[27] It is the "time" of this disjunction that Bhabha tries to circumscribe, a time that interrupts the homogenous, horizontal time of the nation taken as pedagogical object. For Bhabha, both Gellner and Anderson conceive of nations in terms of a narrative of historical emergence and fail to allow for the "in-between time," which he calls the "iterative time of reinscription."[28] What texts such as Aoua Kéita's give us is an example of Bhabha's "national, anti-nationalist histories of the 'people.'"[29] Her rebelliousness with respect to the misogyny, patriarchal attitudes, and political corruption she confronts and courageously challenges is in a sense not the truly transgressive feature of her autobiography, since her role is ultimately reinscribed within the USRDA's male-dominated political structures. Rather, it is her painfully frank account of her struggle to win over the women that renders the "people" irreducibly multiple, and the nation a heterogeneous rather than a homogenous space.

This is not to be understood in terms of "pluralism" or "cultural diversity," which are perfectly compatible with Anderson's "narratives of the nation," but as a rupture in the linearity of historical progress to which her autobiography at first seems to conform. We can see this in her relationship to language at a number of telling moments, or rather as an effect of translation. The text itself is written in an extremely elegant, almost hypercorrect French, but at crucial points this is an avowed source of awkwardness. On one occasion, at a public meeting following her return to Gao, she realizes she has forgotten a lot of her Sonraï and thinks she can get away with using Bambara instead:

Les plus gros reproches concernaient ma façon de parler. Avant la fin de mon premier séjour, je parlais correctement le sonraï, sans accent. C'est ce que toutes mes camarades avaient à l'esprit, aussi, elles engagèrent toutes la conversation dans cette langue si harmonieuse que j'étais peinée de massacrer. Or après treize ans de périple à travers les pays bambara, malinké, kasonké et samoko, j'avais oublié une bonne partie de mon sonraï. Ne voulant ni le bafouer ni perdre mon temps à chercher mes mots, je répondais en bambara. Cela fut très mal pris, car certaines pensaient que ce n'était plus la même Aoua qui chantait si bien en sonraï. Aussitôt, pour enlever l'équivoque, je me mis à parler en sonraï—ce qui les fut toutes rire. (85)

[What they reproached me for most was how I talked. By the end of my first visit I spoke Sonraï with perfect fluency. Since this is what all my women comrades were still thinking, they all began to converse in this most harmonious of languages, which I was loath to ruin. Now after thirteen years traveling around Bambara, Malinké, Kasonké, and Samoko parts of Africa, I had forgotten a good deal of my Sonraï. Not wishing to treat it with disrespect, nor to waste my time searching for my words, I answered in Bambara. This was received very badly, for

some of the women thought that I was a different Aoua from the one
who sang so well in Sonraï. So in order to clear up any confusion I
began to speak in Sonraï—which made them all laugh.]

Later on, this time at a political rally for one of the women's organizations she is trying to set up, she is called away to perform an emergency
childbirth and gives her speech to someone else to read out:

> Mon rapport fut lu au congrès par une militante. A notre première
> rencontre cette dernière me parla des difficultés dans lesquelles mon
> absence l'avait jetée: texte trop long qu'elle dut raccourcir des deux
> tiers au moins, touffu et presque incompréhensible, niveau trop élevé,
> etc. La camarade avait peut-être raison car les dirigeants de Bamako
> ne m'ont ni louée ni blâmée. Ils ne m'ont fait aucune remarque sur
> mon texte. (297)

> [My speech was read out at the congress by a woman militant. At the
> first opportunity we had to talk to each other, she spoke to me about
> the difficulties that my absence had caused her: an overlong text that
> she had to shorten by at least two-thirds, dense and almost incompre-
> hensible, the language was too formal, and so on. The woman comrade
> was perhaps right because the party leaders in Bamako neither praised
> nor criticized me. They made no comment upon my text.]

One could see these incidents simply as examples of her aloofness, her
separation from the people, but at the same time they mark a fragmentation of her identity ("ce n'était plus la même Aoua") and point to a
scattering of the very oneness upon which national narratives rely.

In fact it gives us a very different history, one that is no longer determined by its adherence to principles of testimonial authenticity. Indeed,
in these terms it would be *inauthentic,* if we think of it as a product of
"false consciousness" in Gellner's sense of the term, that is, as an elegant
French "translation" of an African experience. In this respect, it would
be characterized, as we saw, by an avoidance, internally, of intimate revelation, as well as externally, of any mention of the political failures of
the Modibo Kéita regime after Independence, since the narrative is essentially predetermined by its teleology of Malian Independence. However, if we take into account its many disruptive, self-doubting moments,
and its double movement, it can be read in terms of an ambivalence that

interrupts the "homogeneity" of this national narrative. As such, *Femme d'Afrique* is not inscribed within the linearity of the narrative of historical emergence but makes a reinscription of the subject, and of the nation, the very condition of possibility of "history-telling," and autobiography as perhaps its exemplary narrative form. Like Dadié's *Climbié*, it is a performative political act, but one that has a truly feminist agenda to it, what Irène Assiba d'Almeida terms "practical African feminism."[30] In other words, and this is a question that I will explore in greater depth in chapter 6, the process of Kéita's self-discovery as a woman writer is indissociable from her solidarity with all African women.

3

The Ironic
Subject in
Bernard Dadié's
Travel Writing

Between 1959 and 1968 Bernard Dadié published a series of semiautobi-ographical accounts of his travels to three of the centers of Western civ-ilization: *Un nègre à Paris* [*An African in Paris*], *La ville où nul ne meurt* [*The City Where No One Dies*], and *Patron de New York* [*One Way: Bernard Dadié Observes America*].[1] These texts have always been read either in isolation or as source material for more general thematic studies of Dadié's oeuvre as a whole.[2] His accounts of his trips to France, Italy, and the United States echo the common theme within traditional African folktales of the journey of initiation and also reflect an increasingly important preoccupation in Francophone African literature of the 1950s and 1960s, that of the young African going for the first time to the metropolis (writers such as Ousmane Sembene, Cheikh Hamidou Kane, and Aké Loba had written before Dadié of their experiences in France). Dadié's texts are distinctly different, however, in that while his fellow African writers focused on their loneliness, the violence of the clashes between African and European culture, the racism they were subject to, and their miserable living and working conditions, Dadié's narratives are written with a cheerfulness and apparently naive sense of wonder.

What I would like to do is to show how Dadié, through a number of startlingly effective narrative strategies, undertakes a subtle critique of Western civilization. There is an explicit continuity linking the Paris and Rome narratives, even though they were in fact distinct visits, but in foregrounding the fictional reworking of his experiences, he thereby enters into a rather complex negotiation with the rhetoric and ideology of Western travel writing as a genre, which I will try to delineate. *Patron de New York,* while taking up many of the themes of *Un nègre à Paris* and *La ville où nul ne meurt* and repeating a number of their rhetorical gestures, engages with a different range of issues, which produces a distinctly different narrative. In the previous chapter Dadié's irony emerged as an important structural device in *Climbié,* and it will be no less important in his travel writings. In fact the stakes are raised even higher in these narratives, since he engages actively (performatively) with the binarisms of colonialist and racialist discourses. The risk he runs in his ironic engagement with these discourses is that he could potentially undermine his own attempts at subversion. What I will attempt to show, however, is that he moves beyond the constraints of an objective, *constative* narrative precisely through what I have termed a performative reinscription of subjectivity, of which his travel writings are consummate examples.

Paris

Un nègre à Paris is written in the form of a series of long letters by the narrator, named Tanhoe Bertin, addressed to his unnamed friend back in the Côte d'Ivoire, recounting the events of his trip, from the circumstances of his obtaining the plane ticket to the end of his three-week stay in Paris. This first-person narrator marvels with wide-eyed enthusiasm at every detail of the city, at the customs and lifestyle of the Parisians themselves, and also, in more reflective passages, at the history, politics, religion, institutions, and literature of France in general. He attempts to understand the strangeness of the whole experience by constant reference back to, and comparison with, life in his village in the Côte d'Ivoire, concerned as much to establish the characteristics that the two cultures share as to record the differences that separate them. So, for example, there are many observations such as the following: "Sous leur dure carapace, ils demeurent des hommes comme nous [. . .] Je rencontre partout des hommes comme nous: bavards, timides, audacieux . . . " (140) [But underneath their hard exteriors, the Parisians are just like us [. . .] Everywhere I go, I see people like us: talkative, shy, courageous . . .] (97). It is important to note that Dadié was a devout Catholic and an avowed humanist, as well as a French speaker, and we should not be too surprised in one sense at this desire to seek a common humanity beyond racial, cultural, and linguistic differences. Paris comes to represent for him a beacon of universal humanist values, and there are many sentences proclaiming its moral superiority in this regard. Indeed, part of the danger of the seductiveness of Paris, epitomized by what are for him the alluring charms of Parisian women, is that the celebration of, and the accompanying identification with, its life and people at the same time threaten to lead to a troubling *loss* of identity. At one point about halfway through the book Tanhoe Bertin remarks:

> Il est temps que je parte de ce pays. Cessant d'être l'observateur impartial, je risque de me creuser un lit, de ne plus rien sentir. J'ai surtout peur d'être pris dans le tourbillon, dans l'engrenage. Je bois à petites gorgées, je prends du café, je ne crie plus pour appeler un ami, je fais la queue d'instinct, je lis mon journal, mon imperméable ne me quitte plus et je dispute le passage aux autos. Ce sont les signes évidents de mon évolution, de mon intégration, de mon assimilation. (106)

> [I should leave this country now. One of these days, I may find I can no longer be an impartial observer, that I lose utter control. But what I'm afraid of most is being swept up in this whirlwind, thrown out of my usual gear. Already, I find myself taking little sips when I drink, having an espresso at appointed hours, and no longer shouting to get the attention of a friend; I even find myself instinctively lining up, reading my newspaper, arguing with passing motorists, and wearing a raincoat. These are definite signs of my evolution, of my assimilation.] (71–72)

"Assimilation" is obviously a loaded term in this context, and one might suspect Dadié of condoning and submitting to a form of colonialist hegemony, with the cultural self-effacement this implies.

This effacement of differences, whether voluntary or otherwise, has to be read in another light once we remember who is setting the terms of the comparisons. The innocent traveler is not quite as innocent as he at first appears—the device that allows him to see Parisian society through the eyes of an "exotic" outsider is, as readers of the book have pointed out, clearly reminiscent of its well-known literary ancestor, Montesquieu's *Lettres persanes* [*Persian Letters*], and its satirical effect is

no less incisive. As with the *Lettres persanes,* the satire works by a reversal of the Eurocentric (or Francocentric) colonialist hierarchy, so that
what is assumed to be exotic, foreign, other, comes to assume the central position of the familiar, thereby "exoticizing" French civilization. As
this more mischievous, ironic intention comes into focus, we begin to
recognize the mock ethnographic tone of many of the observations. Just
like many early ethnographers, the narrator draws *general* conclusions
about the people known as "Parisians" from the *particularity* of his experiences. He remarks, for example, on the Parisians' emblematic use of
the cockerel, *le coq gaulois,* but deplores their transgression of the respect
normally accorded a totem: "Partout au long des boulevards sont des
rôtisseries, où l'on aperçoit sur broches des poulets bien dorés" (85) [The
boulevards are filled with rotisseries, and in every one of them you find
beautiful golden chickens turning on a spit] (57).

Later on, he tries to find some way of accounting for the immense
power and influence that journalists appear to enjoy in Paris and draws
analogies with the local *génies* from his home, tracing their ancestry back
through writers and poets, who in medieval and Renaissance times seem
to him to have performed a similar function to the village griot. And in
one passage that highlights Dadié's strategy of ironic reversal, he turns
on its head the racist assumption that Western civilization is more "ad-
vanced" than African civilization. Bertin recognizes that many Parisians
would object to the kinds of analogies he is drawing, not because there
may be elements of truth in them, but

> parce que je semble les ramener à notre niveau, en arrière, oubliant du
> coup les millénaires d'effort [. . .] Qu'ils ne me fassent pas rire! S'ils
> étaient aussi vieux qu'ils le prétendent, ils auraient eu la peau noircie
> par le temps. Or à peine sont-ils bronzés! (126)
>
> [because I seem to be taking them backward, forgetting in one fell
> swoop the thousands and thousands of years of hard work [. . .]
> Why, it's enough to make me laugh! If they were as old as they think
> they are, their skin would have darkened with age. But they're barely
> even tan!] (85)

Although Dadié's irony is humorous in its effect, it is also, just as with
Climbié, a key to the narrative structure of the text.[3] Irony implies two
simultaneous and contradictory positions, which in this case might be

said to foreground the text's double origin, drawing its inspiration both from a very sophisticated French literary tradition (which Dadié at once inhabits and subverts from the inside) and from an African oral tradition, whose techniques the narrator is constantly employing (e.g., the use of the present tense, the direct address neatly achieved by using a letter form, the inclusive "nous," the exclamations, the digressions, the rhetorical embellishments, and the insistent rhetorical questions which, in addition to reminding us constantly of the presence of the friend to whom the letters are addressed, implicitly draw us in as readers too).

Does this ironic technique work simply by inversion? This question might be best addressed by thinking about the differences between Montesquieu's text and Dadié's. The first and perhaps most obvious thing one might say is that both texts work by what Roger Caillois, in talking about Montesquieu's strategy of adopting the position of being a stranger to the country one lives in, termed a "sociological revolution," that is, looking at France, and specifically Paris, from the inside out. But while the *Lettres persanes* may employ a clever narrative device, Dadié's text is written by someone who is in fact a stranger to the country he is in, and whose ambivalent relationship to the culture he has inherited in some senses also makes him, by the very conditions of his existence, a stranger to himself. Montesquieu's text, while satirizing the genre of the travel narrative and implicitly questioning exoticized eighteenth-century French representations of geographically distant and culturally distinct lands and peoples, does not really challenge the fundamental assumptions underpinning what V. Y. Mudimbe calls the "colonializing structure" of Western discourse about other cultures, which he sees as running through different forms of writing from the texts of early explorers right up to present-day tourist guides. As Mudimbe describes it, anthropological and ethnographic exploration was in fact a continuation of the Enlightenment tradition of seeing Africa as backward, primitive, savage, and so on, but with the difference that "the discourse on 'savages' is, for the first time, a discourse in which an explicit political power presumes the authority of a scientific knowledge, and vice versa." Mudimbe goes on to say: "Travelers in the 18th century, as well as those of the 19th and their successors in the 20th (colonial proconsuls, anthropologists, and colonizers), spoke using the same type of signs and symbols, and acted upon them. During the colonial era, these consistently involved reduction of difference into a Western historicity."[4] In writing about *Un nègre à Paris,* Elisabeth Mudimbe-Boyi has described Dadié's text as forming a "counter-discourse that actually challenges the ideological function of Western discourse about the Other," a function she defines as follows: "Exotic, missionary, and colonial discourse continue to pervade the social discourse of the West [. . .] Presented as a perception, Western discourse, in its rudimentary state, is in reality a projection: it creates, invents, and orders everything in terms of itself."5

Dadié's ironic appropriation of this discourse is thus not simply a matter of repetition, and the rhetorical operations of assimilation, borrowing, or inversion seem inadequate to account for its full critical effect. One might turn for a more sophisticated elaboration of this question to the work of two postcolonial theorists, Mary Louise Pratt and Homi K. Bhabha. Pratt reads travel writing, and accounts of European explorers, as having produced, as she puts it, "the rest of the world" for a European readership. Her *Imperial Eyes: Travel Writing and Transculturation* deals largely with accounts of European travelers to South America and with Anglophone explorers of West, Central, and South Africa, but the general theoretical terms she deploys, precisely because they are so firmly rooted in particular contexts and periods of history, make her book equally valid for Francophone Africa. Travel writing for her functions also as a means of self-representation and is organized in the service of the metropolis's imperative to "present and re-present its peripheries and its others continually to itself."6 She thinks it is important to go beyond binary oppositions of colonizer and colonized and to reread writings by both Western and non-Western authors from what she calls a "contact perspective," that is, according to how subjects are constituted in and by their relations to each other. She uses the concept of "transculturation" to look at how subordinated or marginal groups select and invent from material transmitted to them by a dominant or metropolitan culture, and one form of this, which she terms "auto-ethnography" (that is, self-representation by engaging with the colonizer's own terms, by collaborating with the idiom of the conqueror), seems very useful in thinking about Dadié's particular strategies. While this might be said to be true of all Francophone African writing, which necessarily either assimilates, negotiates, or resists the heritage of the colonial encounter, it is Dadié's gesture of a determined subjective reappropriation that makes his writing unusual in this regard. Nowhere is the force of this more apparent than in the *language* of Dadié's texts.

Bhabha, in the essay "Of Mimicry and Man," in *The Location of Culture,* focuses on the concept of "mimicry" (adopted from the title of V. S. Naipaul's *The Mimic Men*) to articulate the ways in which colonial discourse represents to itself its colonized other. "Mimicry" captures the ambivalence of the relationship the colonizer entertains with its own colonized, which is supposedly created "in the image" of the colonizer but which must also be essentially *not* the same; as he puts it, "to be Anglicized is *emphatically* not to be English."[7] The very ambivalence of mimicry creates a slippage, a rupture in the homogeneity of the representations of colonial subjectivity, producing forms of *partial* self-representation, what Bhabha terms a "flawed colonial mimesis."

To return to *Un nègre à Paris,* we could now attempt to articulate more precisely the relationship of Dadié's text to the tradition and the culture it is ironizing. Montesquieu's *Lettres persanes* can be seen, despite its clever subversiveness, as one more example of Western exotic discourse and thus a form of mimicry. Tzvetan Todorov, in *Nous et les autres,* underlines Montesquieu's complicity with colonialist ideology by pointing out that, despite his principled declarations in the *Lettres persanes,* he demonstrates later, in his *L'esprit des lois* [*On the Spirit of Laws*], that his images of others (Africans, Indians, Japanese, and Chinese) are "purely conventional and ultimately degrading."[8] What Dadié does in repeating Montesquieu's strategy, and in situating himself in an ironic relationship not only to French literary history but to the entire legacy of travel writing, is to repeat the same process of colonial mimicry, but from the point of view of the colonized. As a Francophone writer, and one who is finely attuned to the nuances of the French language as well as to French literary history in general, he is both inside and outside. What he is doing in *Un nègre à Paris* is in effect *mimicking* the mimicry of colonialist discourse, in a gesture that can no longer be understood simply as an inversion (which would imply a continued dependency on the model from which it was derived) but that takes this model apart—from the inside out, as it were.

What, then, is Dadié's relationship to French culture and language? Just as he waxes lyrical about the endlessly surprising charms of Paris and its inhabitants, so his explicit statements about their language appear to be unreserved in their praise. French is said to be a language of formidable depth and subtlety: "La langue française est si précise, d'une profondeur si insondable qu'on ne saurait, avec elle, prendre trop de précautions" (16) [The French language is so precise, so very profound, that you can never take too many precautions] (9). Dadié describes the language with an eloquence and verve that betray his supposed linguistic naïveté. He plays throughout on the semantic resonances of the words *franc* and *français*. If French is a language of infinite rhetorical resourcefulness, it is also capable of getting straight to the point: "De ses origines franques, il [= ce peuple] a gardé une qualité essentielle: son franc parler" (94) [From their Frankish ancestors they inherited one absolutely essential quality: speaking frankly] (63, trans. slightly modified). This admiration for the directness of the French language is linked to a number of reflections on the moral integrity of the people, above all their *franchise,* their sense of community, and their passionate defense of freedom. Indeed, French is seen to be *the* language of many of the core values of humanist belief: "Parler cette langue, c'est devenir l'héritier de sa culture, un prolongement de son âme, un témoin de son humanisme" (191) [To speak this language is to become a part of their cultural heritage, in effect an extension of their very being, and when you become a part of them, you share their concerns for human dignity] (134).

It is, however, above all the *wit* of the language, *l'esprit,* which seems to attract Dadié, or rather his narrator. Talking with Parisians is said to involve endless verbal sparring, and while Bertin confesses his inability to match the sparkling conversation of his company, his discussion of wit again demonstrates all the qualities that he claims are the trademark of the Parisian's language. The passage is an extended commentary on the Parisian's love of salt, which develops through a playful exploration of the metaphorics of *le sel* (which is used idiomatically in French to connote the piquancy of wit):

> La consommation de sel dans ce pays est effrayant [. . .] Et pour relever le goût de la conversation apportera-t-il [= le Parisien] son grain de sel [. . .] L'étranger ignore le secret du Parisien: le grain de sel. Et on ne sait jamais où il le cache. Dans la bouche? Dans la tête? Il n'en parle jamais, feignant d'ignorer l'effet magique du grain de sel [. . .] Je l'ai essayé. Le mien a fondu dans ma bouche. (91–92)

> [The amount of salt used in this country is frightening [. . .] And when they want to spice up a conversation, they throw in a grain of salt [. . .] Foreigners forget the Parisians' secret: the grain of salt. And you never know where they hide it. In their mouths? Their heads?

>   They never talk about it, they pretend to ignore the magical effects of
>   that grain of salt [. . .] I tried using some. But mine simply melted in
>   my mouth] (61, trans. slightly modified)

It is not just, however, that Bertin's language is, in spite of his constant
disavowals, every bit as witty as that of the Parisians, such that he might
appear to have "inherited their culture." He never loses sight of the in-
appropriateness of assimilation, both linguistic and cultural, and in
one particularly insightful passage that I'd like to look at more closely,
he explores this very question of cultural identification and cultural
difference.

In the course of talking about how close Parisians are to their pet cats
and dogs Bertin advances the following explanation for their love of
animals:

>   Un hommage rendu à des ancêtres. Eh oui, les Parisiens prétendent
>   [. . .] que l'homme est tout juste un peu supérieur au verrat et au
>   bouc, par exemple, mais nullement au singe dont il descendrait [. . .]
>   L'homme aurait pour ancêtre, le singe. Ils sont tellement convaincus
>   de cette ascendance simiesque, mais aussi tellement imbus du progrès
>   accompli qu'ils vous disent volontiers: «Oh! pas d'histoire, ne fais pas
>   le Singe». C'est-à-dire ne singe pas notre ancêtre le Singe, un peu de
>   respect pour lui; son âge l'exige. (63)

>   [To pay homage to their ancestors. Yes, it's true [. . .] Parisians have
>   no trouble seeing man as superior to the boar and billy goat, but not
>   to the ape they descended from [. . .] Yes, they believe the ape is their
>   ancestor; in fact, they're so convinced of their simian ancestry, so
>   caught up at the same time with the progress they've made that you'll
>   often hear them say: "Oh, come on now. Quit acting like a monkey!"
>   What they really mean is, don't ape our ancestor the Ape. Show some
>   respect for it] (42, trans. slightly modified)

Bertin continues this line of thinking, rendering more clearly visible the
underside of much of the apparently unequivocal praise of Western civilization and its humanist values, that is, their complicity with evolutionary theories of racism. The ironic play of reversals, whereby Parisians
are said to have the same type of ancestral respect as Africans do for certain animals, quickly gives way to the suggestion of an assumption of

innate cultural superiority based on skin color, and that this "respect" is
at the same time a kind of protective barrier keeping Western civilization safe from its own barbaric past, a "savagery" that it would equate
with African and other colonized cultures. This fear of the uncivilized
"other" of the Western world is then described in terms that also evoke
the history of colonialism and slavery:

> Cette horreur pour le Singe ancêtre est telle que dès qu'on dit à un
> enfant: ne fais pas le singe, il redevient homme, ne se gratte plus, ne
> sautille plus, ne grimace plus. A un ancêtre aussi respectable, ils met-
> tent la chaine aux reins. Drôle de façon de l'honorer tel que le com-
> mandent leurs lois. Il est vrai que le Singe est seulement un ancêtre et
> qu'à ce titre on ne peut l'honorer comme un père ou comme une
> mère. Et plus, jusqu'à quel point, le Parisien ne pense-t-il pas avoir
> mis les chaînes aux reins de notre ancêtre Singe, à nous, Noirs, Jaunes,
> Rouges, puisque jusqu'ici, on n'a vu nulle part de singe blanc? (63–64)

> [This fear of the ancestral Ape is such that whenever they tell a child
> to stop acting like one, the child turns into a human being. He doesn't
> scratch himself any more, he doesn't turn somersaults or make funny
> faces. They consider their ancestor so special they've even put chains
> around it. A strange way, indeed, to honor one's origins! In truth the
> Ape is simply an ape; it doesn't demand the same reverence a mother or
> father does. But sometimes I catch myself wondering if the Parisians
> haven't put chains around our simian ancestor as well—the ancestor of
> those who are black, yellow, red. And after all, up to now, no one has
> ever seen a white monkey.] (42–43, trans. slightly modified)

Bertin then forces the question still further by wondering how theories
of evolution, upon which French colonialism depended in order to justify its "civilizing mission," can be compatible with theories of divine
creation, which formed the religious basis for imperialist expansion. If
"man" was created in the image of God, and "man" as a universal term
originally meant "white man," then how can Bertin account for his own
existence? This line of reasoning seems to give Bertin some clue, at any
rate, as to why he gets so many odd looks in Paris: "D'aucuns, en me
voyant, se demandent s'ils ne viennent pas de rencontrer le diable en
personne [. . .] J'étonne. C'est le terme exact; et ils doivent se deman-
der quelle fantaisie avait pris Dieu de se tromper de couleur en me bar-

bouillant de goudron" (65) [Some people when they see me think they've encountered the devil himself [. . .] I catch them by surprise. That's the problem. They must wonder what in the world possessed God to get the colors wrong and smear me with tar] (43). The whole passage is, of course, wickedly satirical and extremely witty. If Parisians suffer from a cultural interdiction barring them from being able to clown around and "make a monkey of themselves" (*faire le singe*), this is precisely what Bertin does, clowning around with the Parisians, with their language and with their wit, mimicking or aping their mimicry, beating them at their own game, and effectively *out*witting them.

The sight of a black person created "in God's image" leaves the Parisians, according to Bertin, dumbfounded, while he, never lost for words, finds a brilliantly apt and witty idiom: "Un casse-tête, pas facile à résoudre, et *sur lequel ils perdent leur latin,* un héritage du temps des Romains" (65, emphasis added) [I'm a problem for them, a puzzle, and they can't make heads or tails of it—something they haven't been able to do since they lost touch with their Roman past] (44). More than just a clever turn of phrase, "ils perdent leur latin" (lit. "they lose their Latin") suggests a disruption of the foundations of French culture, which Bertin has caused *by his very presence.* It also raises for him the perplexing question of the extent to which French is "his" culture and language, and in the context of the discussion of ancestry—whether the ancestry leading back to the shared origin of Adam and Eve or the one playfully evoked at several points in the book when he alludes to the absurdity of the French teaching the Africans about "our ancestors the Gauls"—it asks the question of just how much he can claim French history as his "own." I would argue, listening to the resonances of the "Latin" idiom Bertin singles out, that these questions determine the subsequent destination of Dadié's travels, that is, to Rome.

Rome

The narrator of *La ville où nul ne meurt* is no longer Tanhoe Bertin, although the text is explicitly addressed to a "tu" who is the narrator's friend, and the satirical style and the themes of the many long reflections are much the same as in *Un nègre à Paris. La ville* was written three years after the Paris book, but starts out with the narrator still in Paris and picks up where Bertin left off. Now, however, the narrator has become disillusioned with Paris, and his opening diatribe against Paris and the Parisians stands in stark contrast to the descriptions in *Un nègre à Paris,* since he now states openly much of what had remained between the lines or subtly hidden within its irony:

> Ah, ne pas comprendre les autres! Ne même pas tenter une approche, mais toujours et sans cesse ne considérer que sa situation privilégiée [. . .] Car tout ce qui porte le label parisien ne saurait être une panacée universelle. Et le ridicule ne serait-il pas d'imiter Paris dans ses fastes, ses grandeurs et ses petitesses, dans ses rires, ses colères et ses rêves sans les avoir compris? (15)

> [Ah, not understanding others! Not even trying to get close, but only ever considering one's own privileged situation [. . .] For everything that is marked "Parisian" cannot be a universal panacea. And wouldn't it be ridiculous to imitate Paris in its pomp, in its grandeur and its little details, in its laughter, its anger and its dreams, without having understood them?] (41)

The narrator's impatience with Parisian culture and the prejudices of its citizens replaces the gently mocking tone of the earlier narrative, such that similar examples of mock ethnographic irony become particularly biting. He is astonished at the cultural *immaturity* of Parisians—"Ils ont conservé, malgré leurs immenses progrès incontestables, une mentalité des ancêtres de nos arrière, arrière, arrière-grand-pères" (19) [They've maintained, in spite of their immense and incontestable progress, the mentality of the ancestors of our great-great-great-grandfathers] (43)— and finally loses his temper with the customs official who embarrasses him publicly by asking him how much money he has: "Allons! Allons! Suis-je dans un pays civilisé? Quelle curiosité malsaine! [. . .] Quelles moeurs étranges!" (30) [What! What! Am I in a civilized country? What sick curiosity! [. . .] What strange customs!] (48). Rome calls out to him with the promise of a city that is more ancient than Paris and where Western civilization can possibly be found in a purer, more uncorrupted form: "Il me faut toucher du doigt le socle sur lequel les hommes d'ici bâtissent leur société, socle à comparer au nôtre" (10) [I must touch, with my fingers, the pedestal upon which men from here have built their society, a pedestal comparable to our own] (39, trans. slightly modified). The journey from Paris to Rome is thus intended to be not just geographically and culturally enlightening; it is one in which the stakes are high, since the narrator will be holding the very source of Western civilization up to its own claims. It is at the same time a journey back to his "own" roots, as a French speaker and a Roman Catholic, and also one that will involve taking his comparative ethnographic mind "upstream," as it were.

In fact, as travel writing goes, the book leaves a lot to be desired. It is not until page 68 (of 205) that the narrator finally gets to Rome, and when in Rome there is little of the description of people and places one might expect, although he does wax lyrical about the Romans and their city, much as Tanhoe Bertin did with Paris. The traveling seems to be more a pretext for the narrator to reflect on the history of Roman civilization and its impact on Europe, with places and incidents providing the catalyst for him to pursue his meditations further. The plane trip from Paris to Rome, in which he is sitting next to a Jewish rabbi and a young Jewish girl, is dominated, for example, by his thoughts about the relationship of Judaism to Christianity and comparisons between the respective histories of Jews and Africans as the victims of Western barbarism. When the narrator finally visits some of the ruins of ancient Rome, he is singularly unimpressed by their superior claims to antiquity. Using the same mock ethnographic argument as Bertin, he points to his skin color as irrefutable evidence that "his" civilization is far older. As was the case for Bertin with Parisian culture, while he is drawn in by the seductive power of Roman history, he stresses the importance for himself and his fellow Africans of resisting forms of assimilation or imitation:

> Gardons-nous des imitations et des caricatures. Ne nous fions pas à la façade des monuments; ils ont des fondations dont l'importance nous échappe. Oh! Rome m'effraie, autant que Paris! Comme je suis inquiet à cause de leur pouvoir de séduction! Sommes-nous armés pour une lutte éventuelle? Oui, si nous prenons conscience des fondements de ce que Rome et Paris appellent la civilisation. (130)

> [Let us protect ourselves from imitations and caricatures. Let's not put our confidence in the façades of monuments; they have foundations whose importance escapes us. Oh! Rome frightens me as much as Paris! How uneasy their seductive power makes me! Are we armed for

an eventual struggle? Yes, if we become aware of the foundations of what Rome and Paris call civilization.] (96)

This "becoming aware" ("si nous prenons conscience") of the foundations of Roman civilization is in fact what much of the text is concerned with, and it takes the form of a fascination with its ruins, with the history of its origins and the mythology surrounding them. Not only does the narrator relish recounting the legend of Romulus and Remus, but he lingers significantly over the idea that Rome itself was founded upon a legend. What is more, there are different and conflicting versions of this legend and much that remains open to question, which leads him to comment that it might be compared to the African oral tradition, in which the transmission of history and mythology is inevitably subject to the fallibility and distortions of human memory. His accounts of the Roman Empire, of Jesus' life and the establishment of the Christian Church, are then narrated in a similar oral style, as if their status were exactly the same as that of the Romulus and Remus myth. In the same way that he recalls the contradictory versions of this legend, he dwells upon the historical uncertainties of Christianity and the perplexing motivations of the Roman emperors, making ample use of rhetorical questions. These function at one level simply as an engaging oral device, vivifying the tale he is telling and actively involving his "listeners," but at another level have the effect of further destabilizing the supposed factuality of Western history, and by extension the "foundations" of Western civilization.

One aspect of imperial Roman history that not surprisingly appeals to the narrator is the conquest of Gaul. As someone whose country was invaded and colonized by France, what better way for him to undermine French colonialist preeminence than to point to the time when France was itself in the position of the colonized? This reminder of France's own "foreign" roots also deconstructs the myth of a pure French national identity, a myth that was essential to France's colonial expansion. The narrator's language cleverly reflects this focus on France's own subaltern past by using not just an extremely classical, elegant French but one that constantly echoes or mimics Latin, both syntactically and lexically: the use of declamatory phrases and compact adjectival clauses, throwing in the odd Latin phrase (*alea jacta est, urbi et orbi*), and peppering his

French with as many particularly Latinate words as possible (e.g., *famélique, belliqueux, glèbe, auguste, indélébile, cécité, minime, infime, pérenne, pie*). This is not just to draw the attention of the French to the impurity, or otherness, of their origins, but it is an important strategy in Dadié's attempt to stake a claim to the French language, as well as to its history and culture. If French civilization is in effect founded upon its own otherness, then metropolitan French citizens who describe themselves as more authentically French by dint of a family history that stretches back some time, *les Français de souche,* have no more rightful a claim to their national heritage than do their colonial subjects, whose relationship to France is in theory more marginal or extrinsic.

The temptation, of course, is to then join ranks with the Romans "against" the French and feel a closer affinity with Rome and its people, obeying the imperative, in effect, to "do as the Romans do." "*Civis Romanus sum!*" the narrator exclaims at one point, "La porte est là, sans battant, sans gardien. Il suffit de passer sous la voûte, de faire acte d'allégeance pour que Rome vous accueille" (161) [The door is there, without a clapper or a guard. It's enough to pass under the arch and pledge allegiance, for Rome to welcome you] (110, trans. slightly modified). Elsewhere he is less enthusiastic and more wryly skeptical: "Me romaniser! Est-ce possible? Nous pouvons dire les même prières au même Dieu, mais sortir de moi—pour arborer un autre visage, acquérir une autre attitude me paraît très improbable" (146) [Make myself Roman! Is it possible? We can say the same prayers to the same God, but to give up one's own skin, to wear another face or acquire a new attitude seems very improbable] (103). The improbability of this identification with the Romans is then acted out in several humorous scenes toward the end of the book: the narrator and his friends, wanting to go dancing with the locals, are directed by a local policeman to an *American* night club; he is later fleeced by an unscrupulous salesman; and in the most humiliating episode of all, he is defeated in his attempt at winding spaghetti onto his fork, so he cuts it into small pieces and eats it with his spoon, to the horror and astonishment of the other Italians in the hotel restaurant. He is subsequently stigmatized by the hotel staff, who refuse to change his tablecloth, leaving the stain made by his spaghetti sauce as a sign both of his inability to act like a Roman and of their collective shunning of him: "chacun m'avait classé: le barbare dans la Cité" (194) [everyone had classified me: the barbarian in the city] (126).

Although this experience is described as being similar to several other moments in the book where the narrator is made aware of his otherness because of his blackness, his embarrassment here comes not from being black but from being non-Roman, or "unromanlike." This is a critical point in his sense of self, but he calmly turns it to his advantage by again reversing the terms of the equation. The Romans are seen in the end, like most Europeans, to be unable to think beyond the circularity of their own self-representation: "ils ramènent tout à leur mesure" (195) [they measure everything according to their own standards] (127, trans. modified). Ironically, it is the weight of their own history (which the narrator is free to take or leave) which acts to block their ability to think in terms of difference and otherness, and which is seen as a sign of cultural immaturity and, implicitly, of a kind of barbarism: "Nous aurons un jour à les aider à se ranger, à se contenir, à faire place aux autres. Ce sera difficile certes, après tant de pérégrinations, d'autant plus que Caton l'Ancien revit dans chaque citoyen" (195) [One day we will have to help them get settled down, get a hold of themselves, make room for others. Certainly this will be difficult, after so many conquests, and all the more so since Cato the Elder lives again in each citizen] (127, trans. slightly modified). Rome is thus seen ultimately as not much better than Paris as a choice of culture, and an object of identification:

Ne serait-il pas paradoxal que du jour au lendemain, toi et moi devenions parisiens ou Romains? Que représenteraient pour nous les aigles romaines, la louve, Auguste César, le Tibre, l'Assembléee nationale, la Seine, le château de Versailles? [. . .] Pourrions-nous jamais aimer Rome ou Paris comme les aiment ceux qui y sont nés? [. . .] N'aurions-nous pas le sentiment parfois d'être en marge quelle que soit la place qu'on nous accorde? (127)

[Wouldn't it be paradoxical for you and me, from one day to the next, to become Parisians or Romans? What would the Roman eagles, the wolf, Caesar Augustus, the Tiber, the National Assembly, the Seine, and the Palace of Versailles represent for us? [. . .] Could we ever love Rome or Paris in the same way as those who were born there? [. . .] Wouldn't we sometimes have the feeling of being on the outside whatever status were granted to us?] (94, trans. slightly modified).

This is not to say that Tanhoe Bertin or the narrator of *La ville où nul ne meurt* rejects either the French or the Italian language and civilization. Far from it, they embrace them, and even glorify them, with rare enthusiasm and good humor. In valorizing positively both Paris and Rome, Dadié avoids the accusation that his discourse is simply one of opposition, which would therefore potentially have nothing to say *to* the French. But by ironically challenging the very foundations of their cultures (chosen strategically for their importance to Western civilization as a whole) *from within*, Dadié is doing more than giving the colonial oppressors a taste of their own medicine. This would merely repeat the structures of identification, assimilation, and mimicry upon which colonialism depended for its own self-representation and self-propagation. This is more than a recognition and inversion of colonialism's overlaying its civilization on the civilization of the people it colonized. By writing accounts of his visits to Paris and Rome that ironically subvert the genre from which they derive, Dadié unmasks the complicitous manner in which European travel writing served the ideology of colonial imperialism. Thus it is not the "same" as European travel writing, nor is it outside or "other." This ambivalence is in a sense "like" the mimicry Bhabha articulates, being both the same but also other, so in this sense a partial or flawed imitation. But this "same-other" ambivalence is not the "same"; it is quite deliberately "other," mimicking colonial mimicry and interrogating not just the foundations of Western civilization and its humanist values but the very strategies it employs to represent and contain otherness. A strikingly different version of this same performative reinscription can be seen at work in the New York text.

New York

Although published before *La ville où nul ne meurt, Patron de New York* is chronologically the last in the series of Dadié's travel narratives, giving an account of six months he spent in New York, from October 1962 to April 1963. It thus represents by far the longest period abroad for him, a fact that is reflected in the composition of the text, which is less the account of a hurried and harried traveler, with an emphasis on the reactions of an (ironically) enthusiastic and wide-eyed stranger, than that of a more settled and reflective temporary resident. In other respects it follows the same pattern as the Paris and Rome travelogues: the first-person narrator spends several pages recounting the preparations for his journey and the plane trip; his observations about America and Americans are extremely sharp and witty, and they often serve as pretexts for long, meditative passages. He has much to say, not surprisingly, about the history and the contemporary situation of black Americans. Even though New York is culturally and geographically the most distant location of the three trips, the plight of African Americans in a predominantly white, and at that time still largely segregated, United States offers him a more immediately obvious focus for his mobile identifications. Dadié's humor at the expense of American culture is at times heavily sarcastic, but rather than producing a more somber and bitter text, given the historical and political context of American slavery and racism, the result is more complex in its narrative form than *Un nègre à Paris* and *La ville où nul ne meurt,* and richer in the wit and poetic resources it draws upon to explore this complexity. So while the text deals thematically and objectively with what the narrator witnesses and experiences during his time in the United States, it also invites a more careful consideration of the narrative strategies he employs and the function and effect of the pervasive linguistic playfulness.

The America Dadié presents to us with such declamatory verve is the stuff of myths and legends (cowboys and Indians, tall buildings, youthfulness and brash overconfidence, the relentless pursuit of wealth and individual freedom, patriotic and religious excess, and so on), but the text is essentially about race relations and will address the question of how, as he puts it, "deux fleuves peuvent couler ensemble, dans le même lit, depuis des siècles sans jamais se mêler" (7) [two rivers can share the same bed for centuries without ever mixing] (3). Dadié's comments on the American way of life primarily take the form of ironic ethnographic inversion: almost every section begins with some variation on "L'Américain est . . . " or "L'Amérique est . . . ," as if all Americans were reducible to a single type. While this may initially seem naive and uninformed, the deliberately clichéd and subjective nature of his comments is in fact part of Dadié's strategy, repeating as it does the gesture of drawing general conclusions from particular observations which is part of the ethnographic method he satirizes in his other travel narratives. Indeed, the problematic status of the term *American* is very much what is at stake in the text and is an issue that he comes back to again and again. As the text progresses, an emerging pattern connects the metaphors Dadié uses to describe American society, so that far from being made up of randomly selected images, the text is constructed as a rich and complex linguistic fabric.

We can see this, for example, in the way he weaves together his discussion of religion and economics. If gold is said to be the supreme object of worship in the United States, "the reflection of the white god" (79), then the dollar is its everyday manifestation, "the favorite offspring of gold" (82). This association between money and religion is more than just figurative in nature, as Dadié goes on to demonstrate: "Le dollar est du reste une bonne et sainte monnaie sur laquelle est écrite la profession de foi de tout le pays: «In God we trust». En Dieu nous avons confiance. Une monnaie mise au service du Créateur" (78) [The dollar is above all a good and holy currency, whose motto proclaims the faith of an entire nation: "In God we trust"—a currency serving the Lord] (42). There is nothing particularly original or striking about this definition of a capitalism that finds its spiritual and moral basis in New World Protestantism and its avatars, but Dadié forces the metaphorical suggestiveness to show how this materialist religiosity pervades all aspects of American society. He depicts Americans as reanimating the spirit of the centuries of holy wars that exhausted Europe, but with a passion that is allied to economic rather than political or nationalistic interests. Toward the end of his account he paints a picture of paradise overrun by Americans:

> Voyez-vous le visage du paradis peuplé d'Américains? Des one way ici, des one way là; ailleurs des banques, des usines, des buildings reliés entre eux par des ponts étagés; le soir venu, le twist satanique, lubrique, sans oublier que le paradis pourrait devenir une résidence d'été pour millionaires américains! (266)

> [Can you imagine how a Paradise occupied by Americans would look? One Ways here, One Ways there, elsewhere banks, factories, and buildings connected by tiered bridges. At sunset, that fiendish, lustful dance called the twist, not to mention that Paradise could become a summer residence for American millionaires!] (143)

The ironic reference to "one-way" road signs may seem here like a rather random and casual adaptation of a "typical" American icon, but it is in fact a perfect example of Dadié's careful and elaborate technique of exploiting the connotations of a given term. So while he does mention at several points the American obsession with one-way road systems, and by extension with taking the most direct and unhindered route from A to B, the notion of "one way" connects up with other themes he has been developing. The close alignment of a relentless economic drive with a religious conviction means that the one and only way for Americans is upward. Dadié's wit singles out the elevator as a perfect image of this desire for ascendancy (the French for elevator is *ascenseur*) coupled with the efficiency of a well-oiled machine: "les citoyens passent tout leur temps à courir vers le Up, le sommet, le belvédère. Des milliers d'ascenseurs discrets, huileux, conscients du rôle auguste qui est le leur . . . " (106) [citizens are constantly running toward the Up, the summit, the observation tower. Thousands of well-oiled elevators, unobtrusive and proud of their majestic role . . .] (57).

For the American economy to be as successful as it clearly is, it requires a tightly choreographed relationship between the different elements of American society, and Dadié proposes a number of possible metaphors to describe this relationship. The economy is compared on numerous occasions to a machine, and this metaphor is extended to suggest an increasing mechanization and technologization of life as a fundamental characteristic of American society. The "American way of life" is thus dominated by a constant struggle to control the balance between man and machine. Sometimes, it seems, "men and machines live in perfect symbiotic rapport" (48), but at other times machines are characterized by a barely containable and almost diabolical force:

> Gigantesque usine où l'on prend un plat pour résister, continuer à travailler tout comme on met de l'huile et de l'essence dans un moteur. Toujours l'efficience! Les rues par endroits fument comme si un volcan entrait en éruption. Toute l'Amérique bouillonne de fièvre productrice. (80)

> [In this gigantic factory you eat in self-defense, just to keep working, just as motors get oil and gas. Efficiency first! In some places steamy streets resemble volcanoes as all America boils with productive fever.] (43)

The very concepts of "man" and "machine" in America are put into question by Dadié in a number of ways, especially when black Americans are worked into the equation. African slaves brought across to America were comparable to machines insofar as they were subordinate to their white masters, spent all their waking hours in hard labor, and were treated as less than human, or other than human. Although the industrial revolution led to machines in a sense replacing slaves, this increasing mechanization of the world, rather than giving back slaves their humanity and putting them on an equal standing with their former owners, meant a generalized dehumanization of society. In this respect, the American model of the world as a vast economic machine came more and more to dominate rhythms of work and life. This analogy is further complicated when Dadié considers the question in a religious light, and he ironically appropriates the machine metaphor as a way of reasserting the supremacy of man over machine: "L'homme paraît être le seul moteur qui jamais ne cesse de tourner" (276) [Man seems to be the only motor that never stops running] (148). The category of the "human"—especially in relation to black Americans—is clearly central here, and I will come back to Dadié's subtle treatment of it a little later on.

This tapestry of interwoven metaphors is perhaps best exemplified by the master trope of the text, that is, the *patron* of the title, which functions here very much as what Nicole Vinceleoni terms a *mot pastille.*[9] Dadié appears to exploit all the connotations of the word *patron*. In French it is the generic way of referring to the boss, but it can also variously mean an owner, a patron (including a patron saint), the master of a freed slave (in Roman history), a captain of industry, a knitting or sewing pattern, a stencil, and a kind of template for any artistic creation. It is the meanings of "boss" and "pattern" which predominate. Dadié typifies the American boss as follows: "Le patron américain est un homme de cran, un homme qui a conscience de sa force dans le monde" (72) [The American boss is a man with plenty of pluck, aware of his power in the world] (38). So the American *patron* is not just any boss but the capitalist par excellence, who will not be satisfied until he reaches the very top. His intention is thus to become the boss of bosses, through relentless economic competition:

> La compétition engagée avec les autres nations est donc toute économique. C'est à qui couvrira le monde de ses produits, de son drapeau, de ses idées, de ses tics. Qui sera le patron, le tuteur des autres peuples? (139)

[Competition with other nations is all economic. Who will blanket
the world with her products, her flag, her ideas, and mannerisms.
Who will be the boss, the tutor for other peoples?] (75)

Patron as boss and *patron* as pattern or model come to be closely con-
nected in the rhetoric of Dadié's text. By conflating the metaphors of
design, creation, and mass production (particularly of clothes) with the
various modes of social and financial superiority that the *patron* as boss
suggests, Dadié presents American bosses as those who employ a strategy of economic domination and assimilation in order to impose their
own cultural values on others: "Pense-t-il pouvoir tondre tous les mou-
tons du monde, les vêtir sur le même patron, les nourrir selon les mêmes
normes?" (130) [Does he think he can shear all the sheep in the world,
dress them according to the same pattern, feed them according to the
same standards?] (69–70, trans. modified); "Mais qui à notre époque, ne
veut tailler ses habits sur le patron américain? Qui ne veut passer pour
Américain?" (95) [But who nowadays doesn't want to tailor his customs
to the American pattern? Who doesn't want to pass for an American?]
(51, trans. slightly modified). This in turn merges with the depiction of
Americans as self-appointed torchbearers of godliness and the conjunction of religious and architectural ascendancy:

> Le nouveau patron produit par le nouveau monde, un patron mod-
> erne aux idées larges. A ce titre, il n'aime pas avoir les pieds sur terre.
> Il ne se trouve à l'aise qu'au trentième ou quarantième étage, sur sa
> propre montagne d'où il peut parler à Dieu. (199)
>
> [A new boss produced by the new world, a new open-minded role
> model? In this capacity, she dislikes having her feet on the ground, at
> ease only on the thirtieth or fortieth floor of her own mountain
> where she can converse with God.] (106)

So we come back around to elevators and to "one-way" systems. Now,
however, the "way" in "one way" not only indicates a direction but also
suggests the idea of manner or of a model; the *patron* is thus a boss to
the extent that he imposes his own (only) way of doing things on others. If this is essentially a definition of cultural imperialism, it is already
implicit in the term *patron,* which might be said, in Dadié's text, to be
more or less synonymous with "American" in general, insofar as being

American involves conforming to the model, the *patron,* and at the same time participating in the exportation and imposition of that model. In essence, "America" ultimately means uniformity.

Unless, of course, you happen to be black. The "image" of America Dadié presents is deliberately reductive, not only because it is part of his strategy of ironic ethnographic inversion but because the very process of condensation or reduction of difference is precisely what (white) America is all about. Its identity is predicated upon the powerful unifying myths of freedom, equality, the pursuit of individual dreams, greatness, brotherly love, and so on, but Dadié's text skillfully exposes their status as myth. The effect of the irony is to reveal the underside of these myths, and nowhere is this more apparent than in his portrayal of black Americans.[10] His comments on the situation of blacks in the United States intermittently interrupt his narrative in the first half of the text but come to dominate more and more toward the end, and this increasingly pervasive presence is, as we shall see, very much part of the overall cumulative effect. The American pattern doesn't seem to be made for blacks: "The American straitjacket does not suit them" (96). In fact, they actively disrupt the model; they are "disconcerting beings" (112) and "unassimilatable products" (75). They were clearly different from other immigrants, as Dadié poignantly remarks, since unlike voluntary settlers they were uprooted from their homeland against their will, and the African is "indisputably the only citizen who never got letters from home" (38).

Dadié points out that, from a historical and economic point of view, blacks could not have benefited from the massive creation of wealth in America because as slaves they were in fact the producers of this wealth, ensuring the survival of the system that so ruthlessly exploited them:

> Les capitaux, il ne pouvait en avoir puisqu'il les produisait pour d'autres [. . .] Sous tous les cieux, par leur sueur et leurs chants, ils poussaient à l'avènement de nouveaux systèmes de vie qui les écrasaient, les broyaient ensuite. (71)

> [As for capital, he could never have any because he was making it for others [. . .] Under every sky, by their sweat and songs, they strived for the advent of a new system that crushed them and then pounded them.] (38)

In this respect it is African Americans who made America what it is. In terms of the metaphors of mechanization, they are the motor of the enormous machine that is the American economy: "They're one of the largest turbines making America run" (163). This situation has not substantially changed since the abolition of slavery and the advent of industrialization, for "there are black sweat and white sighs on many American cars" (96). Dadié devotes several passages to descriptions of the poverty and depressed living conditions of black Americans in the ghettos of Harlem and the Bronx, noting both the *fact* of their marginalization from mainstream America and the way this fraying at the edges has the effect of threatening to pull apart the fabric of the myth of American uniformity.

Dadié is particularly drawn to those spaces of contact and conflict between white and black in America. He sees the place of black music (Negro spirituals, gospel music, blues, and jazz) within American culture as highly symbolic in this respect. For black Americans music is an important means of self-expression and self-affirmation, as well as of contesting their situation within the white world, and yet it is also an artistic form that white America (as well as Europe) found very attractive and quickly assimilated: "Sans doute, les mélodies de Harlem aident-elles les machines à tourner dans la concurrence effrénée que l'Amérique livre au monde" (141) [No doubt Harlem's tunes help machines running in that unbridled competition which America delivers to the world] (76). In terms of its political effectiveness, jazz consequently has an ambiguous status, since it is precisely through this kind of appropriation that white America is able to exoticize and defuse (defuse by exoticizing) the threat that is smoldering at its edges, and at the same time to enjoy the reflected glory it brings to America as a whole: "Harlem l'exotique, prospère dans ses ordures qui la rendent très pittoresque et en ajoutent à l'opulence des quartiers environnants" (141) [Exotic Harlem prospers amidst its garbage—a picturesque complement to the opulence of neighboring areas] (76).

This cultural assimilation, which we have seen to be operative through the figure of the *patron* as both imperialist or capitalist, and as a reproducible model to which all Americans are expected to conform, elsewhere takes more literal forms, perhaps most controversially and problematically when Dadié tackles directly the question of skin color. In 1964, to be a "dyed-in-the-wool" (49) American ("de bon teint" [92], lit.

"of the right shade") meant to be white-skinned, and Dadié seizes on the opportunity for ironic linguistic playfulness when talking about the range of skin-lightening products available in the United States: "Ailleurs on naturalise, c'est-à-dire on anoblit votre couleur, on la blanchit par un texte pour l'étudier à loisir; ici, il faut réellement montrer patte blanche" (93) [Elsewhere they naturalize, that is, dignify your color, lighten the situation a bit by a document to be perused at leisure, but in America, you really have to prove you are acceptable] (49, lit. "to show a white paw"]. From this perspective, at the point of intersection and interaction between white and black, it seems not only that white America successfully contains and assimilates black culture but that many blacks themselves are happy to accept the model of social "integration" that is presented to them, to "troquer leur couleur contre la couleur modèle blanche" (241) [barter their color for the model white color] (129). I would like to come back to the ways in which we can read this play between black and white in *Patron de New York,* but it is important first of all to explore its political and theoretical resonances, since it is a recurrent focus throughout Dadié's writings, from legends such as *Le pagne noir* [The black cloth] to *Climbié,* and from his poetry (see, e.g., "Je vous remercie Dieu de m'avoir créé Noir" [I thank you, God, for having made me black]) to the other travel narratives.

As we saw in the previous chapter in discussing *Climbié,* the opportunities for inverting and subverting the positions of black and white can in fact be read as "shorthand" for the ethnographic irony we find in Dadié's travel writings. Just as he does in *Un nègre à Paris,* Dadié here presents Western culture (and a fortiori American culture), because of its relative infancy, as lagging far behind Africa, with its older civilizations and more deeply embedded traditions. African references thus become benchmarks against which to measure Americans, and Dadié presents Americans as a strange species of animal to be observed and studied in quasi-scientific fashion. "L'Américain est un homme très compliqué qu'il faut étudier avec une extrême patience" (193) [You need enormous patience to study the American, a very complicated person] (103–4). Unlike people in more mature cultures, they are impatient to get things done, to have everything now, and have not learned to take time over important things like meals. The economizing of time also involves an analogous condensation of language, and in another mischievously witty passage Dadié takes the example of the shortening of "Hello" into the monosyllabic "Hi!":

> Le «Hello!» était encore trop long et faisait perdre du temps. L'Amérique lentement nous reconduit à l'ère des onomatopées. Elle tient à démontrer que l'homme descend du singe et que le temps est proche où le frère gorille, le cousin chimpanzé, la tante guenon, le tonton zèbre, vont fêter le retour de leur parent longtemps égaré sur le chemin de l'aventure évolutive. (278)

> ["Hello!" is still too long and time-consuming. America is slowly leading the way back to the era of onomatopoeia, intending to demonstrate that man is really descended from apes and that the time is near when brother gorilla, cousin chimpanzee, aunt ape, and uncle zebra, can welcome their long-lost relative—a malingerer on the path of evolutionary adventure.] (149)

The allusion to monkeys and man's place on the evolutionary ladder is reminiscent of the scene in *Un nègre à Paris* in which Tanhoe Bertin suggests the racism inherent in colonialist discourses of "savagery" and "barbarism." Here, however, the positions are reversed, and it is Americans who, with their animal-like brevity of expression, appear to be returning to a kind of "precivilized" state of being. In stark contrast to their linguistic contractions, the language of Dadié's text is full of repetition, elaboration, and digression and takes all its time to work out the resonances of its metaphors.[11] The ironic inversion of the cultural values associated with black and white is thus always at the expense of the whites, and insofar as Dadié privileges Africa as the standard of civilization by which white America is judged, his discussion of black/white relations within the United States occurs by way of identification with black Americans and of a deeper bond uniting Africa of the 1960s with the condition of blacks in the United States. This is clearly a subjective position, and deliberately so, since it both functions as a reversal of Western ethnographic objectification and also underlines his own subjective investment in the plight of American blacks. Such an identification is not as straightforward as it might seem, though, and Dadié's ironic strategy is not without its dangers.

At the time of his visit, during the civil rights movement in the mid-

1960s, racial tensions were of course high, but Dadié avoids journalistic-style references to specific events or people and prefers to use historical facts as points of departure for often elaborately woven general observations. It might be argued that starting out from cultural clichés weakens the political dimension of his text, especially given that his irony runs the risk of being too playful for the seriousness of the subject matter. If blacks, in the economy of Dadié's narrative, disrupt the homogeneity of myths about America, and if irony is a devastatingly effective tool of demythification, this irony can also structurally turn out to be a double bind, insofar as it establishes or reinforces a relationship of dependency toward this ironized object. It binds the two contradictory points of reference—African to American, that which would escape the *patron*'s subjection to the *patron* itself. This was the dilemma of the ethnographic inversion of *Un nègre à Paris* (which depended for its irony on the model from which it was derived). How does this double bind work within the terms that Dadié elaborates? In aligning himself with black Americans, Dadié is thereby subscribing to the pan-Africanist ideology that was prevalent in the 1950s and 1960s, while at the same time seeking a resolution to racial conflict in the name of a nonracial Christian humanism. The dilemma is a classic problem of antiracist politics—does one make difference or common humanity the basis for political action?—and Dadié's text seems to be no exception. It is caught between arguing for a humanism that transcends race, and—following Mudimbe's archaeological uncovering of the racism buried within the Western concept of Man—critiquing the white American myths of individual freedom, brotherhood, and so on, for their complicity with colonialist discursive subjection and reduction of difference. It makes the problem of racial oppression appear either insuperable (since any militant political action, however mild, seems destined to be reabsorbed into mainstream America by the "uniformity" machine) or resolvable only by an ultimate denial of race (Christian humanism).

Of course, this is not a dilemma that emerged only with the black consciousness movement in the United States in the 1960s or with the increasing contact between Africa and America. Kwame Anthony Appiah, in the chapters "Illusions of Race" and "Going Nativist" in his book *In My Father's House,* has explored the ideological origins of pan-Africanist thinking in the texts of the early African American writers W. E. B. Du Bois and Alexander Crummell. His readings focus on the different manifestations of "racialism" during the nineteenth and twentieth centuries. These range from its more extreme racist versions to the "scientifically" and politically sanctioned forms of racialism that underpinned colonialist ideologies. Appiah is particularly interested in the ways in which racialist thinking was assimilated into the early pan-Africanist manifestos of Du Bois and Crummell. Du Bois's answer to racial oppression was to "respond to the experience of racial discrimination by accepting the racialism it presupposed."[12] Rather than deny the categorization of humanity by race, what he did was to shift the axis of relationships between the races from a vertical to a horizontal one, seeing Negro races as complementing, instead of being inferior to, white races. Du Bois's pan-Africanism in fact necessitated assuming some form of collective racial identity if the term was to have any meaning or political usefulness. He argued that this identity was founded upon the idea of a common descent and a "shared history," binding, for example, African Americans to Africans. In "Illusions of Race" Appiah shows, by a rigorous process of logical elimination, that whatever the basis upon which one argues the point (genetically or according to "grosser morphological features" such as hair and skin color) not only is race largely insignificant as a means of explaining cultural differences and the historical evolution of peoples, but it ceases to be a valid basis of classificatory systems and thus of collective identification at all. From this perspective, the "Africa" that serves as the term of ultimate reference not only for early pan-Africanists such as Du Bois but for later movements inspired by his thinking (such as *négritude*) is essentially an invention and moreover an ideological construction that is, according to Appiah, an "outgrowth of European racialism."[13] Thus the danger for pan-Africanist movements is that the "Africa" to which they subscribe may be as mythical as the ideals underwriting American culture, as Dadié defines it. Since Dadié also, by identifying with black Americans, appears to be accepting the notion of a common racial ancestry, this clearly poses a problem for his attempt to undermine and escape, through ironic ethnographic inversion, the *patron* of Western discursive subjection. So where does this leave him?

Whether he seeks to transcend racial discrimination through projecting a future nonracial harmony, or whether he sides with his American "brothers and sisters" in a gesture of pan-Africanist solidarity, either way he runs the risk of eliding his agency as a narrative subject. In this respect *Patron de New York* is unlike the accounts of his travels to Paris and Rome (where he has no immediately obvious object of identification) in that the subjectivity of the narrator is literally submerged and consumed for the greater part of the narrative by "objective" (if rhetorically complex) commentary. The text seems to be the most straightforwardly nonfictional of the three travel narratives, precisely because the "je" is hardly ever mentioned (and my own analysis of the book bears this out, since I have throughout assumed Dadié and the narrator to be one and the same). However, the narrator does surface at a number of crucial moments, which have a significant bearing on the question of Dadié's "racialism."

On those few occasions in the text when he does pull the narrative back to his own subjective experience, it is usually to present himself as hopelessly (and thus quite humorously) unable to cope in conversation with Americans. In one scene from toward the end of the book, the narrator recounts an experience at a reception he attended at an American university. It recalls those situations that the narrators of both *Un nègre à Paris* and *La ville où nul ne meurt* found themselves in all too often and that marked them decisively (because more visibly so) as outsiders.[14] In *Patron de New York* the narrator—after drawing attention to himself for overenthusiastically applauding a speaker he didn't really understand—takes his turn in a queue to shake the university president's hand. When he reaches the president he suddenly seems to lose his bearings, and to lose his grip on the English language:

> Donc le bon Président me tient la main, me pose quelques questions. Pour moi, il avait changé d'ordre des questions et me voilà désemparé, perdu, dans les «Was», les «don't», les «did», les «I am», les «U» prononcés A, les «O» jouant aux A. Je me noyais. (250)

> [The good president extended his hand and asked me several questions. For me, he rearranged the questions, so there I was in distress, utterly lost in the "was," the "don'ts," the "did," the "I'm," the "U" pronounced "A," the "O" pretending to be "A." I was drowning.] (134)

The situation goes from bad to worse as he circulates among the other American guests. One man asks him how he is. He replies "thank you," and the man lets go of his hand and brusquely turns away. A woman offers him a fruit juice which he reluctantly takes, too self-conscious by this point to tell her that he finds most food and drink in America far too sweet for his taste. Then a Mexican American woman accosts him and starts helping him with his pronunciation of the English "th." To his momentary relief, she speaks French and is able to help him feel at ease for a while; however, his respite is short-lived and merely reinforces his status once she leaves him: "Grâce à elle, je restais Noir" (255) [Thanks to her I remained black] (137, trans. modified). He is a black precisely to the extent that he is out of place. At this moment of linguistic "drowning" and of fundamental cultural alienation, he experiences America in the same way as he imagines American blacks do, and his efforts to bridge racial differences through a kind of humanistic generosity seem to founder as he is forced into the position of racially excluded other.

Yet this representation of subjective disempowerment is precisely the moment of the narrative subject's performative inscription within the text. If the irony at one level condemns Dadié to the same cultural alienation as American blacks, at another level the writing subject in effect emerges by virtue of this ironic doubling (that is, Dadié and his narrator). Far from being a source of existential anguish, this apparent cultural and linguistic alienation is the pretext for the dazzling linguistic virtuosity we in fact get as an effect of the narrator's subjective intervention. Just as with the accounts of the travels to Paris and Rome, feigned "incompetence" doubles as mischievous and very deliberate playfulness (he shows his hand at one point when he talks of "their language which I deliberately butcher to tease them" [108]). Examples of this exuberant linguistic wit abound on almost every page. We have seen how this functions with *patron, ascenseur,* "one way," and so on. This playfulness takes on a deeper resonance when the subject is racial differences and the condition of American blacks. A discussion of the black ghettos surrounding many American cities becomes a pun on judo "black belts": "Nombreuses sont les cités portant des ceintures noires" (241) [Many cities wear black belts] (129). A description of blacks working in factories where goods are mass produced ("à la chaîne") leads to an analogy with the literal chains that bound African slaves to the slave ships. The evidence elsewhere of his command of English, and the subtlety of his cultural references, give the lie to his claim to linguistic and cultural naïveté. His puns are in fact often cross-cultural and translinguistic in nature. Referring again to the "simian" monosyllabic quality of American English, he mentions the popularization of "OK," remarking that "dans n'importe quel pays du monde, il faut avoir ce qu'on appelle le hoquet" (102) [in any country whatsoever in the world, it's necessary to have what is called the *hoquet* (= hiccoughs [but pronounced OK in French])] (54). And he has no end of fun with expressions for different kinds of relationships: "«To make a good match!» Faire un bon mariage! Marquer un but. Vous avez gagné la compétition [. . .] Mais «dear» n'est pas très loin de «deal»—affaire, marché—et de «death»—mort" (232) ["To make a good match!" To make a good marriage! To score a goal. You've won the competition [. . .] But "dear" is not very far from "deal"—business, the market—or from "death"] (124). This leads to further ironic comment about divorce: "Marriage avec un «r» de plus contenait le «R» de rupture" (233) [Marriage with an extra "r" contains the "R" of rupture] (124–25).

The linguistic playfulness with respect to relations between black and white reaches a kind of climax toward the end of the narrative. If white America, in the various rhetorical tensions of the text, seems to predominate by marginalizing, assimilating, and absorbing blackness through the various operations of "patronage," "black resistance" grows stronger as the narrative progresses. The textual buildup of this resistance parallels the historical struggle for self-affirmation of American blacks. In several brilliantly condensed passages the narrator draws together the various images of black and white which he has been developing in the course of the narrative: day and night; light and darkness, with all the established ideological associations that set European and European-based civilization in opposition to the dark continent of Africa; the white stars on the American flag; metaphors derived from the sea and sailing which contrast ships carrying voluntary immigrants with slave-bearing *négriers,* and so on. Previously Dadié had imagined Manhattan and its skyscrapers shaped like a huge ship. This image is taken up again toward the end when he writes, "La galère américaine a des soutes ténébreuses que voilent la lumière des mâts" (290) [The American galley houses dark holds hidden by luminous masts] (155). New York become a slave galley, with its huge buildings as the masts and its "dark holds" as both its excluded, hidden blacks and the dark underside of the history of American slavery. In this formulation, though, it is the "light" of these "white" buildings—or the sails ("voiles") on the masts—that paradoxically hide or veil ("que voilent") the darkness. Earlier Dadié had combined the chiaroscuro imagery with the symbolism of the stars of the American flag as a way of explaining, with poetic concision, white fears about black Americans: "Le jour a-t-il peur que la nuit ne lui réclame ses étoiles?" (262) [Does day fear that night will claim her stars?] (140), the irony being, of course, that the stars truly belong to the night.

Passages such as these signal a shift in the balance of power between black and white, with blackness being more and more positively valorized and whiteness less so. The only solution Dadié can see to certain problems afflicting white Americans is for them to become more black ("Best to wait until Americans become blacks . . . ," 150). The balance between black and white now takes the form not so much of the simple reversal of values we find with the ironic ethnographic inversion but rather of a deeper synthesis of cultural values, which in effect transfigures the terms black and white and their associated values:

> Oui, attendons qu'ils soient mûrs, c'est-à-dire assez noirs pour livrer des secrets de famille assez importants. Il faudrait toutefois qu'ils manifestent le désir de rester nègres. A ce propos, il serait souhaitable que la nuit se fasse sur l'Amérique, une nuit de cent ans et que Blancs et Noirs mêlés dans cette obscurité totale, se retrouvent au grand jour après ce siècle pour dire qui est Blanc, qui est Nègre! Oui, il manque de la nuit à l'Amérique, une bonne nuit de repos, de relaxe, de réflexion, une nuit pendant laquelle la lumière pourrait se faire dans les coeurs et les esprits.
>
> Cette nuit providentielle d'où naîtrait une nouvelle conception des rapports humains pourrait s'étendre à d'autres continents. (282–83)
>
> [Yes, it's true, we have to wait until they're mature, that is, black enough before we tell them such important family secrets. In any case, they'd have to want to remain black, and for that to happen, night would have to fall on America, a night of one hundred years from which whites and blacks, mixed together in total darkness, would emerge into broad daylight to announce who's white and who's black! Indeed, America needs nighttime, a good, restful night of reflection for the enlightenment of hearts and minds.
>
> This providential night—possibly heralding the birth of a new conception of human relations—might spread to other continents.] (151)

This new light that emerges out of the darkness, and not in opposition to it, gets Dadié's full approval as a potentially global force for good, which would supplant the imperialist spread of American capitalism.

This is more than a kind of idealistic wish for universal peace and harmony, even though the images of light and of coming into the world do bring Dadié back around to his own Christian beliefs (in a typically witty sequence he wonders what it means to be born—"voir le jour" [lit. "to see the light of day"]—in the nighttime, which is of course the Nativity scene). The power and full impact of the narrative lie less in *what* it says than in the interpenetration or artful weaving together of its themes and the cumulative rhetorical energy of its images. By "borrowing" and ultimately rewriting the American myth (that is, the *patron* and his global ambitions), Dadié ensures that the narrative form itself becomes a decisive statement. In what is perhaps the most unexpected irony of all, linking the text's cumulative effect to the economic model of which it offers such a devastating critique, the narrative can be read according to a capitalist logic (the model of the *patron*). What Dadié does is to invest his linguistic capital, putting it into a kind of high-growth savings account that accrues interest over time. By the end it has clearly produced a substantial return on his investment.

He has, of course, not simply "sold out" to capitalism and its values, any more than he has "bought into" the Western genre of travel writing, with the assimilation that would imply. The act of reappropriation and reinscription of the form he is ironizing is the key to the originality of Dadié's entire trilogy. With this reinvestment, irony is released from the static relationship of dependency which threatened to immobilize it. The text's "value" is no longer simply determined in opposition to an already fixed or determined value (say, the model or genre of Western travel writing) but is a function of the subjective investment of its narrative agency. Like the narrator of *Un nègre à Paris* mimicking colonial mimicry (and thereby producing a radically *other* narrative), the narrator of *Patron de New York* writes a text that generates its own value, its own identity. If it necessarily takes as its point of departure the clichés not only of American culture but also of the discourse of racialism itself, it effectively escapes falling back into the essentialism it ironizes because of this subjective inscription. The effects of Dadié's wit and linguistic playfulness are far-reaching and, I would argue, have a profoundly political dimension. One could say, in fact, that it is precisely by deconstructing conventions of race and color that Dadié is able to deessentialize and deontologize race relations. In this sense Dadié's *Patron de*

New York itself serves as an exemplary model, and what better way to read the final words of his narrative?

> Donner un coeur, une âme aux productions des usines, les con- traindre à remplir scrupuleusement leur rôle, qui d'autre que le Patron de New York pouvait réussir une si belle prouesse?
> Est-il étonnant que le monde entier se mette à son école? (308)

> [To give heart and soul to factory products, to compel them to fill their role scrupulously, what better way to accomplish such a beautiful feat than the One Way?
> No wonder the whole world is signing up for America's school.]
> (165)

The text itself—or rather the narrative performance, and a reading at- tentive to its performative and transformative effects—might thus ulti- mately be seen as a kind of *patron:* a blueprint, in a sense, for a future that is no longer projected as uniformly American, but one in which Africa plays a decisively influential role.

4

Subjectivity, History,
and the Cinematic
Ousmane Sembene's
Guelwaar and
Tierno Monénembo's
Cinéma

Ousmane Sembene wrote his novel *Guelwaar,* published in 1996, *after* his 1992 film of the same name, prefacing it with a few highly suggestive comments about the relationship between literature and film in Africa as it enters the new millennium.[1] It has become something of a commonplace in talking about Sembene's artistic development to see his shift from writing novels and short stories in French to producing films in which a large proportion of the dialogue is in Wolof or Diola as logically consistent with his enduring commitment to the Senegalese people and to the political function of both writing and filmmaking. As if to confirm the "value-added" dimensions of film over writing, he begins his novelistic adaptation of *Guelwaar* by reminding us again in the preface of the advantages of making a film from a previously existing written text:

> Because he has a book to draw on, the scriptwriter [*le scénariste*] [. . .]
> has at his disposal everything contained in this book. His work as a
> kind of geologist is facilitated because the ground (that is, the situation
> of the characters and dialogues) is already porous. The filmmaker pos-
> sesses tools that yield to his desires . . . High-angle shots, low-angle
> shots, tracking shots, the duration of a shot, the descriptive silence of
> the horizon. In the cinema, scenes of poverty-stricken dwellings are
> as beautiful as paintings produced by African artists, with their exces-

sive taste for bright colors. A close-up of a face is the limitless horizon of a soul, changing like the sea. As for the gaze (the eyes), it is an open door. This fleeting visualization is an effect (voyeurism) that the script-writer can invoke and that gives him a definite advantage over the writer.[2]

These distinct *artistic* advantages for the filmmaker have a corresponding *didactic* value for an African public: the wider accessibility for an illiterate audience, the powerful impact of cinematic images, the incorporation of traditional or more contemporary African music, the visual humor of films such as *Xala,* the more effective transposition of the oral dimension of traditional African narratives, the vividness of historical dramatizations, and the use of African languages in addition to, or instead of, French, all of which suggest that cinema can provide a far more authentic representation of the sociohistorical reality of African culture and is thus more appropriate to its political exigencies.[3]

This valorization would seem to be underlined all the more emphatically in the film *Guelwaar* given that, as the African critic Sada Niang has argued, the film seems to be making a forceful case against the repressive nature of writing and official written documents (taken as emblematic of colonial and neocolonial abuses of political and legislative power) and for the "socially enabling" potential of oral communication. As he puts it, "Through orality, the marginalized characters in society redefine themselves as citizens, charting a new course for themselves against the literate law-makers."[4] The empowering nature of indigenous language orality, represented by marginalized, subaltern groups, is in fact a thread running through many of Sembene's novels and films, but it is given more explicit expression in his films. Far from indicating a clear split between the two artistic practices, however, this empowerment through orality permits an ever wider expressive range in the presentation of the complex negotiation of positions within Senegalese society, and also opens the way for a mutually enriching relationship between film and fiction writing.

It is in this vein that Sembene continues his preface by recognizing, conversely, literature's "trump card" vis-à-vis cinema, which is its potential for narrating with greater depth and subtlety what is going on "behind" the image and the infinitely resonant silence of the character's face or eyes: "But on this precise point, the writer of literature has a trump card. He sculpts and paints with words (his tools) the shape of the face, and explores in depth the psychology of the subject. Where the film (its director) privileges spectacle and the spectacular, the writer [*le plumitif*] carves out and incises his reliefs, sentence by sentence." This reversal of priority produces what Sembene terms "une bigamie créatrice" [a creative bigamy], and he proposes this differently conceived relationship between the cinema and the novel as a new genre of sorts, one that might be linked to Africa's expression of its own modernity, its self-expressive and creative future (the subtitle of both the novel and the film *Guelwaar* is "Fable africaine de l'Afrique du XXIème siècle dédiée aux enfants du continent" [African fable of 21st-century Africa dedicated to the children of the continent]).

In this chapter I would like to follow up Sembene's suggestion of a creative interpenetration between cinema and literature by looking first at his novel *Guelwaar* as a significant rereading of the film, and then at a novel by the Guinean writer Tierno Monénembo, *Cinéma* (published in 1997), which explores some of these questions from a different perspective and in a very different cultural and historical context. I am not so much interested in weighing up the competing merits of the two media in contemporary African culture, or in discussing the cinematic adaptation or representation of legends or epics of (mostly colonial) history or of preexisting literary texts, although these are all important objectives for Sembene and other Francophone African filmmakers. Rather, I'd like to try to circumscribe the particularity, and the particular effects, of a literature that *proceeds from* the cinema, taking it as a theme as well as exploiting its specific qualities. In theoretical terms, this will coalesce around a reflection on the relationship between subjectivity, history, and the visual or cinematic imagination in a postcolonial African context.

A Twenty-first-Century Legend

The story of *Guelwaar* is based on an actual *fait divers*. Pierre Henri Thioune, also known as Guelwaar, one of the elders of a Christian community in Thiès, east of Dakar in Senegal, is killed in suspicious circumstances. To make matters worse, his body disappears. We learn, following investigations by the local police chief, Gora, aided by Guelwaar's expatriate son, Barthélémy, that it has been mistakenly delivered

to Muslims in a nearby village, who have buried him in a Muslim ceme-
tery according to Islamic traditions. The Christians seek to recover his
body, but the Muslim hierarchy argues that this is unacceptably sacri-
legious and refuse to allow Thioune to be disinterred. We sense a cover-
up, and one that involves collusion with the deputy of the region,
Amadou Fall. The answer to the puzzle of Guelwaar's death gradually
becomes clearer as we learn, through several flashbacks, that he had been
a militant figure, defending the rights of the Catholic Association of
Women to political freedom of speech, strongly denouncing as a form
of begging Senegal's continuing reliance on food aid from Europe, and
exposing the corrupt collusion between the neocolonial local government and the Islamic community. It is because of his dramatic and very
public intervention during a food aid distribution "event" designed to
express Senegal's gratitude to Europe that Thioune was murdered by
members of the corrupt Islamic hierarchy, acting under orders from the
deputy. Guelwaar's burial in Muslim sacred ground is thus no mistake
but a deliberate plan intended to prevent any subsequent incriminating
autopsy. The standoff between the Christian and Muslim communities
almost results in a full-scale riot, which is averted only by Gora's skillful
mediation between the various parties and by the courage and integrity
of Birame, the imam, who in a ferocious outburst disowns those of his
community responsible for the murder and cover-up—that is, Mor Cis,
the brother of the person supposedly buried in the grave, and his
cronies. The body is recovered and the Catholics transport it home.
Both the novel and the film end as the Catholics intercept a truck of
food aid heading for the Muslim village and proceed to break open the
bags and boxes and scatter their contents over the ground.

Guelwaar extends and reworks many of the themes of Sembene's earlier films and written texts, especially his fiercely critical attitude toward
the abuse of power of the Islamic community in Senegal (*Ceddo*), the
corruption of the neocolonial elite (*Xala*), the defiant insurrection and
transformative journey by disempowered social classes, and the need to
reconceive and renegotiate national identity (or rather its unwarranted
primacy) in order to explore social and economic tensions underlying
this nationalism.[5] This last point has determined an important shift in
Sembene's cinematic style away from the single point of view or cen-
trally focalized narratives of his early films, such as *Borom Sarret* (1963)
or *La noire de . . .* (1966), to what Philip Rosen terms the "decentred col-

lective narration" of the larger scale films such as *Emitaï* (1971), *Ceddo* (1976), or *Camp de Thiaroye* (1989).[6] This shift involves an abandonment of the use of single characters whose plight is intended to reflect a collective, national fate and a movement toward a more fragmented social vision. In these later films, and *Guelwaar* would be included among them, the narration is no longer focalized through individual subjectivities but via multiple, competing, and partial perspectives, which foreground the problem of conceiving of the nation in terms of any unitary harmony. Yet even in the early films, which seem to dramatize the psychology of a subjectivized narrator, there is already a deliberate distancing effect at work that contradicts the primacy of subjectivity. As Rosen astutely observes: "The ultimately insufficient knowledge of any individual character is a key epistemological provocation. The films imply the necessity of supra-individual, relational, collective perspective, even as they seem to make individualized consciousness a privileged object of representation."[7]

The emphasis Sembene places on the "psychology of the subject" in the preface to the novel *Guelwaar* thus seems all the more surprising, since even in his written fiction he is usually less interested in characterization as such than in the dynamic or dialectical interaction *between* characters, who are themselves often representative figures in the service of a broader sociopolitical vision. Yet Sembene is insistent on this point and identifies individual subjectivity as the pivotal point of articulation that tips the balance back in favor of literature ("on this precise point, the writer of literature has a trump card"), a subjectivity that is, as he goes on to say, relayed through the *look* or the gaze ("le regard"). Literature appears to recover the upper hand on the very ground—"le voyeurisme"—that one might assume to be cinema's inalienable artistic privilege. How, then, does the novel *Guelwaar* bear out this claim, and what does Sembene the *plumitif* do to Sembene the *scénariste* in this particular narrative?

On a cursory reading, the novel is quite faithful to the film in that it follows more or less the order and detail of the film's narrative. The novel includes many evocative descriptions of the landscape and weather and also several dialogues between the characters, such that it appears to be close to a screenplay, which Sembene himself openly admits: "I respected the framework of the script" (10). He provides additional background to the history of the various characters and their motivations and even begins chapter 7 as follows (an intervention I will come back to later): "A mi-récit, je dois vous ramener en arrière, pour vous narrer ce qui s'était passé, bien avant le soleil de ce funeste jour. Conteur, je ne dois omettre personne et situer chacun à sa place, même minime dans cette fable" [In mid-narrative I have to take you back to tell you what happened before the sun rose on this fateful day. As a storyteller I have to leave no one out, and to situate everyone, however minimal their role in this fable] (56). There are also several explanatory footnotes and authorial asides, such as the reference to the Regional Agricultural Cooperative, "which swallowed up a billion of our francs before the devaluation of 11 January 1994" (24). The descriptions of the suffocating heat and the stinging har- mattan winds that hamper the Catholics' efforts to recover Thioune's body have an intentional poetic effect in the novel, whereas the corre- sponding imagery of the film does not have the precise function of the language of the text, whose metaphors constantly echo the themes of oppression and of literal as well as figurative covering over. A few exam- ples (emphasis added): "Du nord, le *mboye* soufflait [. . .] *noyant* la zone d'un boubou de brume" [The *mboye* blew from the north [. . .] *drown- ing* the area in a *boubou* of mist] (103); "les derniers rayons du soleil auraient *englouti* avec voracité la concession mortuaire" [the last rays of the sun would have *swallowed up* voraciously the burial ground in the concession] (96); "Un souffle *suffocant oppressait* les narines" [A *suffo- cating* wind made it very *difficult to breathe* through one's nose] (30); "La grande concession des Thioune était *avalée* par la sombre silhouette du caïlcédrat" [The Thiounes' large concession was *swallowed up* by the dark silhouette of the cailcedra tree] (14); "La fine poussière se dégonfla avant de *retomber sur eux comme une voile* de barque" [The fine dust billowed up before *falling down on them like the sail* of a fishing boat] (129). Like the film, the novel uses the technique of flashbacks to gradually connect the dots of the story. But the novel makes a far more extensive and sub- tle use of individualized flashbacks, so we gain considerable insight into the personal memories of almost all the main characters.[8]

This is in fact part of a more widespread feature of the narrative, which constantly directs our attention to faces and to looks, and moves back and forth between *external* descriptions of visible expressions and commentary on what is going on *internally,* "behind" this expression.

This often takes the form of the conventional cinematic interplay of shot and reverse shot, such as when Barthélémy, Thioune's *évolué* son, first enters the police building:

> Barthélémy Thioune entra dans la grande salle [. . .] Il balaya d'un regard distant l'intérieur de la pièce avec l'air de dire: «Qui est votre responsable?» [. . .] Sa désinvolture attira l'attention. Le jeune gendarme de la table du fond l'épiait. Il était fasciné par le costard [. . .] En connaisseur de fringues, il se répétait: "Celui qui se nippe de la sorte n'est pas un cul terreux." (24–25)

> [Barthélémy Thioune entered the large room [. . .] His distant gaze swept around the inside of the room, as if to say "Who is in charge here?" [. . .] His offhand manner called attention to him. The young policeman at the desk at the back stared at him. He was fascinated by his suit [. . . .] He had an eye for fashion and kept saying to himself: "Anyone who gets dressed up like that is no country cousin."]

Pierre Henri Thioune's earlier visit to Gora, described in a flashback that is triggered off when Barthélémy gives his patrilinear name, is a tense eyeball to eyeball affair. The description of his eyes captures perfectly Thioune's imperturbable conviction:

> [L]es yeux de Guelwaar ne quittaient pas ceux du gendarme [. . .] A travers la fente des yeux ourlés de poils blancs surgissaient des prunelles humides, aux éclats de mercure. L'oeil droit plus grand, immobile, traquait et écoutait les pensées du gendarme. (32)

> [Guelwaar's eyes did not leave the policeman's [. . .] His moist, sparkling, mercury-like pupils glared through his narrowed eyes which had white hairs around them. His larger, immobile right eye tracked and listened to the policeman's thoughts.]

This emphasis on faces and looks is evident in the depiction of the other characters, too. René, one of the Catholic elders (who are collectively known as *Guelwaar-yi*), makes a joke at one point: "Son visage révélait une gaieté intérieure qui se reflétait dans ses yeux noyés de larmes" [His face revealed an inner gaiety which was reflected in his tear-soaked eyes] (62). Baye Aly, the Muslim village chief, is initially very wary of Gora: "Du coin de l'oeil, il épia le gendarme avec méfiance en pensant: 'Lorsque tu parles, tu sais ce que tu dis. Mais tu ne sais pas comment l'autre va l'entendre'" [He stared mistrustfully at the police-man out of the corner of his eyes, thinking: "When you speak, you know what you're saying. But you don't know how the other person will take it"] (84). The profound relief of Nogoye Marie, Thioune's widow, once his body is finally discovered is described thus: "Délivreé de ses afflictions, les yeux clos—un profond regard intérieur—, elle égrenait son chapelet" [Liberated from her suffering and with her eyes closed—a profound inner gaze—she counted the beads on her rosary] (158) .

Finally, there are two decisive descriptions of looks toward the end of the novel. First, the most respected elders of the Christian and Mus-lim communities, Gor Mag and Birame, who as young boys, along with Thioune, had been circumcised together, reaffirm a friendship that tran-scends religious differences. In a triumph of mutual respect and toler-ance over mistrust and intolerance, they are able to look at each other with complete openness: "Les deux septuagénaires se dévisagèrent, si-lencieux, sans haine, ni rancune" [The two seventy-year-olds gazed at each other in silence, with no hatred or bitterness] (155). Then Nogoye Marie, called upon by the Catholic priest to stop the destruction of the food aid, instead pronounces a damning judgment on the Catholic elders' willing subservience to the politics of collusion, a verdict that is preceded by an all-powerful look: "Nogoye Marie scruta les visages, coula un long regard sur le chemin coloré, et répondit:—Gor Mag, ce qui est un péché, c'est ce que vous, *Guelwaar-yi,* avez fait" [Nogoye Marie stud-ied their faces, turned and looked long and hard at the colored path, and answered: "Gor Mag, it is what you, *Guelwaar-yi,* have done that is a sin"] (161–62).

This technique of looking behind the looks—whether by directly recounted interior monologue, descriptions of thoughts and feelings, or looser variations of free indirect discourse—is of course not new to the novel and could be seen, rather than as an innovative adaptation of cin-ematic conventions to novelistic ends, as a return to a traditional realist narrative form, with its distanced, objective, omniscient narrator. This would be to forget, though, that this technique has to be read in con-junction with the infinitely suggestive power of the cinematic close-up and the look that it is rewriting, the "fleeting visualization" and the "lim-itless horizon of the soul." What the novel does is to demystify one of cinema's most potent effects—the mesmerizing promise of a perfect correspondence between inside and outside, between the gaze and the soul—or to "read" this effect, to put down finite boundary markers on the potential infinity of what the look conveys. When Sembene admits in the preface to *Guelwaar* that the psychologization of the look has been creatively productive for him ("It has enriched me"), he is not shifting the emphasis away from the sociopolitical resources of decentered collective narration in the film to the psychological inner world of his characters in the novel, since individual psychology continues to function as a structural device, rendering explicit what is often alluded to or implied in the film. What Sembene does in cinematic terms, according to Rosen, is to challenge the convention in Western film whereby point of view connotes individual psychology and to reinscribe this convention into a postcolonial African context.

A good example of this in the film is the scene in which Nogoye Marie addresses her dead husband, or rather his clothes laid out on the bed. It is cinematically "coded" as a private address to Guelwaar, that is, as a monologue revealing to us her inner emotional state, the intensity of her love, and her despair at the heavy burden of the legacy she is left to bear. Yet it is filmed ironically in shot/reverse-shot, thus indicating that this "individual psychology" is determined by the limitations of her public role as Guelwaar's wife. As Rosen puts it: "That she will never reveal her disputes with her husband publicly insures, as usual in Sembene's work, that the narration does not anchor itself in an individual character, and simultaneously poses a sociopolitical analysis of her problem."[9] The novel not only makes this level of sociopolitical analysis more explicit—describing, for example, Nogoye Marie's social embarrassment about her daughter Sophie's prostitution—but also importantly extends her criticism of Thioune in a way that I will return to.

What is significant about Sembene's "omniscient" comments is that he submits himself to this same movement away from individual psychology, so that we have to read authorial interventions such as the opening of chapter 7 ("A mi-récit, je dois vous ramener en arrière . . .") in terms of decentered collectivity. These comments are always *engagés,* he always demonstrates solidarity with his people, as in the earlier remark about the devaluation of "our" money. Just as he often appears as a minor character within his films, so he includes himself as part of the collective history that he uncovers. In fact, Sembene leaves many loose ends and at several points in the narrative lets certain characters' words or actions remain enigmatic. When Gora mentions to Barthélémy that he has never visited Europe, Sembene's narrator wonders himself what motivates this statement: "Sentiment d'envie? Reproche de celui qui n'a jamais quitté l'Afrique? Rêve de connaître un ailleurs plus clément?" [Is it a feeling of envy? The reproach of someone who has never left Africa? The dream of discovering a more temperate "elsewhere"?] (30). At other points he openly turns the responsibility for completing the story over to the reader: "Le reste, à vous de le découvrir" [The rest is for you to find out] (76). In drawing the reader into the narrative, and downgrading his own role as omniscient author, Sembene reinscribes his objectivity as one more subjective perspective within the multiplicity of partial outlooks. Rather than designating a position of control, subjectivity is thus, as Rosen puts it, "a symptom of the characters' limitations."[10] This is already implicit in Sembene's early films and becomes increasingly explicit. In films such as *Xala,* which Rosen describes as a "relatively focalized narration," situated between the early and later films, this theoretical stance is already fully in place: "Subjectivity is ultimately conceived as an objective sociopolitical force among other objective sociopolitical forces shaping and limiting the centrality of any individual subject."[11] One might well ask—if Sembene is in fact "always already" working with a model of the subject as sociopolitically determined—whether the question of individual subjectivity needs to be posed at all. Or alternatively, whether the few gestures he makes toward divesting himself of authorial responsibility are sufficient to achieve this desubjectivization. This might best be answered by considering more directly how Sembene considers the creative act itself, and the implications that the shift from the film to the novel has for his broader conception of the relationship between literature or cinema as a means of political intervention.

In the film, the powerful indictment of the neocolonial political elite and the theme of continued dependence on foreign aid, as well as criticism of the collusion between local government and the Islamic community, are channeled through the charismatic figure of Pierre Henri Thioune, who, already dignified by his identification with the Wolof traditional nobility (who are known as *Guelwaar*), becomes something of a martyr following his death. His chosen association with the traditional *Guelwaar* underlines Sembene's conviction that true collective autonomy can best be achieved by looking beyond the boundaries imposed, and the divisions wrought, by the various "imported" religious beliefs and ideological values, and coupling this with a shared political vision for the future. As with his other historical films, Sembene demonstrates the necessity of returning to the past in order to understand the present, of digging up what has been buried, of rewriting official histories as a contemporary political act and as a step toward transforming the future. Significantly, it is Thioune's young followers—in particular Etienne and Yandé—who carry his ideas forward with the most courage and conviction, who initiate the tearing up of the food sacks, and who actively espouse a kind of syncretism of Catholicism and traditional African religion. Although the novel subscribes as unconditionally as the film to Thioune's political convictions, it nonetheless offers a telling critique of his methods and, by extension, of the potential dangers of cinema as a vehicle for historical revisionism.

As we have seen, the novel's probing exploration of different characters' thoughts and emotions underlines the decentralization of subjective positions we find in the film and enables us to read subjectivity more clearly as objective symptom. An important consequence of this narrative technique in the novel is that we learn more about Thioune's less savory past, in particular when the narrative is focalized through the women characters. They know more than anyone about the notorious womanizing of the *Guelwaar-yi,* and indeed we learn that Anna, one of the young members of the Catholic Association of Women, is pregnant with Thioune's child. It emerges that "Thioune's" ideas are not his at all but originated with one of the women, Angèle, who was the first to refuse Western food aid and who moreover refused it from one of Thioune's contemporaries, Guigname, as part of her revenge against him for taking a second younger wife (hardly consistent with his Catholicism!). She launches into a ferocious verbal attack on the phallocratic mentality of all the *Guelwaar-yi* and their submissive acceptance of Western aid. It is her act that is in effect the source and inspiration of Thioune's, and the women are thus well positioned to "see through" the hypocrisy of the Catholic elders, culminating in Nogoye Marie's summative judgment of them at the end. As we saw, the women's condemnation of the elders' hypocrisy is hinted at in the film but given far less emphasis.

Likewise, his wife criticizes the selfishness of Thioune's uncompromising stance because he has made no provision for her and their children after his death. Whereas in the film, the scene in which she castigates the *Guelwaar-yi* for not being as courageous as her husband suggests her espousal of Thioune's ideas, her willingness to carry them forward, in the novel this emphasis shifts, and her intervention is reencoded within the more explicitly profeminist speeches by the other women characters. Her criticism of her daughter's prostitution (which Thioune was willing to overlook, since for him it was better than accepting foreign aid, and it allowed her to financially support her brother, Aloys) is realigned with Yandé's wish for a future in which young women will no longer have to resort to prostitution at all. Indeed, as with other films and novels of Sembene, it is the women who are the real catalysts for the action, who see clearly, and who get the men to come round to their point of view. All the characters, in fact, are willing to compromise and are transformed to some extent, including Barthélémy, who at the beginning defines himself as a French citizen but by the end is speaking Wolof rather than French. As he proudly proclaims, "I have always been Senegalese" (54). All, that is, except Thioune, who dies for his stubborn absolutism. He may be a hero, but his mistake is to believe in his own heroism, his incarnation as a *Guelwaar.* He wants to speak for his people, a role that is emphasized in the film, whereas in the novel his people all speak for themselves and come to understand the need to reconceive political cooperation and action in terms of mutual respect and compromise (not toward the West, of course, but toward each other, whatever the other's religion, social status, or political belief).

The multiple subjectivities that the novel provides space for suggest a collective African historical memory that is made up of the sum of its parts and is not derived from a single authoritative version. Thioune is very much a filmic character, one who is in a sense stuck in a kind of historical imaginary; it is no accident that he makes use of the very public spectacle of the food aid distribution event, that he should choose the visual resource of the spectacular, in order to get across his political message. In the film, he is the one character who is truly mesmerizing, his look is the most direct and visually powerful, but of all the faces and looks described in the novel, his remains the most opaque, the least open to scrutiny. Thioune's "vision" of a politically and economically autonomous Africa would appear to be at the opposite end of the spectrum from his expatriate son's idealized cinematic image of Dakar ("an enchanted universe," 28), of which Barthélémy is gradually disabused as the story unfolds. However, they are both versions of the same desire to view a complex, mobile, heterogeneous sociohistorical reality through the lens of a reductive visual imagination. And this might be the very risk that cinema itself runs, and to which Sembene refers when he says in his preface, "The arbitrariness of cinematic norms is a pitfall" (10). While the case for a politically committed cinema as a means toward reconceiving national identity is for Sembene a compelling one, *Guelwaar* the film needs *Guelwaar* the novel to remind it of its aesthetic risks, to save it from being coopted and reassimilated by the very ideology and monolithic view of history it seeks to challenge.

Films and fiction writing are equally important for Sembene, and both allow him to express his own vision of Africa in the twenty-first century. In their different ways, the film and novel versions of *Guelwaar* are both necessarily open-ended in the kind of future they advocate for Senegalese society. This is not a kind of utopianism, since as we have seen, Sembene is less interested in *representing* sociohistorical reality than in using cinema and literature as catalysts for the *transformation* of social relationships. Although cinema, particularly around the language question, may seem to be the artistic medium that can mold itself most authentically to African cultural contexts (that is, Sembene the *cinéaste* as the "cinematic griot" par excellence), it may ultimately be the case that literature is a more faithful descendant of the art of the griot. As Sembene himself has pointed out, since cinema is *not* in fact interactive but instead imposes its subject, leaving nothing to the imagination, it should not be confused with orality, even though it has been able to exploit the resources of indigenous traditions in rich and startling ways. In the novel *Guelwaar,* but not in the film, there is a public performance to rival Thioune's own at the food aid distribution event—Angèle's diatribe against Guigname, the "original" version of Thioune's speech. The sheer force of her language proves irresistible to all those present in the concession:

> En vraie *mbadakatt,* Angèle avait l'adhésion du public. Débordante de vitalité tant sa haine était puissante, elle déplaçait son corps volumineux avec souplesse. Ses bras courts accompagnaient l'avalanche de son verbe riche et coloré. Ses propos déchaînaient l'hilarité générale. (60)

> [Angèle captivated her audience like a real *mbadakatt.* Her hatred was so strong that she burst with vitality as she gracefully swung her voluminous body around. Her short arms accompanied the avalanche of

her rich and colorful speech. Her words triggered off a general feeling
of great mirth.]

A footnote gives us the definition of *mbadakatt,* which could indeed
describe Sembene's own artistic performance in producing the "creative
bigamy" between the film and the novel versions of *Guelwaar:* "a type of
actor or satirical storyteller. He is his own author, actor and director. He
is rewarded for the elegance and beauty of his speech." The *mbadakatt*
is in fact very close to the "new griots," those who have adapted their
art to the entertainment business. Angèle's performance is not that of a
traditional griot and does not point to a revalorization of indigenist
authenticity in the novel. Her act is quite transgressive, perhaps even
more radical than Thioune's, since like Sembene, she is breaking new
ground, culturally speaking. In her own way she seems to be suggesting
a possible syncretism—a creative bigamy?—between tradition and modernity, grounding her performance in the tradition of the griot's art but
without its social parasitism, which is ultimately very much of the same
order as the food aid "begging" Sembene condemns so forcefully.

So one might say that the novel's dramatization of the interplay
between what appears to be a fairly traditional individual authority
and a broader, socially determined "subjectivity-as-symptom" does not
merely reproduce a common tension present in European realist fiction
from Balzac onward. If this debate typically plays itself out at the level
of representation, in Sembene's terms the representative value of creativity is overridden by its power to bring about social transformation,
and it is thus its performative effect that comes to the fore. Read performatively, the novel also demonstrates the extent to which *Guelwaar*
enacts its own allegory, as a story about African cinema today, its conditions and potential, its continuing financial and technical dependence
upon the West, and its struggle to establish its own identity and autonomy in the face of the continued overwhelming dominance of imported
films.[12] This theme is also at the heart of the novel I would like to turn
to now, Tierno Monénembo's *Cinéma.*

Voyeurism and History

Monénembo is not a filmmaker, but his text is an intricate psychological drama in which the cinema both serves as a central theme and also

informs the narrative itself, making it very much "creatively bigamous," in Sembene's terms. The novel is set in a small town, Mamou, in the Fouta Djallon region of Guinea. The main events take place in 1958, immediately before Independence, and are focalized through the impressionistic memories of the first-person teenage narrator, Binguel. It is written in the form of an autobiography recalling Binguel's early adolescent years and the trials of his life at home and at the Koranic and French schools.[13] Two older friends, Ardo and Benté, offer him an escape route and introduce him to the world of the cinema run by the Lebanese Seïny-Bôwal, where the big attractions are the Westerns he shows. Binguel idolizes Benté in particular, who represents for him a form of independence from various social constraints; freedom from the relentless surveillance of his father, the Koran master, and the head-teacher; and an initiation into a more exciting world of young adulthood. This is seen—with some irony, as it will turn out—as a liberation from other people's looks: "C'était bien la première fois que je voyais deux êtres humains libres de leurs soucis ainsi que du regard des autres" [This was really the first time I had seen two human beings free from their own worries as well as from the looks of other people].[14]

In a kind of relayed relationship of hero worship and identification, Binguel looks up to Benté as if he were a screen idol, just as Benté himself identifies with many of his favorite movie characters. Both live their lives as if they were in a film (Binguel: "When things would get really rough, I imagined I was in a film," 46). Their heroes are Gary Cooper, Rod Steiger, Burt Lancaster, and John Wayne; and Benté and Binguel each adopt screen personae, the "Oklahoma Kid" and "L'Homme de l'Ouest" [The Man of the West], respectively. The association between archetypal Hollywood Western characters and Binguel's own "Western-ization" is in fact heavily overdetermined in the novel. His father, Môdy Djinna, is an import/export merchant who has done very well for himself under French colonial rule; he lives in a spacious *pavillon,* wines and dines on imported French food, dresses himself and Binguel in French clothes, and is the most European character in the novel. In a further extension of the analogy between the Wild West and Western colonialism in Africa, Mamou as a place takes on the aspect of a frontier town, one of the countless far-flung outposts of civilization which, as in the American Far West, sprang up as the railway was developed. The town is very much a product of colonization, "a small town built under the fateful auspices of the railway" (157), and is populated by a collection of outcast or outlaw characters, both African and French, that are typical of Monénembo's fictional world.

Binguel's account of this crucial period in Guinea's history in thus filtered through his vivid filmic imagination, such that his Hollywood-inspired adolescent fantasies become a screen that also serves to conceal the political reality of the time, the impending dictatorship of Sékou Touré. Binguel's is a subjectivity that is not yet formed, that is still extremely impressionable and malleable, as his initially rather one-sided friendship with Benté demonstrates. That history and fantasy should merge and be confused in his mind is not at all surprising, given that any information he possesses about the current political scene is likely to have been gathered from the French-produced, and therefore ideologically controlled, newsreels that accompany the main attraction at the cinema.[15] His fantasy version of history is also an immobilization of history and deprives him of any true historical consciousness or agency.[16]

The point, though, is not just that Binguel is incapable of any historical understanding because of his immaturity, of which his fantasy life is symptomatic. Monénembo suggests that Binguel's subjective impressionism is related metaphorically to the wider question of collective historical memory in the novel. Binguel's perspective is both singular, individual, and also representative of how the political maneuverings of the key players were perceived at the time by the population of Guinea. General de Gaulle and Sékou Touré also become actors nicknamed "Général" and "Boubou Blanc," and in the run-up to the 1958 referendum the supporters of Independence and of continuing attachment to France are transformed into "Eléphants" and "Flèches" [Arrows] respectively. As with other scenes in the novel, such as the opening chapter, and the drunken row in the bar where Binguel shoots Bambâdo, a well-known local troublemaker, the historic meeting between Sékou Touré and de Gaulle is described in terms of a Hollywood drama, with both protagonists confronting each other in a kind of showdown. If the story is essentially about Binguel's passage from childhood to adulthood, "my fragile awakening to the world" (45) as he says, his life also stands in an allegorical relationship to Guinea at an equally pivotal turning point in its history. Written as an autobiography, and with the true nature of Sékou Touré and his regime known in hindsight, the novel presents the transition to Independence as a spectacular failure, and Guinea as still in its political adolescence, in a state of "arrested development," as it were. The country under Sékou Touré, the novel suggests, moved into a phase of cultural regression that was every bit as ahistorical as the imaginary projections of the Hollywood-style colonialism it replaced. So how does the novel develop this problematic identification with the colonizer, and what does it tell us about the relationship between subjectivity and the cinematic imaginary?

Homi Bhabha, in his essay "The Other Question," discusses stereotyping and the imaginary fixity that structures and motivates colonial discourse, but he claims that not enough attention has been paid to the process of subjectification, of both the colonizer and the colonized. Focusing on the psychic processes involved in the encounter between colonizer and colonized, he describes the identification it involves as structurally ambivalent, an ambivalence that disrupts the clear-cut opposition of colonizer and colonized as fully constituted subjects.

> In the act of disavowal and fixation the colonial subject is returned to the narcissism of the Imaginary and its identification of an ideal ego that is white and whole. For what these primal scenes illustrate is that looking/hearing/reading as sites of subjectification in colonial discourse are evidence of the importance of the visual and auditory imaginary for the *histories* of societies.[17]

He goes on to relate the panoptic surveillance necessary for the exercise of colonial power to the scopic drive of psychoanalytic theory, and more specifically to the relationship of narcissistic identification which structures Lacan's Imaginary Order and the voyeurism of the primal scenes in which it is played out. Much film theory that uses psychoanalytic models describes the spectator's position as an essentially voyeuristic one.[18] This voyeurism is not restricted to particular conventions in narrative film that sometimes address an implied hidden viewer, but is determined by the necessary (and therefore necessarily fetishistic) relationship to the always hidden camera. Binguel's fantasy-driven subjectivity is an assimilated version of the colonial imaginary as represented by the archetypal Hollywood cinematic product, the Western. He thus appears to repeat the very Imaginary closure and fixity that characterize the narcissism and panoptic voyeurism of the colonial subjugation of the other. He is not in fact alone but is merely reproducing the same colonial imaginary order that Benté had already assimilated before him, and the same constant surveillance to which his father subjects him: his father's room is described explicitly as a kind of panopticon, a "tanière [. . .] d'où mon vieux loup de père surveillait son monde" [a lair [. . .] from which my old dragon of a father kept watch over his world] (52).

There are in fact several scenes of voyeurism in *Cinéma,* but I would like to focus on one in particular.[19] This is the opening chapter of the novel, which in terms of the chronology of the story takes place somewhere in the middle of Binguel's friendship with Benté. He is past the initial phase of blind adulation, which occupies the early part of the narrative, and is beginning to rebel against the total subservience Benté demands and to assert his own identity. He has stolen Benté's gun, which he will use toward the end of the novel to kill Bambâdo. Benté is unaware that his gun is missing, nor does he know that Binguel is watching him from his hiding place at the top of a pole in the town dump next to the marketplace. The scene is recounted as a reversal of fortunes; Binguel is now the one literally occupying a position from which he can look down on Benté—"how pitiful he looks seen from so high up!" (23)—and he carefully plans the moment at which he will leap out and assert his new-found power, which he does at the end of the chapter: "Je bondis comme un lièvre, le vise sur la nuque et hurle: —Bouge pas, Oklahoma Kid! Cette fois, c'est moi qui mène le bal!" [I leap out like a hare, aim my gun at the back of his neck, and yell: "Don't move, Oklahoma Kid! This time I'm running the show!"] (28). Binguel is in no hurry, however, but relishes his invisibility, remaining silent to Benté's pleas that he reveal himself and exploiting to the full the pleasure afforded him by his panoptic view; like a camera tracking its object, he follows Benté's every move as he walks around the empty market stalls and abandoned cars. His interior monologue, which vents in somewhat sadistic language his contemptuous feelings for his former mentor now that he is in a position to express them openly, provides a kind of voice-over to the filmic images. In fact the whole scene, like the meeting between de Gaulle and Sékou Touré, is narrated with the drama of a Western gunfight in which a knowing calculation of motives, and anticipation of actions, are crucial.

Binguel's bid for independence from Benté is not, however, one that will provide a way out of the circuit of narcissistic identification. His feelings toward Benté fluctuate constantly between enmity and friendship, revenge and pity, hard-heartedness and compassion. He is caught between distance and identification, and this ambivalence toward Benté is in fact precisely how the Imaginary functions in Lacanian terms, that is, simultaneously as narcissism (seeing myself in the other) and as aggressivity (to counter the threat of self-alienation and absence). Furthermore, in this act of fetishistic disavowal of Benté, Binguel continues to imagine himself as one of his screen heroes, yearning to be the object of the same adulation and to acquire the same legendary status he had bestowed on his friend: "Voilà comment que je veux qu'ils réagissent, et que même dans les brumes de la sénilité ils se souviennent encore des prouesses de l'Homme de l'Ouest" [That's how I would like them to react, and even in the mists of their senility, I would still like them to remember the exploits of the Man of the West] (20–21). Rather than establish his own identity, he is intent merely on occupying the "same" position as Benté. The twist at the end of the novel, when he is congratulated by the police rather than punished for murder, acts as a kind of "suturing" of the wound of alienation and appears to confirm his ultimate reassimilation as something of a hero within the community. It also seems to give the narrative—which, like Binguel's fate and the relatively predictable world of life in Mamou, is fast disintegrating and losing its coherence—a final and satisfying closure, which is consistent with the moment when, in psychoanalytic terms, the split subject of the Imaginary Order recovers its plenitude in the Symbolic Order.

The opening scene could thus be read as emblematic of the novel's subtle weaving together of its themes of subject-formation, the recuperative power of colonial discourse, and the cinematic imagination. Binguel and Benté naively believe that they are, in their adolescent rebelliousness, subverting the panoptic surveillance of the various authority figures, yet Monénembo suggests that it is precisely the substitutable nature of this narcissistic or fetishistic denial of difference which underpins the ensuing political immaturity of Guinea under Sékou Touré. More than this, it immobilizes history, in true Hollywood style. This is very much what is happening in the opening scene, which is in fact hard to locate temporally within the rest of the story. So although it makes effective use of a number of cinematic techniques (such as the dramatic entry in medias res into the story, the camera eye of Binguel following Benté, his interior monologue "voice-over," and a kind of narrative present, from which we begin to get fragments of the events leading up to this present via short flashbacks), it also points to the potential ahistoricism of classic cinematic representation. As if to underline this, Binguel states at one point in his commentary: "Time no longer has any meaning after what I have decided to do" (18).

Yet there is more to this opening scene. What Binguel does in making Benté the object of his own voyeuristic pleasure is to expose him by catching him off guard and glimpsing the human reality behind his tough persona. He cannot help feeling moved by this spectacle: "Tiens, je ne l'aurais jamais imaginé aussi songeur et dubitatif! A présent, son visage exprime quelque chose de touchant, de terriblement fragile et solitaire" [Well, I would never have imagined him so pensive and skeptical! Right now the expression on his face is quite touching, he seems terribly fragile and solitary] (12); "Cette fois, j'ai bien envie de descendre l'embrasser" [This time I really wanted to climb down and kiss him] (23). Although suppression of feelings and insensitivity to others are preconditions of their bravado image—Binguel talks at one point of "la mare des émois nuisibles et des scrupules inutiles qu'il me faudrait assécher" [the pond full of harmful emotions and useless scruples that I have to drain out] (91)—by exposing his friend's defenseless humanity he also lays bare his own vulnerability and fragility. The question of gender is of course paramount here, which is consistent both with the psychoanalytic basis of the subject-positioning of cinema spectatorship and with the extension of this articulation into the area of subjectivity in colonial discourse. His masculinity is predicated on a rejection of the "feminine" qualities of sensitivity of feeling and empathy toward others. Binguel's identification is exclusively masculine, just as the narcissistic investment of the spectator's subjectivity in classic Hollywood cinema involves a kind of complicitous externalizing and objectifying of woman as Other,[20] and indeed he goes through a necessary phase of rejection of his mother. His imagined manliness is also a repetition of the patriarchal structure of the colonizer's objectification of the colonized other, and the most vividly symptomatic illustration of this assimilation is his participation in the degrading treatment of the most abject and helpless character in the town, King Kong.

As Monénembo implicates our position as spectator/readers, we become the *voyeurs* watching Binguel watch Benté, and this more vulnerable Binguel—not "L'Homme de l'Ouest" or the surprise local hero of the end—is the one we in fact see throughout the novel. More important, we are watching Binguel watch himself, not only as an adolescent struggling to find some kind of identity but as the older, post–Sékou

Touré narrator looking back on this decisive transitional time of his life. This other "look" is perhaps the crucial one in a reading of *Cinéma*, since it brings into play a very different historical memory from the apparently dominant model in the novel, that is, the cinematic immobilization of history, with all its political and psychoanalytical ramifications. The older narrator intervenes at one point near the beginning of the novel to comment on the quality of his friendship with Ardo, the shoeshine man, who ultimately turns out to have a far more significant and lasting influence on him than Benté:

> Maintenant que les jeux sont définitivement faits, pour ce qui est de mes illusions tout au moins, je me demande si, de tous mes instants vécus, je ne préfère pas ceux-là, certes fugaces et rarissimes mais combien riches et sauvegardés dans le film de mes souvenirs. Je m'y étais fait un ami, aujourd'hui disparu: Ardo, le vertueux cireur de chaussures, le conteur infatigable. Ses paroles me captivaient, j'en oubliais mon essence et ma raison ainsi que les foucades de cette ville si forte dans l'art du mensonge que le diable s'en porte mal. L'écouteur me guérissait de tous les maux, réels ou imaginaires . . . (29)

> [Now that the die has finally been cast, at least as far as my illusions are concerned, I wonder whether, of all the moments I have lived through, I don't prefer those that are of course fleeting and extremely rare but oh so rich and preserved in the film of my memories. I had made a friend who is no longer with us: Ardo, the virtuous shoeshine man, the indefatigable storyteller. His words captivated me, and made me forget my essence and my reason, as well as the whims of this town, so skilled in the art of deception it would make the devil himself ill. As he listened to me, Ardo cured me of all my ills, real or imaginary . . .]

These fleeting moments have a very different quality in his "memory film" than the cinematic illusions that deprived him of the possibility of determining either his own destiny or that of his country ("Now that the die has finally been cast"). Although these moments are themselves described as cinematic, they also suggest a more potent, transformative historical memory that is bound up with narration and writing: Ardo is a consummate *conteur* and also something of a psychoanalyst for the young Binguel ("As he listened to me, Ardo cured me of all my ills"), a role that the older Binguel assumes in writing the autobiographical text he does. It is the older narrator who is the true writing subject, the one who in writing makes visible the "invisible" subject of his early voyeuristic fantasies, and by association the invisible subject of colonial discourse. More important, this writing involves a kind of dissolution of this illusory subjective identity ("made me forgot my essence and my reason"), as well as of the colonial world of pre-Independence Guinea, but suggests renewed contact with a more deeply rooted subjectivity, one that is preserved intact in Ardo's captivating stories and that has its foundation in an enduring orality.

Monénembo does not set up a simple opposition between cinema and literature but suggests that a *writing of* (that is also a deconstruction of) the visual or cinematic is one extremely potent means of reactivating history, and thereby transforming the present. *Cinéma* is a novel that both dramatizes and problematizes the aesthetic (narcissistic) pleasure specific to films; it is a text whose narrative complexities also work to resist a sense of closure and to unsettle any easy imaginative identification, whether between the characters, between the narrator and his younger self, or between the readers and the text. In this respect—to return to my point of departure—it is consistent with Sembene's insight into the creative potential of a literary rewriting of the cinematic when he says at the end of his preface: "When we set up our own School of Cinema [. . .] we will have to [. . .] exploit this method for the writers and filmmakers of the future."

5

The Gendered
Subject of Africa
Mudimbe's
Le bel immonde and
Shaba deux

In her well-known if not always well-understood essay on the subaltern woman's inability to "speak," Gayatri Spivak succinctly describes the historical fate of disenfranchised women, showing how they are the ones most consistently exiled from both a colonial and a postcolonial episteme. As she puts it, "Both as object of colonialist historiography and as subject of insurgency, the ideological construction of gender keeps the male dominant. If, in the context of colonial production, the subaltern has no history and cannot speak, the subaltern as female is even more deeply in shadow."[1] Although Spivak's cultural reference in the context of her essay is rural subaltern Indian women, her critical paradigm is clearly relevant to African women, who have likewise had to contend with this double objectification, oppression and social alienation: as Africans they have been the Other of colonial discourse, but as women they have been the Other of a patriarchal order that operates both internally and externally. What I would like to do in this chapter is to think through the question of the gendered subject of Africa by taking as my point of departure Spivak's discussion of essentialism as it relates to strategies for a feminist contestation of the universal Subject of phallocentrism. I will make some loose but, I hope, theoretically productive connections to Judith Butler's now canonical text, *Gender Trouble,* and then to Mudimbe's account of the discursive violence of colonial and neocolonial systems of knowledge/power in an African context. As well as referring to his essays, I will spend most of the chapter looking more closely at his two novels that explicitly dramatize the question of female subjectivity, *Le bel immonde* [*Before the Birth of the Moon*] and *Shaba deux*.

For Spivak, the colonial "subaltern" has become in postcolonial theory the object of the West's nostalgic yearning for the source of an "authentic" native voice. The subaltern's "inability" to speak, according to Spivak, is a function precisely of the fact that she has no place within the discursive hegemony of the social text in which she is nonetheless sociohistorically implicated. The West's perhaps well-intentioned desire to accord subjectivity and agency to the subaltern classes can thus end up merely consolidating a structure of colonial hegemony, even if on the surface the classes are fully acknowledged and are granted the means to autonomy and self-representation. Spivak summarizes as follows:

> Reporting on, or better still, participating in, antisexist work among women of color or women in class oppression in the First World or the Third World is undeniably on the agenda. We should also welcome all the information retrieval in these silenced areas that is taking place in anthropology, political science, history, and sociology. Yet the assumption and construction of a consciousness or subject sustains such work and will, in the long run, cohere with the work of imperialist subject-constitution, mingling epistemic violence with the advancement of learning and civilization. And the subaltern woman will be as mute as ever.[2]

The "epistemic violence" of this desire for a full, voiced subject that can be retrieved from beneath the multiple layers of discursive objectification and exclusion has direct implications for the question of representation, in the double sense in which Spivak, returning to Marx's original German text, deploys the term: that is, both *Darstellung*, as artistic representation, and *Vertretung*, as political representation or "speaking for" another. If First World intellectuals are discursively bound to perpetuate the silencing of subaltern classes in the very act of attempting to "let them speak," then their task should become instead, in Spivak's view, one of tracing the precise effects of this silencing of the subaltern, coupled with an "unlearning" of the privileged subjectivity of First World discursive hegemony: "This systematic unlearning involves learning to critique postcolonial discourse with the best tools it can provide and not simply substituting the lost figure of the colonized."[3]

The epistemic violence to which Spivak's denunciation of First World nativism testifies echoes Mudimbe's theses on the West's "invention" of Africa and Africanist discourse, and the continuing power of this discursive hegemony even within much African writing and thinking. For Mudimbe, the source of an entire colonialist epistemology (which ultimately incorporates philosophy, political theory, anthropology, psychology, and religion) is to be located within the Enlightenment's promotion of a rational, universal humanism, with the metaphysical subject as its most durable vehicle. If the Cartesian *cogito* represents the epistemological starting point, as it were, Mudimbe's own project involves a return to and radical recontextualization of the *cogito,* rather than a naive rejection of the *cogito* altogether. Descartes's mind/body dualism generated a whole range of oppositions that structured this colonialist epistemology, and from a feminist perspective this separation of mind and body, reason and emotion, is determined by a phallocentric assumption about man's innate predisposition to philosophical thinking and the assignment of "bodiliness" to women. This is famously taken to absurd extremes by Kant, who obsessively regulated his body and its functions in order to minimize its interference with the exercise of his rational mind.[4] Women are in this schema excluded from the "universal" subject of philosophy by virtue of their anatomy. Diana Fuss summarizes it neatly when she says: "Anatomy becomes the irreducible granite at the core of woman's being. This, then, becomes her essence, and paradoxically, her route to nonessentiality [. . .] it is the essence of woman to have no essence."[5]

Judith Butler and Diana Fuss have both elaborated strategies for moving beyond the impasse of the debates opposing essentialism and determinism in feminist theory. In *Essentially Speaking,* Fuss argues that the opposition is rendered unworkable if one entertains the notion that essentialism, rather than suggesting a quality or entity that exists independently of constructedness, is itself dependent on a process of cultural determination. She also argues, conversely, that "social constructionists do not definitively escape the pull of essentialism, that indeed essentialism subtends the very idea of constructionism."[6] The logical consequence of exposing this complicity between constructionism and essentialism is to see, as Fuss does, a covert essentialism operating even within the most apparently antiessentialist of theoretical discourses, such as deconstruction or Lacanian psychoanalysis.[7] Butler has a different though complementary formulation in rethinking the category not only of gender but also of biological sex. Her book *Gender Trouble* is an extended critique of the homology underlying the conventional wisdom according to which sex is essentially biological and gender the product of social construction. According to her, sex (or what is taken as natural) is in fact cultural through and through, and feminism has to be wary of falling back into another form of biological determinism or essentialism in reaffirming women's "bodiliness." A truly self-critical feminism can only stand to gain, she argues, in effectively *dissociating* agency from subjectivity, and in attending to what she terms the "performative subversions" of the constructed body, considered itself as agency in the formation of gender. As she says toward the end of her study: "Just as bodily surfaces are enacted as the natural, so these surfaces can become the site of dissonant and denaturalized performances that reveal the performative status of the natural itself."[8]

This has direct implications for feminist identity politics generally, and for female African subjectivities in particular, since the latter dramatize, stereophonically as it were, the subversion of both colonialist and phallocratic discursive hegemonies. Butler, though, voices the following caveat: "Feminist discourse on cultural construction remains trapped within the unnecessary binarism of free will and determinism." Given this, "the critical task for feminism is not to establish a point of view outside of constructed identities; that conceit is the construction of an epistemological model that would disavow its own cultural location and, hence, promote itself as a global subject, a position that deploys precisely the imperialist strategies that feminism ought to criticize."[9] This is in fact close to Spivak's own concerns about the nativist desire to "let the subaltern (woman) speak," and her own strategies for moving beyond the "essentialist" trap of overfacile "antiessentialisms." These are most clearly formulated in the course of the various interviews collected together in *The Post-colonial Critic.* In several of these interviews she vigorously defends the importance of deconstruction's contributions to a more radical postcolonial critique, not because of its status as an antiessentialist theory, but rather, as we saw in chapter 1 when discussing Masolo's reading of Mudimbe, because of its ability to account so rigorously for the *inevitability* of essentialism. As she says in the interview with Walter Adamson, "But it is not possible, within discourse, to escape essentializing somewhere. The moment of essentialism or essentialization is irreducible. In deconstructive critical practice, you have to be aware that you are going to essentialize anyway."[10] Likewise, she argues that any theory of subjectivity invoking a decentered subject is operating in bad faith: "For, the subject is always centered as a subject. You cannot *decide* to *be* decentered and inaugurate a politically correct deconstructive politics. What deconstruction looks at is the limits of this centering, and points at the fact that these boundaries of the centering of the subject are indeterminate and that the subject (being always centered) is obliged to describe them as determinate."[11] What she thus advocates is the deployment of a certain strategic essentialism, as least provisionally, a move that Diana Fuss herself comments on approvingly and subscribes to.[12]

This strategically and productively ambivalent essentialism can be aligned with Mudimbe's own position. He makes a point of emphasizing his "critical position against all essentialisms" in an interview with Faith Smith in 1990 and supports it by referring to the famous paradoxical statement by Jean-Paul Sartre, "I am what I am not, and I am not what I am." Does this amount to an endorsement of Sartrean existentialism? As we saw in the opening chapter, although he is critical of the political homogenization of Sartre's "Orphée noir," he also sees Sartre as an important African philosopher, one who opens the way for an effective political philosophy and who stakes out the arena in which many of the debates in African philosophy are being played out, the necessity of a reaffirmed subject being the particular focus for Mudimbe. Mudimbe's ambivalent appropriation of Sartrean existentialism could thus be rephrased as a strategically essentialist deployment of existentialism. This may appear to have minimal relevance for the question of African women, but in his interview with Smith, Mudimbe himself makes the connection between this particular theoretical crux in his work and the two novels in which he explicitly deals with an African female subjectivity, *Le bel immonde* and *Shaba deux*.[13]

Mudimbe and the Female Abject

The central female characters in *Le bel immonde* and *Shaba deux* are both shown to be victims of circumstances and external forces that are beyond their control and that appear to make a mockery of their attempts at subjective self-affirmation. In *Le bel immonde* a prostitute, named Ya, or

Belle, falls in love with a government minister in Kinshasa, but the political intrigues she finds herself embroiled in lead to the death of her male lover and her woman friend. In *Shaba deux* an African woman, Marie-Gertrude, joins a Franciscan order in the Shaba region in what was formerly Zaire to fulfill her personal quest for spiritual salvation, but she is caught in the middle of the civil war between the national military and the rebellious separationist guerrilla army of the Katanga province, and the novel, in the form of a journal, ends with her death. In a sense, both women are caught in particularly brutal versions of traps opposing free will and political overdeterminism. Furthermore, the characters Mudimbe presents seem literally to typify the virgin/whore binarism of phallocentric objectification and sublimation of women. It is important to remember, however, that virginity and prostitution have very different connotations in an African setting than they do in the myth-ridden ideology of European phallocentrism. In Sembene's films and novels, such as *Guelwaar* and *Les bouts de bois de dieu* [*God's Bits of Wood*], prostitutes have a far greater degree of social acceptability and indeed play a much more active social role. Mudimbe likewise emphasizes the *narrative* agency of both his female characters, and he is interested in exploring the counterdiscursive effects of this agency, setting it off against the dominant, male-centered historical discourse into which it is inscribed.

Despite Mudimbe's assertion in a note at the end of *Le bel immonde* that the story and its characters are entirely fictional, his novel is nonetheless given an actual historical context (taking as its pretext the rebellions in 1965 while Kasa-Vubu was in power in what was the Congo Republic), and the two main characters, Ya and the government minister, are actively involved in the unfolding political drama. The events are narrated from a number of different objective and subjective positions, and the first, second, and third persons are used for both the minister and Ya; the constant pronominal shifts have implications for the question of female subjectivity, to which I will return. The novel begins with the prostitute Ya waiting for a client in a smoke-filled bar in the shadowy urban night world of Kinshasa, and it traces her love affair with the minister, the manipulation of her and this affair by the rebel forces in order to gain access to plans of the government's actions and movements, and her ultimate betrayal of the minister to the government, which realizes that he is now a danger to them and arranges for his "accidental" death. *Le bel immonde* can be read at one level as a portrayal of the violence and despair of life in what Mudimbe has termed the "marginal space" of underdevelopment in Africa, by which he means the "intermediate space between the so-called African tradition and the projected modernity of colonialism."[14]

At other levels the novel again clearly brings into play some of Mudimbe's central theoretical preoccupations, but with an interesting twist. The metaphor of defying and getting rid of "l'odeur du père" can be seen most obviously in Ya's relationship with her own father, a chief of the rebel tribe, who has been murdered by the government forces but who represents the African past, loyalty to tradition, and so on; it is her father's followers who force Ya to engage in what amounts to a kind of political prostitution. But the minister is also shown to be part of this same "patriarchal" order when he turns for help to a tribal "maître," who makes him a "fils" and forces him to make a sacrificial killing of Ya's woman friend. In much the same way, the government uses her to get rid of the minister, and she is subjected to a violent and humiliating police interrogation. The methods of the government and the rebels are equally brutal, and the *immonde* of the title is clearly meant to extend beyond what might appear to be its obvious association with Ya's prostitution and treachery—toward the end the police inspector interrogating her calls her "une immonde p . . . " [a filthy whore]—to include the other characters as well. The extreme limit of her timid attempts at subjective affirmation, the fourth chapter of the last section of the book, is also the moment of the most brutal repression of the freedom she had glimpsed for a while, such that her "je" is trapped within the net, or network, of intersecting determinations that is inexorably closing in upon her: "J'étais au croisement du déversement de multiples coïncidences" [I stood at the point where a whole series of coincidences converged] (162).[15] As she returns to the bar, and after the cultural, political, and ethical determinations of the book have been exhausted—like the "truth" that is finally eked out of her by the government representatives—one wonders what is *left over*, what remains for Ya.

The question of what is left over is crucial in determining the space of female subjectivity in this novel. Ya is in every other respect defined by the patriarchal system and by her subjection to male political subterfuge, violence, and abuse of power. The ending takes us back to the same bar she was in as the novel opened, and Ya seems to have been even further diminished as a result of the loss of her friend and her lover. Yet the *immonde,* like the *écart* of Mudimbe's novel of that title, could be taken as an important act of epistemological resistance, a defiant assertion of subjectivity that takes the form of a rejection of the *monde* to which the competing political ideologies have consigned her, in the same way that Nara's "madness" in *L'écart* is a rejection of the *ratio* that defines him. *Le bel immonde* ought thus to be read not in terms of a kind of symmetrical reversibility of male and female subjectivities, in which the oxymoron of the title suggests a certain indeterminacy about whether the impurity or immorality is on the side of Ya or the government minister, but as the subtle subversive effect of an apparently subservient female subjectivity on male discursive power.[16] It also suggests a number of connections between this novel and *Shaba deux.*

These affinities are even clearer if we look beyond the female characters' respective symbolic roles to their experiences before the time of the main events of each narrative. Ya was in fact brought up by nuns, and both she and Marie-Gertrude had university educations but abandoned them, or were forced to abandon them. They both also express a need for absolute love—Ya's a physical passion that is doomed from the start, Marie-Gertrude's a spiritual craving that goes unanswered—but are left with existential choices that turn out to be no choices at all. Perhaps more important, both women have significant relationships with other women: Ya with her prostitute friend who is sacrificed, and Marie-Gertrude with Sister Véronique. These relationships suggest the possibility of a desire that can bypass, or at the very least challenge, the various patriarchal discourses that motivate the tragic endings of each text. Lesbian desire has a powerful subversive effect in these novels, one that can be usefully theorized by returning to Butler's discussion of ways of destabilizing the socially constructed contours of the allegedly "natural" body. For Butler, homosexual erotic practices disrupt the hegemonic order of the heterosexual body, which itself serves as a synecdoche for social bodies and how they define themselves against that which is not allowed to permeate them.[17] Butler links this to Kristeva's notion of the "abject," the repulsion and expulsion of the "Other" as a necessary moment in the constitution of the subject. The subject thus requires stable boundary lines, and as Butler says, "this coherence is determined in large part by cultural orders that sanction the subject and compel its differentiation from the abject." However, when the abject seeps back into the subject, it can radically disrupt this stability: "When the subject is challenged, the meaning and necessity of the terms are subject to dis-placement. If the 'inner world' no longer designates a topos, then the internal fixity of the self and, indeed, the internal locale of gender iden-tity, become similarly suspect."[18]

The *immonde* of *Le bel immonde* is precisely this kind of disruptive abjection. Ya's body is *not just* a prostituted body (which is, socially and sexually, a perfectly acceptable form of *immonde*) but a lesbian body that radically transgresses socially sanctioned gender roles.[19] In fact, the move-ment from third to first person for Ya is relayed through her love for the woman friend she calls her "little sister," which initiates the shift to the second person at this point in the narrative: "Tu te sentais seule, triste. Elle est venue, t'a parlé, t'a introduit dans sa vie [. . .] A présent, tu l'adorais, convertie, convaincue que ton amour pour elle était un en-chantement permanent, aussi éloigné des mâles que des regrets" (21–22) [You were feeling lonely, sad. She came, spoke to you, ushered you into her life [. . .] At this point you worshipped her, you were converted, convinced that your love for her was a permanent state of rapture, as remote from the male as it was from any regret] (28–29). This second-person address by the implied narrator blends in with a direct quotation of the words her friend uses in consoling Ya soon after they first meet: "Je t'aime. Beaucoup. Vivre avec toi. Nous retrouver après le travail. Ne ressens-tu pas ce besoin d'une ombre pure, lumineuse, un abri loin des sécrétions masculines?" (22) [I love you. Very much. Just to live with you. To meet after work. Don't you feel this need for a pure, luminous spot of shade, a hiding place far from masculine secretions?] (29). Immedi-ately after this passage Ya watches her friend in the bar and feels a more overtly sexual attraction to her: "Elle rit et ses dents [. . .] jaillissent [. . .] Tu voudrais les sentir, en ce moment, contre les tiennes" (23) [She laughs and her teeth [. . .] flash [. . .] Right at this very moment you would like to feel them against your own] (30). This attraction triggers off an abrupt rejection of the male client she is with at the time. The second-person narration thus functions as a crucial intermediate zone, signaling an added intimacy that takes her out of the desperate solitude she suffers in her first-person narrative, and the abandonment to her fate of the distanced third-person objectification.

The destabilizing effects of the lesbian body have more far-reaching implications, as Butler points out. Taking as her frame of reference Fou-cault's analysis in *Discipline and Punish* of the discursive regime that subjects and subjectifies criminals, Butler emphasizes the process by which "inner truth," indeed the very inner space of subjectivity itself, is effectively *inscribed upon* the bodies that are subject to this disciplinary law: "There the law is manifest as the essence of their selves, their conscience, the law of their desire." This has the rather disconcerting consequence of making the soul, traditionally invisible and "enclosed" within the body, one of the effects by which the body is discursively signified: "In this sense, then, the soul is a surface signification that contests and displaces the inner/outer distinction itself, a figure of interior psychic space inscribed *on* the body as a social signification that perpetually renounces itself as such."[20] When this schema is disrupted, as it is with the lesbian body's rewriting of the heterosexual order and its "body politic," not only is the opposition between body and soul further displaced but the status itself of the soul, with its guarantee of a subjective inner space, is no longer secure.

Mudimbe's formulations of the West's "invention" of Africa—that is, the primitive as a kind of "abject" Other that is simultaneously produced and expelled—demonstrate how this process of constitution of the subject and its body works for a colonialist epistemology. In his book *Tales of Faith,* Mudimbe explicitly deploys Foucault's concept of "docile bodies" from *Discipline and Punish* in order to describe the conversion to Christianity of young African seminarians and the carefully regulated procedures by which this was achieved.[21] The seminary is a version of Foucault's panoptic surveillance and as such serves as a paradigm for a whole range of Christian institutions in Africa designed to educate nuns, catechists, and lay Christians, as well as priests: "Yet, it is the seminary that convincingly illustrates a meticulous programme of an absolute conversion and spiritual normalization, which systematically wishes to erase the distinction between 'us' and 'them' and produce new individualities inscribed in both the election of Christianity and 'civilization.'"[22] One such new individuality, or "docile African body," appears to be Marie-Gertrude in *Shaba deux,* about which Mudimbe has stated that it was an attempt "to write a novel in which I could speak from an African woman's voice, in which I could describe a woman's subjectivity which is relatively independent from, let's say, male power."[23]

Indeed, *Shaba deux* seems to dramatize well the overpowering effects of the three closely interlinked orders that Mudimbe analyzes extensively in such theoretical texts as *The Invention of Africa* and *Parables and Fables.*

In the chapter "Revelation as a Political Performance" in *Parables and Fables,* these orders are described as overlapping powers—the colonial state, science, and Christianity—which ground three principal "arenas of conversion," these being "the colonial commissioner's transmutation of 'savage species' into 'civilized settings'; the anthropologist's codifying of humans, institutions, and beliefs by their particularity vis-à-vis a functional model; and the Christian missionary's self-sacrifice among 'primitives' in the struggle between the 'true light' and local tradition."[24] This essentially paternalistic order was, as we have seen, derived from the ideological foundations of Enlightenment epistemology, with its "universal humanism" a far-reaching agenda suited to the white, male, European subject's *Weltanschauung.* In focalizing the events of *Shaba deux* through the subjective diary of an African nun, Mudimbe both illustrates the mechanisms by which the "political performance" of Christian conversion is achieved and subjects these repressive operations to a more subversive critique, which he describes as follows in the preface: "The novel of the powerless and the saints thumbs its nose at the history of the powerful and at the diabolical arrogance of politicians."

By making his narrator an African nun who has chosen to separate herself from the world, he is able in theory to isolate and insulate her from patriarchal systems of power, and so in this respect she seems to be at the opposite end of the spectrum from Ya in *Le bel immonde.* Sister Marie-Gertrude is one of only a few African nuns in a Franciscan order in the town of Kolwezi. As in *Le bel immonde,* the unequal struggle between subjective freedom and subjection to religious, social, and historical forces is fleshed out by giving the story an actual political context, one that ultimately destroys the female character. As its title suggests, and as Mudimbe himself makes clear, the narrative takes place during the second invasion in 1978 of the province of Shaba by Katangais rebels who had been based in Angola since 1968. The mother superior of the convent, Mother Laetitia, fearing for the safety of her compatriots, evacuates the convent and flees the region, along with the other Europeans living there at the time, leaving Marie-Gertrude in charge of the few nuns who remain behind. Marie-Gertrude rises to the challenge, and in the process her understanding of what Christian spirituality represents in an African context is radically transformed. Her initial willingness to submit to the detachment, discipline, and dogmatic conformity of the Franciscan order, with its insistence on obedience, prayer, and meditation, gives way to a deepening concern to help those who are left behind. She makes an active commitment to her fellow Africans who are suffering as a result of the conflict, a real if eventually futile act of existential *engagement*. As Josias Semujanga puts it, "She opposes an ethics of action to the morality of 'duty', which uses Church dogma to support its spirituality."[25]

This "reconversion" to existentialism occurs as Marie-Gertrude becomes aware of her difference within the religious community, and of what she represents for the European sisters. As she says, "Je semblais, pour elles, n'être qu'une curiosité" [To them I seemed nothing but a curiosity].[26] Even though she is the product of the conversion program, the other nuns do not accept her on an equal basis: "pour certaines de mes consoeurs, j'étais simplement un prétexte exotique [. . .] la petite négresse du groupe" [for some of the sisters who were with me I was simply an exotic pretext [. . .] the little negress of the group] (39). This is, of course, a version of the colonial "abjection" of the Other, which Marie-Gertrude explains to Sister Véronique as follows: "Votre peur, celle des Soeurs que vous rencontrez à longueur de journée, c'est la peur de la nuit, la peur de l'Afrique [Your fear, the fear of the sisters you spend all day long with, is the fear of the night, the fear of Africa] (91). And as she says in the middle of her disbelief at being put in charge of the convent: "Un objet, c'était cela ma prédestination" [An object, that was what I was always destined to be] (96). In this respect, the existential choice she is forced into resembles that of Pierre Landu in Mudimbe's *Entre les eaux,* and testifies to the failure of Christianity to respond adequately to the reality of historical contingency in Africa. Yet her fate would be meaningless if it were readable only as a symbol. Insofar as she is defined by her exceptional status within the order, one might say she is also deliberately "deessentialized," and her singularity can be taken not as a negative "singling out" but as the singular chance of her existential freedom (an opportunity she embraces, albeit with great reluctance initially). She in fact refuses to "take sides" in the conflict, and her refusal throws into stark relief the complicity between the discourses of politics (whether that of the neocolonial government or the insurrectionist rebels) and religious conversion.

Her nonrepresentative singularity is in fact evident throughout the text. It takes the form of a questioning of both religious precepts and political ideology, and an emphasis on her own subjectivity as a counterpoint to her "predestined" objectification. She does not believe, for example, in the sanctity of virginity. As she says early on, commenting on the departure of one of the novices:

> Oui, il y a probablement un homme derrière ce départ. Et même s'il en était ainsi, qu'est-ce que cela prouve, sinon que nous sommes des femmes et que l'ordre de la nature a ses lois? En nier l'existence ne nous rapproche pas nécessairement de Dieu. La vénération de la virginité peut, en effet, avoir quelque chose de malsain qui, je le crains, ternit la beauté du don. (20)

> [Yes, she's probably leaving because of a man. But even if there were one, what does that prove except that we are women, and that the natural world has its own laws. Denying their coexistence does not necessarily bring us any closer to God. The worship of virginity can have something unhealthy about it which, I believe, tarnishes the beauty of the gift.]

Throughout the novel she is constantly attentive to her body, from her memory of being an object of sexual desire as a young woman ("Why should I be ashamed of it? I found I was worthy of interest. I liked it . . . ," 20), to an unashamed acceptance of menstruation as a natural fact of being a woman ("Blood is part of my everyday life, and I have learned to live with it," 44), to a profound physical anguish when her mother dies, which shatters the serene indifference to her corporeal existence that she had vowed upon entering the convent ("When I was over the initial shock, I understood that my celibacy was a rupture of my bloodline," 65).

Her spiritual path is anything but easy, and the Franciscan order seems to offer her little hope of ultimate salvation. She goes from seeing the worldly and the spiritual as coexisting ("I identified human progress with spiritual growth," 12) to a realization of the spiritual poverty of a world in which God is conceived of as *Deus Absconditus,* a hidden God ("My spiritual poverty, an absolute poverty, progressively replaced the privileges of reason," 13), and her notebooks present the anguished but vain search for some revelation. She tries to "lose" herself in communion with God but cannot ("I will go through the motions of contemplation, since the joy of His presence is not given to me," 83), and significantly it is only in her final diary entry, when she wakes up from a "blasphe-mous dream" in which she refuses to take Holy Communion and is definitively excommunicated, that she has an experience of spiritual sal-vation, one that moreover is emphatically physical ("I awoke, my body soaked in cold sweat. This morning I was, however, surrounded by the certainty of His love for me," 147–48).

The very act of writing her diary has an ambivalent but crucial sta-tus, since although the diary is an account of loss and of spiritual empti-ness, at the same time the writing of it is radically transformative. By refusing the Franciscan denial of her body, she challenges the equation of Christian conversion with the "docile African body," and this chal-lenge effectively becomes the space for a performative reinscription of her own subjectivity. To refer again to Judith Butler's discussion of the relationship between the body and the soul as a metaphor for the social order and its possible reconfiguration: Marie-Gertrude's writing rede-fines the boundaries of Christianity as a "political performance" in Africa and disrupts the discursive complicity between religious and political powers. Her subjectivity is doubly suppressed: for her European sisters she is the exotic Other of colonialist discourse, and according to her Fran-ciscan vows she has given herself up to God. But at the same time, within the space of her writing, this subjectivity acts as a kind of supplemental excess. The private confessional mode of the diary functions in the same way as a supplement to the religious duty of the *confiteor,* which by rights should monopolize her subjective space.

This subjective reaffirmation is not for all that simply a reemergence of her African identity, even though this is suggested in her recollections of her childhood and her solidarity with the victims of the conflict: "Je suis infirmière, et africaine. Je ferais mon nid au milieu des blessés. Ils sont, probablement, de part et d'autre, des miens" [I am a nurse, and an African. I will build my home among the wounded. They are probably almost all my own people] (75). The description of the convent as "an African place," once it becomes a refuge for the African nuns of the differ-ent religious orders, should be taken as a reconfiguration of the Christ-ian "map" of Zaire rather than as an indigenist reclaiming of a decolo-nized space: "Il y a cependant, en ce capharnaüm, une sorte de triomphe paradoxal: le couvent est devenu un lieu africain. Je trouve de la joie à imaginer la permanence de cette nouvelle communauté surgie d'un accident" [There is, however, in this shambles a sort of paradoxical triumph: the convent has become an African place. It brings me joy to imagine that this new community which emerged by accident could become permanent] (113). Her acceptance of this *accident* of fate underlines her existential commitment to aiding those who have been removed from the religious and political equations—who have in short been subalternized—and is a powerful response to the *calculability* of the discursive objectification to which she is "predestined." Like Ya in *Le bel immonde,* Marie-Gertrude threatens, from the inside out, the order to which she is subjected, and pays a heavy price for this disruption. But although at one level they both fail, their success is to force a rift within the homogeneity of these respective orders and to undo the oppositional structures (body/soul, self/other, subjectivity/subjection, European/African, essentialism/antiessentialism) that circumscribe them.

So do these two African female subjects, so marginalized in their very local political and sociohistoric contexts, have anything to offer African feminism at a more general, collective level? Mudimbe has written most explicitly about feminism and the liberation of African women in his recent intellectual autobiography, *Le corps glorieux des mots et des êtres* [The glorious body of words and things], touchingly framing his comments within a confession of his love for his partner, Elisabeth Mudimbe-Boyi.[27] He admits to being conditioned by the misogyny that characterized his early education and tells how Mudimbe-Boyi gradually instilled feminist convictions in him. He mentions the suspicion aroused by his defense of the feminist cause: "How can I truly understand what it means to be a woman, and especially what it means to be an African woman?" (108). In defending himself he once again turns to the analogy in his reading of Sartre's essay "Orphée noir," that is, the need to make the distinction between being and understanding ("I cannot, and never could, identify with the conscience of another, nor with another's being," 109). His point is that any generalized and abstracted concern for others, of the order of international feminist movements, loses sight of the particularity of an individual existence, and this is especially the case for African women. As he says:

> African women are alone, absolutely alone. No messianic alibi from outside of them could reconcile them with themselves. It will not, cannot hold. If they sincerely want to take their fate into their own

hands, liberate their potential, affirm themselves as humans, they have to find their own way. The idealism of international feminist discourse has little to do with them. (113)

Nevertheless, he sees women as the source of a real transformation of African societies, a genuine hope for Africa's future. This is precisely because of their exclusion from the two great ideological movements that have dominated the social, political, and economic landscape of post-Independence Africa, that is, African socialism and neocolonial capitalism, which have both easily accommodated patriarchal myths of tradition and indigenous authenticity. African women's inclusion would have the effect of challenging not only these orders but also the very oppositional logic that has kept them in place. Echoing Ousmane Sembene (and Werewere Liking, whose work I will turn to in the next chapter), Mudimbe talks of the untapped reserves of strength, discipline, and patience of African women and sees in them the potential to succeed where African men, in the aftermath of the "petit-bourgeois revolution" of the 1960s, have lamentably failed: "I believe firmly that only African women could, soberly and responsibly, reform the African institutions of power and of knowledge" (115). In this respect, he sees individual self-affirmation and liberation, and collective strategies for social transformation, as going hand in hand: "First of all: knowing one is a woman, living it, knowing one is part of a world and a culture that have been denied, being proud of this culture as well as openly critical of it. Second, consciously applying this experience to the creation and promotion of a self-managed 'global society' that is egalitarian and essentially socialist by vocation" (117).

This global society from the ground up, as it were, with the female African subject as an absolute starting point, is thus entirely, radically different from the high theoretical internationalism of what Mudimbe terms "Euramerican feminism," which so often makes African women into a reobjectified pretext and remains stuck in precisely the oppositional logic that needs to be dismantled. And Mudimbe is quite clear that African women are crucial to this process, and thus at the heart of his entire theoretical project: "One could object on the following grounds: by linking a feminist revolution isomorphically with a qualitative transformation of African realities, am I not putting off women's liberation to an ever later time? I do seem to be linking the two 'causes,' and what is more, I make them dependent on the critique of 'reason' and its norms in the social arena" (117).

The fact remains, nonetheless, that Mudimbe's two African female subjects, for all their credibility and theoretical power, are characters in novels written by a male African author. In addition, Mudimbe appears to have a clear sense of his priorities, and to be subordinating African feminism to his larger critical project of decolonizing or deconstructing Africanist discourse generally. He would probably be the first to acknowledge that only African women writers themselves can actually perform the reaffirmation of female African subjectivity that he so cogently and powerfully theorizes. Two well-known texts which achieve this most successfully, to my mind, and which I will explore in the following chapter, are *A vol d'oiseau,* by Véronique Tadjo, and *Elle sera de jaspe et de corail,* by Werewere Liking.

6

Reinscribing
the Female African
Subject
Véronique Tadjo and
Werewere Liking

It is hardly surprising, given the history of African women's multiple and deeply rooted subjection, that they should have only "come to writing," to borrow Hélène Cixous's term, in the last two decades or so.[1] As the literary production of African women writing in French has gathered momentum, and the number of volumes of critical studies and anthologies has grown, it seems that Francophone Africa is finally beginning to redress the balance in recognizing the literary talents of its women writers, giving them a status equivalent to their famous male predecessors.[2]

Women in Africa have traditionally had significant social, economic, and sometimes political roles, as well as being performers in different oral modes, although usually only in comparatively "minor" genres.[3] Material factors, such as greater access to education and employment, improved socioeconomic conditions, and increased financial autonomy, have, of course, been crucial in enabling more and more women to be published and read, but this is only a preliminary, though necessary, stage. Once in a position to write, being able to say "I" is by no means straightforward, which is why many of the pioneering texts take the form of a searching for self, or a creative self-affirmation, and why autobiography is such a significant literary paradigm, as we have seen. The example of Aoua Kéita demonstrates the subversive potential in women's writing as it distinguishes itself from male African autobiography, to which it might appear simply as an appendix. In the course of discussing Kéita's autobiographical account of the history of Mali's movement toward Independence, we saw how her text, despite its emphatic focus on the narrator's "exemplarity," disrupts the allegorical conflation of individual destiny and of nation characteristic of much early African writing by male authors. Kéita's stated aim of giving us an objective historical narrative is undone by the irruptive movement of its own inscription, which led me to hypothesize that it could be seen as a "feminist" text almost in spite of its more apparent intentions.

This early demonstration of the critically productive potential of an attempt to articulate the relationship between subjectivity and gender in a Francophone African space is borne out in writings by African women since the publication of Kéita's groundbreaking text. The diverse modes of renegotiating subjectivity which I have been exploring in the previous chapters have been almost exclusively male, and rather than "paving the way" for women writers, they have perhaps had the effect of establishing a further tradition that women have had to contest, or from which they have had to extricate themselves. For it is the texts of the male writers, from the early *négritude* generation, through the anticolonialist writings of the 1950s, to the post-Independence novels of the 1960s and '70s, which have set out the terms in which all of the major questions have been articulated and addressed. It is thus no accident that the reaffirmation of the (male) African subject has been bound up with parallel discourses of liberation and emergent nationalism. Several feminist critics have pointed to a systematic engendering of Africa that is present, implicitly or explicitly, in much Francophone African male writing, as exemplified by the "Mother Africa" trope given such expressive value by Senghor and others. Florence Stratton, for example, has shown how all the political ideologies of the 1950s and '60s are constructed according to what she calls a "Manichean allegory of gender," that is, these allegories determine the discursive possibilities of a female subjectivity. As Stratton says:

> For underlying the trope that is embedded in all of the texts is the same old Manichean allegory of gender we uncovered in Negritude poetry. In other words, the ideological function of each text is identical. For each reproduces in symbolic form the gender relations of patriarchal societies. The trope elaborates a gendered theory of nationhood and of writing, one that excludes women from the creative pro-

duction of the national polity or identity and of literary texts. Instead, woman herself is produced or constructed by the male writer as an embodiment of his literary/political vision.[4]

In this chapter I would like to look at the different ways in which Francophone African women negotiate the passage from enforced silence to speech and narrative agency, and what happens to the female subject in the process. After an introductory theoretical section, I will look at two well-known texts that have recently appeared in English translation: *A vol d'oiseau* [*As the Crow Flies*], by Véronique Tadjo from the Côte d'Ivoire, and *Elle sera de jaspe et de corail* [*It Shall Be of Jasper and Coral*], by Werewere Liking from Cameroon.

A Theoretical Preamble

As I outlined in the introduction to this study, the apparently neutral category of the "human subject" is in fact heavily overdetermined when read, to borrow Mudimbe's phrase, as a Western invention that operates by a principle of simultaneous appropriation and exclusion. Exported with the various colonial expansions, and consolidated by its discursive domination of anthropology, philosophy, religion, and political theory, the Western subject's domestication-by-objectification of the Other served as a paradigm for a whole range of parallel oppositions—subject/object, self/other, white/nonwhite, civilization/barbarity, reason/nonreason, soul/body, and so on—into which the dichotomy of gender seems to fit all too easily. If Spivak's subtle and powerful analysis of the subaltern's inability to "speak" uncovers the West's nativist desires, for the colonized, or formerly colonized, woman writer the problem is clearly of a different order. As a subject determined by the "social text" of both colonial history and patriarchal traditions—and her life is the one that in fact "counts"—her subject-constitution is the central focus to which we should be attending. So how would this apply to a specifically (Francophone) African context?

Patricia Hill Collins, in her essay "Mammies, Matriarchs, and Other Controlling Images," argues that it is this dichotomous or oppositional thinking itself which keeps these overlapping forms of discursive oppression in place. Although her point of reference is African American women, her analysis is equally applicable to African women, as we shall see: "Denying Black women status as fully human subjects by treating us as the objectified Other in a range of such dichotomies demonstrates the power that dichotomous either/or thinking, oppositional difference, and objectification wield in maintaining interlocking systems of oppression."[5]

The problem of articulating a gendered African subject might best be broached by thinking about how attempts to lay claim to a female African subjectivity, and thereafter a meaningful agency, avoid several pitfalls or recuperative mechanisms. Put very simply and schematically, these pitfalls could be listed as follows: (1) the female subject would simply adopt the rational, universal subject provided by Western epistemology, or mimic the vociferous male subject of *négritude* and its avatars, which would be tantamount to staying in the same place; (2) one might privilege a kind of genderless, transcendental consciousness in a way that would abstract the material and historical aspects of actual "lived experience," including the painful realities of gender differences and discrimination; (3) even operating at the level of gender difference would not necessarily displace the dichotomies generated by a Cartesian dualism, whether the strategy was to negate bodiliness or to reinscribe the body as the basis for a subversive or transformative agency; (4) finally, just as early pan-Africanist ideologies tended to be unicentric in their subordination, marginalization, or simple exclusion of women's issues, and just as patriarchal models (the masculine appropriation of Mother Africa, for example) led to male-centered metaphors of culture and cultural liberation in the anticolonialist political and philosophical writings of the 1950s, one might make further imperialistic or totalizing moves in developing a Western-style feminist agenda for Africa.

These last two points are emphasized by Sara Suleri in her rather exasperated critique of Trinh Minh-ha's "postcolonial feminism" in the latter's *Women, Native, Other,* which in Suleri's view effectively sidesteps any genuine engagement with historical materialism through its phantasmatic recourse to "biologism." To quote Suleri: "A work that is impelled by an impassioned need to question the lines of demarcation between race and gender concludes by falling into the predictable biological fallacy in which sexuality is reduced to the literal structure of the racial body, and theoretical interventions within this trajectory become minimalized into the naked category of lived experience." She continues a little further on: "When feminism turns to lived experience as an alternative mode of radical subjectivity, it only rehearses the objectification of its proper subject."6

Given the many potential traps that any attempts at theorizing an African female subjectivity are likely to encounter, what are some of the strategies that critics and writers have adopted? Carole Boyce Davies, in her book *Black Women, Writing and Identity: Migrations of the Subject,* redeploys the term *black* "relationally, provisionally and based on location or position" to cover the multiple diasporic experiences of all women of African descent.7 Writing by black women becomes for her an experience of crossing boundaries, of permanent transition, of a migrating subjectivity, such that none of the oppositional terms that have historically predetermined black women's place is allowed to remain stable or to gain any kind of permanent foothold. As we saw earlier in discussing contemporary African philosophy, the neutral "subject" of Enlightenment epistemology seems to function as a placeholder for the opposition itself between agency and constructedness, and it is this double bind that Davies sees the "migratory subject" as overcoming: "Employing a variety of meanings of subjectivity, I want to pursue the understanding of the resisting subject and apply it in different ways to the diasporic elsewheres of a radical Black *diasporic* subjectivity. As 'elsewhere denotes movement,' Black female subjectivity asserts agency as it crosses the borders, journeys, migrates and so re-claims as it re-asserts."8

Other critics talk about African and African American first-person women's writing as similarly relational, mobile, and unconstrained by unitary conceptions of identity. Sidonie Smith, for example, analyzes the constant shifting of narrative voice and idioms that one finds in the texts of Zora Neale Hurston as a "condition of radical subjectivity." As she says, "Through her linguistic practice, Hurston declines participation in the univocality and the consequent linguistic exclusions necessary to consolidate a coherent, monadic autobiographic identity [...] We might call this wandering, slippery, word-changing 'I,' the diasporan subject."9

Françoise Lionnet, in her *Postcolonial Representations: Women, Literature, Identity,* takes postcolonial narratives by women as paradigmatic expressions of identities formed from the negotiation of competing cultural influences, a process she refers to as *métissage,* adapting the French anthropologist Jean-Loup Amselle's term of *logique métisse.* Amselle opposes the particularism, and consequent relativism, of anthropological circumscriptions of cultural identity, stressing instead the originary mixing of cultures throughout history. Likewise, Lionnet describes the effect of the cultural interweavings that typify writings by postcolonial women as deconstructing the oppositional structure that defines the Third World as the Other of the First World: "What these writers illustrate instead is the dynamic and creative processes mobilized by subgroups as means of resistance to the 'victim' syndrome. They use their transformative and performative energies on the language and narrative strategies they borrow from the West."[10] In a formulation that echoes the strategies advocated by Mudimbe, Lionnet makes the postcolonial female subject the locus of this transformative creativity:

> My interest in using these novels to understand cultural configurations studied by social scientists is grounded in my belief that literature allows us to enter into the subjective processes of writers and their characters and thus to understand better the unique perspectives of subjects who are agents of transformation and hybridization in their own narratives—as opposed to being the objects of knowledge, as in the discourse of social science.[11]

Despite the differences of theoretical approach and terminology adopted by these critics, and the vastly different array of cultural practices taken to illustrate their theories, there does seem to be a fairly consistent set of recurring narrative tropes—relationality, polyvocality, *métissage,* diasporic movement, and the destabilizing of fixed gender identities—associated with female African subjectivity. One can see all these in practice, to a greater or lesser degree, in the texts by Tadjo and Liking.

Subjectivity and Desire in Tadjo and Liking

As its title suggests, *A vol d'oiseau* is about flight and migration, and in simple geographical terms this is how we can read the "story" we are told by the female narrator, an African woman who, like Tadjo herself, travels to the United States and elsewhere with a freedom of movement one associates with birds. The narrative structure of the text is highly innovative and marks a significant departure from the writings of other contemporary African women authors, as Micheline Rice-Maximin has pointed out.[12] It is organized as twenty-one larger units, which are subdivided, not according to any obvious mathematical symmetry, into ninety-two "chapters" designated by Roman numerals. Although they vary in length from a single line to several pages, each chapter is dieget- ically and semantically coherent and self-contained, and the challenge for the reader becomes one of searching for connections and patterns of meaning between the textual fragments.

The narrative begins with a fairly traditional third-person account of a brief affair the narrator has with the father of her American host fam- ily in Washington, D.C., which takes a catastrophic turn when his wife discovers the affair the very day he and the narrator decide to end it. Thereafter the text seems to break free from any conventional moorings: the voice goes back and forth between first, second, and third person; the events take place in unspecified locations in Africa, North America, and Europe; and the language is continually shifting in tone or genre and includes graphic sociorealistic descriptions, oral tales, myths and legends, allegories, intimate confessions, and passages whose style bears the mark of magical realism. The narrator seems to be not only on a trip across space and time (via memory) but also on an emotional and imag- inative journey in which the blurring of the boundaries between the different narrative components implies a correlative confusion (albeit a productive one) between objective fact and subjective fiction, history and myth, outside and inside, reality and fantasy. The metaphor of the subject as a bird is clear, since it is the ability to move effortlessly across borders ("There are no frontiers," as the narrator says at the end of the first unit) which is exploited narratively and imaginatively.

This scattering and fragmentation of the text is anticipated in the narrator's short preface in which she explains, in the form of a dialogue with herself, the inadequacy or irrelevance of traditional narrative struc- tures to fully account for her experiences of loss and dispersion:

> *Bien sûr, j'aurais, moi aussi, aimé écrire une histoire sereine avec un début et une fin. Mais tu sais bien qu'il n'en est pas ainsi. Les vies s'en- tremêlent, les gens s'apprivoisent puis se quittent, les destins se perdent.*

> *[Indeed, I too would have loved to write one of those serene stories with a beginning and an end. But as you know only too well, it is never like that. Lives mingle, people tame one another and part. Destinies are lost.]*[13]

How then is the new narrative form more appropriate to the emo- tional and imaginative trajectory of the novel, and what are we as readers to do with it? The mosaic of textual fragments could be seen as a kind of multilayered, mythopoetic attempt by the narrator to make sense of, or come to terms with, the devastating effect of the brief affair she has in the opening story. Many of the tales, whether recounted in the first, second, or third person, and despite the eclectic mass of largely anonymous characters that appear in them (in addition to "l'homme" [the man] of the opening tale, there is "the deaf child," "the old man," "the boy," "the daughter," "the son," and another lover, seemingly back in Africa), deal with the joys and anguish of love and the loss of loved ones. So, for example, chapter 31 tells the short, highly lyrical story of a man who is unable to say good-bye to his dying lover, whom he transports around the world to find the most suitable final resting place. In another chapter, a young woman, like the main narrator, searches for an answer to an enigmatic puzzle and believes a magician may hold the key: "His knowledge of secrets knew no bounds" (81). She confesses to the magician: "Je ne connais pas la nature de ma joie. Elle apparaît et disparaît. Rien ne semble statique. Tout est mouvant et je suis prise dans un tourbillon. Je ne vois plus la différence entre rêve et réalité" (75) [I do not know the nature of my joy. It comes and goes. Nothing seems to remain static. Everything is shifting and I am carried in a storm. I can no longer tell the difference between dreams and reality] (82). In a sequence that again calls to mind the magical atmosphere of African oral tales and legends, the woman spends more and more time inside the magician's skull, which contains a dangerous and frightening battlefield.[14] She eventually crosses the battlefield and reaches a lake in which she is finally submerged at the end of the chapter.

This tale, like many others, is clearly allegorical, and as Rice-Maximin points out, can be seen to parallel the narrator's confusion following her first traumatic love affair, her struggle to understand what has happened to her, and her attempts to reemerge from an emotional labyrinth. The narrative dispersion thus gradually goes from being a symptom of loss and despair (the narrator is a "shattered" subject following her experience in Washington, and the textual confusion mirrors this state) to a kind of aesthetic precondition for a "cathartic rebirth," as Rice-Maximin puts it.[15] By the end of the text, the narrator has come to a clearer understanding of the transformative power of this artistic process. She says at the beginning of chapter 85, in a series of phrases that serve as a kind of literary critical template: "Je réarrange le puzzle de ma vie, déplace les moments, récupère les souvenirs [. . .] Je juxtapose les destins, enregistre les sensations [. . .] Je dépasse les années, opère des flash-back et analyse les gestes. Je cherche la connaissance du ciel quand les destins se croisent" (91) [I rearrange the puzzle, move moments, recover memories [. . .] I juxtapose destinies, record feelings [. . .] I scan years, deploy flashbacks and study gestures. I look to the sky to find out where destinies meet] (99).

This "connaissance du ciel," or bird's-eye perspective, is how the narrator comes to make sense of the fragmented "puzzle" of her life. So we have a double movement, of falling apart and coming together again, in which the very process of writing comes to assume the power of a redemptive act and allows the narrator to reassert her subjectivity. As she says toward the end of the text:

Déjà, j'ai presque oublié son visage. Une multitude de regards s'entremêlent, s'échangent. J'ai même perdu sa voix. Et je suis là, dépossédé de tous mes biens. Il ne me reste que l'écriture. Ces mots sur du papier blanc. Ce sont eux qui me disent à l'oreille les souvenirs. (90)

[I have almost forgotten his face already. A host of glances intermingle. I have even forgotten the sound of his voice. And here I am, bereft of all my belongings. All that remains is my writing. Words on a white sheet of paper. They whisper memories in my ear.] (98)

Her reaffirmation of self is thus achieved in part by a filtering out of the dominating presence of "l'homme" in her life, a fading of his image within her memory, a process I will try to articulate a little more precisely within the context of a female African subjectivity.

The flight of the bird-narrator represents not only the freedom to traverse geographical and temporal boundaries but also a means of escaping from "l'homme," and by extension from the phallocratic world of male desire. The movement across narrative genres involves their decomposition and recomposition into a new hybrid genre and is closely bound up with the question of gender. The text scatters its pronominal points of reference such that we are unable to say for sure who the "je" or "tu" or "il/elle" in the various story fragments are meant to be. We cannot in fact be sure how much they are meant to be allegorical palimpsests of the first narrative or indeed of each other.

The dispersion of the male subject of traditional narrative and of desire (the "Mother Africa" trope and the "Manichean allegory of gender" it supports) are part of this same process. The Mother Africa trope is in fact reinscribed so that the poverty and want now afflicting the African continent are allied metaphorically to the hunger of the narrator's own desire ("Ma salive se gavait de sa force et de son énergie, et je découvrais la famine de mon désir" (80) [I lapped up his force and energy, and discovered how famished my desire was] (87). The "je" of the bird-narrator is by the end able to synthesize the textual bits and pieces through a creative rebirth and resubjectification, and an affirmation of female desire. Indeed, there are sections where desire itself becomes one of the characters in the narrative. One chapter takes the form of an African riddle addressed first to an unknown "tu":

Qui es-tu?
Toi—qui frappes à ma porte . . .

[Who are you? / You—who knock at my door . . .]

This unknown object then itself replies:

Je vole en éclats
J'ai envie de
Courir/courir/courir . . . (35)

[My mind shatters into fragments / And all I want is to / Run, run, run . . .] (39)

The object is finally revealed at the end as "Desire."

This particular section highlights one of the important narrative elements that comes to the fore in this affirmative rearranging of the puzzle of textual fragments, that is, the constant invocation of orature. I have already mentioned the otherworldly atmosphere of many of the stories, which clearly evoke an oral antecedent. The narrator at several points indicates, just as a traditional African storyteller would do in recounting a legend or tale, that she is merely transmitting what has been passed down to her: "On m'a raconté cette histoire, et c'est ainsi que je vous la livre" (23) [Someone told me the following story, which I will recount to you as I heard it] (23). This has the effect of reconnecting her with the generations of storytellers that have preceded her, and of submerging her individual identity within a far larger collective identity. Orature thus becomes a means of linking the personal, often very intimate elements of the narrative with the more public passages of social commentary. The limited perspective of the conventional male-centered narrative at the beginning is taken over by the limitless roaming of the bird's-eye perspective of orature, which in effect informs the hybrid genre that is capable of synthesizing the other genres. This new genre is identified with female subjectivity and desire and is more inclusively universal than the restricted, hegemonic "universalism" of the male subject, since it listens to and represents all those who are marginalized or excluded by this limited discourse.

This inclusiveness is in keeping with the aerial, even cosmic, connotations of the text's main themes and is "higher" than a mere worldly, political, or ideological version of universalism.[16] If this bird's-eye view allows the narrator to rise above the abjectness of everyday life, and the abuse and violation to which women in Africa are subjected (described graphically in many of the vignettes), Tadjo is not for all that advocating a kind of elitist idealism. Her projected liberation requires not turning away from the painful realities of contemporary Africa. The female narrator's reaffirmation of her subjectivity is also a reclaiming of her body, in which she takes great sensual, even erotic, pleasure, since it is necessary to take control of her own body and sexuality in order to take control of her destiny. The means by which she can achieve this is by freeing herself from the hegemony of phallocentrism.

It is toward the end (chapter 84) that the narrator realizes that she had idealized "l'homme" and that it was her entrapment within his imaginative and discursive world, the hold that masculine desire had on her, that was preventing her coming to an understanding of her own desires and asserting her subjective and imaginative freedom: "J'en ai fait un poète-génie, un esprit fantastique. J'ai construit ses silences en montagnes dorées, bâti ses paroles en arcs de triomphe" (90) [I have turned him into a genius, a fantastic mind. I built his silences into golden mountains, his words into triumphal arches] (98).

Nonetheless, Tadjo does not exclude men from the transformative process or from the new inclusiveness that she envisages. In chapter 9 (unit 3), one of the more "down-to-earth" sections of the narrative, we are presented with an uneducated young male actor working for the theater company of a radical director. The actor is introduced in French simply as "quelqu'un" [someone] and remains unnamed throughout the chapter. Indeed, he could almost be genderless, were it not for a few masculine past participle agreements in the French. The young man is first described as the people's representative (recall Spivak's discussions of the two meanings of *represent*), acting on behalf of those with no voice: "Je représente le peuple. Symboliquement" (15) [I represent the people. Symbolically] (15). Then toward the end of the section he is a character allegorically playing "the people" in a dramatic artistic performance. Yet in "real life" he does not hesitate to intervene on behalf of those who are victims of social or political injustice. After one performance, he sees two young black men being beaten up by the police, and he and a girl are so moved by their plight that they attempt to stop the beating, despite being told the men are thieves and it is none of their business. The young man and the girl thus exemplify the kind of all-encompassing representativeness the female bird-narrator is hoping to bring about, and which she describes at the beginning of this chapter as follows: "Il faut entendre la voix de ceux qui se taisent avec des mots qui sortent de la terre. Point de langage aseptisé, mais le tempo de la vie au galop, remodelant les images dépassées, les syntaxes usées, la pensée capitonnée" (15) [You should listen to the voice of those whose voices remain unheard although the wisdom they carry is shaped by their closeness to the earth. No refined language but the pace of life at a gallop, refashions outmoded images, well-worn phrases, and ways of thinking that are out of date] (15).

Werewere Liking's *Elle sera de jaspe et de corail* is similar in many ways to Tadjo's text in terms of subject matter and narrative form, yet Liking's narrative innovations go further than Tadjo's. Her text is also fragmentary in its composition, and she underlines its generically hybrid nature by subtitling it "journal d'une misovire" and referring to it as a "chant-roman" [song-novel]. This reflects Liking's own wide-ranging talents, since in addition to being a novelist, she is also, among other things, a well-known playwright, a poet, singer, actress, painter, and jeweler. Far from restricting herself to individual self-expression, she is committed to the socially and politically transformative power of art, and in her native Cameroon she has set up community-based artistic and theatrical groups, which have merged to form the Ki-Yi village, an important collective venture that is unique in Francophone Africa.[17] *Elle sera de jaspe et de corail* reflects Liking's belief in the transformative possibilities of art, in particular theater. The reference to song in the subtitle marks the importance for her of orature, and the text is indeed, more than Tadjo's, regularly punctuated by highly lyrical poetic passages. The text likewise contains several narrative voices along with that of the principal narrator, the *misovire,* a neologism that at first seems to be a symmetrical counterpart to "misogynist" and translates literally as "manhater." Irène Assiba d'Almeida has shown that, in terms of her overall narrative strategy, Liking's principal technique in blurring the boundaries between genres as a prelude to a radical new identity, and a female subjective voice, is one of *intertextuality.*[18] This includes not only her own experiences, memories, and dreams but also references to the language of early ethnographers and the French colonizers, to the discourse of *négritude,* and to the "classic" male authors of Francophone Africa, such as Ferdinand Oyono.

The text is set in the fictional African village of Lunaï, which is intended to exemplify the abjectness of contemporary Africa, and the narrative has several different main registers or levels: there is, first of all, the *misovire's* own commentary; then there is a directly reported dialogue between two characters—Grozi, a black man, and Babou, a white man—whose intellectual exchanges dramatize both racial stereotyping and supposedly antiracialist counterdiscourses; there is also the voice of the ironically named character Nuit Noire [Black Night], who represents light, clarity of vision, and consciousness; and then occasionally the lyrical interventions of a "Little Spirit." The *misovire* narrator describes the text she is writing as a "texte-jeu" [game-text], and it does formally resemble Tadjo's "puzzle" text. The "game" that Liking is playing does not move toward a solution or resolution in the way that *A vol d'oiseau* does, however, and she employs a quite different narrative mechanism for negotiating the simultaneity of despair and hopefulness and the projected passage from the one to the other. Rather like the temporality of Proust's title *A la Recherche du temps perdu,* Liking's *Elle sera de jaspe et de corail* refers both to the actual text we are reading and to a future text which the narrator sketches out in the course of the narrative but which by the end she is still uncertain of being able to write: "Dois-je vraiment écrire un journal de bord? Serai-je capable de l'écrire? Est-ce utile?" [Do I really have to write a logbook? Will I be able to write it? Is it useful?].[19] In fact, the writing of the text is indefinitely postponed, or at least put off until the conditions she lays down for the "new race" she envisages have been satisfactorily met. So the text exists in a kind of future or conditional perfect, as well as a complex intertextual present, and I will return later to the implications this has for the writing subject. First, though, I would like to look a little more closely at the representation of gender relations within the text, and at the status of the female subject as Liking articulates it.

In contrast to the female "je" in *A vol d'oiseau,* the *misovire*-narrator is far more explicitly and vehemently critical of masculine desire and phallocentrism generally.[20] She sees this as the source of both the (colonial) destruction of African culture and the inherited lack of self-belief or of any passionate commitment to change of postcolonial Africans, of both sexes. The constant circular dialogue between Grozi and Babou demonstrates how the continued articulation of Africa's contemporary predicament—and future—in terms of white and black, African and European, colonized and colonizer, leads to a sterile impasse. Their symbolic role reversal merely serves to consolidate, rather than challenge, this fundamental inertia. In a parodic enactment of Senghor's *négritude* philosophy which essentializes Europeans and Africans respectively as rational and emotional, Grozi (in whose name one hears *gros zizi,* or "big prick") is a black man who "se décrète cartésien commet des thèses sur la raison et en perd sa langue maternelle" (16) [declares himself a Cartesian commits theses on reason and loses his mother tongue in the process] (10), while Babou is a white man whose exoticist imagination leads him to try to become like an African. As a consequence, "Grozi et Babou ont amorcé un transfert de personnalité et réussi un auto-rejet mal assimilé [. . .] Babou rêve d'Emotion-Nègre [. . .] Grozi vise l'Intellect-Blanc" (16–17) [Grozi and Babou have embarked on a personality transfer and have managed to achieved an ill-absorbed self-rejection [. . .] Babou dreams of Black-Emotion [. . .] Grozi aims for White-Intellect] (10).

Rather than furthering the cause of the "new race" that the narrator is setting her sights on in some as yet unidentified future, Grozi and Babou are both shown to be essentially weak and prey to the irresistible and inhibiting forces of their own desires. In the text, male desire is constantly depicted in terms of mental masturbation, both as a metaphor for their self-centered intellectualism and also, more literally, as a form of "thinking with one's penis," such that they are unable to conceive of desire beyond their own orgasm, which becomes an end in itself. Grozi in particular has very poor self-control, and there are several fairly graphic descriptions of him masturbating until he ejaculates, followed inevitably by a rather pathetic shamefulness, which the narrator captures in the repeated phrase "une goutte honteuse pendouille là hésitante: tombera tombera pas" (27) [a shameful drop dangling there shilly-shallying: will fall won't fall] (18). This autotelic quality of male desire is then extended by analogy to describe the phallocratic basis of African society generally:

> Je parie qu'il [Grozi] visualise l'élan de l'âme comme un phallus dressé!
> Et comme toutes ces gens de Lunaï en m'entendant parler de désir il pensera à ce désir phallique caractérisé par son impossibilité d'accéder à l'éternité: un désir s'érigeant constamment en épées en fusils en missiles en monuments architecturaux un désir se vidant avec autant d'aisance en guerres en sang en pus . . . (66)
>
> [I bet that he visualizes the leap of the soul as an erect phallus!
> And, like all the other people in Lunaï who hear me talking about desire he will think of this phallic desire characterized by the impossibility of attaining eternity; desire that invariably becomes erect in the form of swords rifles missiles architectural monuments desire that relieves itself easily in wars in blood in pus . . .] (48)

Female desire is of course excluded, or at best denigrated and assimilated, by this self-perpetuating machine that is phallocratic culture. Yet the *misovire* herself, despite the symmetrical mirroring of misogyny in her name, resists the temptation to consume her energies in a man-hating form of feminist separatism. Her "misovirism" is seen to be predicated on, or derived from, male desire and its misogynist underpinning, since it forces her to define herself against phallocratic culture, and as such it risks leading to the same sterile circularity that characterizes the interplay between Grozi and Babou. Liking adopts a more nuanced, sympathetic approach. As d'Almeida puts it: "She thus exerts force by the act of inventing *misovire,* and yet moderates that force with a certain subtlety through the special definition she gives the word. This is the balancing act that remains at the heart of how women negotiate their demands, indeed their positions, within African societies."[21] In fact, in her more nuanced position, the *misovire* is equally critical of the "pious wishes" of traditional feminist discourse: "Oserais-je parler de la fécondité de la femme [. . .] à l'heure où elle se laisse entretenir tout en se

gargarisant de mots creux: égalité émancipation féminine . . . ?" (93)
[Would I dare speak of women's fertility [. . .] at the time that she
allows herself to be kept as she indulges in hollow words: equality emancipation feminism . . . ?] (67). Her writing is instead, in a similar vein to
Tadjo's, directed toward a new kind of humanism based on female desire, one that would not exclude men but would have to be modulated
differently from male desire:

> J'imagine un désir sinusoïde
> Un désir qui ondule par approches successives
> Et trouve son éternité dans le rythme
> Tel l'océan: il n'est jamais bandé et ne sera jamais flasque . . . (68)

> [I picture a sinusoidal desire / A desire that undulates with successive
> advances / And finds its eternity in rhythm / Such as the ocean: it will
> never be erect and it will never be limp . . .] (49)

This reaffirmation of female desire sets in motion a thematic sequence that goes from the projected theme of "page 2" of the as yet
unwritten text—"the desire for a desire that lasts like the ocean" (52)—
to a reflection on a kind of mythical womanliness on "page 3" (53–69),
to the need to create a new language that would be appropriate for the
"new race" on "page 4" (69–84), and finally to a satire of critical stereotypes of Africa and Africans. In this sequence, a hypothetical artist of the
new race is asked a series of journalistic questions about her practice and
her art, questions intended to trigger off answers that would be acceptable to a Western readership (which the narrator contrasts to a set of
"wrong answers," more truthful but commercially suicidal). This is both
a satire of Western critical discourse, exposing its intellectual and economic appropriation and exploitation of African art, and also in a wider
sense a subversion of the general ethnographic impulse of Western
thinking about Africa. The *misovire* puts herself in the position of the
"Other" of ethnography, suggesting a subtle critique of the West's desire
for nativism.[22]

Liking and Tadjo dramatize the problem of writing "as" an African
woman very differently, but both bring us back to the same tension
between agency and constructedness we have come up against throughout this study. Tadjo's narrator-subject proceeds by scattering the coherence of male-centered narrative forms and conventions as a means of

breaking free of the structure of male desire she was caught within, and she privileges the oral tradition of storytelling in order to hold together the fragments of her life. This double movement of dispersion and reconciliation is in effect a process of resubjectification, in which the metaphor of "je" as bird-narrator functions both as self-representation and as a more widely representative symbol ("Je représente le peuple. Symboliquement"). With Liking there is a more complex narrative structure, a vigilance about being deluded by any false dawns, and a deferred temporality by which she appears to circumvent the problem of writing "representatively" for her people or for African women at a more abstract, symbolic level. She actively attempts to make her narrator "nonrepresentative" in both senses of Spivak's use of the term; this awareness of the rather shadowy consistency of her subjectivity appears in such phrases as "De l'autre côté de moi, il n'y a que l'étrange" (74) [On the other side of me there is only strangeness] (53). Yet at the same time as she makes the narrator-subject essentially nonrepresentable, or rather nonpresentable within the parameters that currently delimit its discursive possibilities, she in fact gives us a subject-narrator, the *misovire,* who is able to write profusely all the while she is claiming to be unable to write. As d'Almeida puts it: "The *misovire* (whose identity is clearly that of a woman) represents the woman who, in spite of the prohibitions placed on her by patriarchal society, is in the process of creating for herself a subjectivity. By claiming not to be a subject, while, in fact, being a subject through the creation of a novel that is a kind of literary Trojan horse, she is able to manage what I call a 'prise d'écriture.'"[23] There is thus, subtending the proclamations of subjective nonrepresentability, a clearly designated female voice who *is* the subject.

This performatively reinscribed subject that we find in different forms in Tadjo and Liking is allied to a redefinition and a transformation of women's social roles, as was also the case with Aoua Kéita and other women autobiographers. It involves nothing less than a deconstruction of gender identities. As Juliana Makuchi Nfah-Abbenyi puts it, "Fixed identity must therefore be de-stabilized and by so doing, fixed relations of power and gender hierarchies can also be dis-organized."[24] D'Almeida structures her study of Francophone African women writers according to a series of concentric circles that have the "self" at the center and move outward through the family and then to society. What happens to this neat model, however, is that it is unable to account for the actual tensions and transgressions she finds within the texts themselves, and she has to change this model to one of intersecting circles instead. I would go further and say that it is the act, or performance, of writing itself which takes apart not only the convenient hierarchies or oppositions into which women have been assigned a place but also any model in which a woman's role can be defined a priori. Indeed, the performative force of this subjective reaffirmation has a *radically* disaggregating effect, but one that has the potential, as Mudimbe rightly says, to bring about profound social transformation.

Ghostwriting
Sony Labou Tansi's
Spectrographic
Subject

The rebel leader Martial, in the fictional post-Independence African nation of Katamalanasie, is arrested along with the other eight members
of his family and brought in front of the brutish neocolonial dictator of
the country, the "guide providentiel" [providential guide], as he sits glut-
tonously devouring his four-hour-long dinner. The guide casually thrusts
his table knife into Martial's throat, barely interrupting his meal. When
Martial, though clearly dying, remains standing, the guide slices his chest
open, "from his plexus to his groin, as if opening the zipper of a jacket,"
then stabs him in each of his eyes. "What are you waiting for?" he asks.
"I don't want to die this death," Martial replies.[1] The guide's ever more
violent and furious attempts to put an end to Martial prove to be equally
vain, and soon only the butchered upper half of his body remains floating in front of the guide, who proceeds to hack it to pieces and to have
it made into pâté and a casserole, which the other family members are
then forced to eat. Those who refuse suffer the same fate, until only
Martial's daughter, Chaïdana, remains. This is the opening scene of the
novel *La vie et demie* [Life and a half], by the celebrated Congolese novelist and dramatist Sony Labou Tansi. As the novel progresses, it narrates
the continuing reign of the guide and his equally barbaric successors in
an absurdly exaggerated style that is both Ubuesque and Rabelaisian in
inspiration. As Chaïdana, her children, and her grandchildren attempt
to exact their vengeance, the bleeding corpse of Martial continually re-

visits both the guide and Chaïdana, hounding the former mercilessly and viciously punishing his daughter for using her sexuality as a weapon of revenge. Other spectral apparitions, too numerous to detail here, abound in the course of the novel, as indeed they do throughout Sony Labou Tansi's theater and fiction writing.[2]

What do I see in Martial's unpredictable (re)visitations in this novel, as well as in a whole range of other such enigmatic spectral presences in some recent writing by Francophone African authors? What do I *think* I see? Not only in Sony's texts but also, for example, in Calixthe Beyala's 1987 novel *C'est le soleil qui m'a brûlée* [*The Sun Hath Looked upon Me*]— featuring a narrator who is a kind of intermittent phantom presence— or Ahmadou Kourouma's acclaimed *Les soleils des Indépendances* [*The Suns of Independence*], which opens with Koné Ibrahima's "shade" heading home to announce his death, prefiguring the death of the main character, Fama Doumbouya, who is throughout the novel literally a "shadow" of his former self. This "other" spectrality, or rather the intimation of a connection between the postcolonial Francophone African subject and its spectral other, will serve as my point of departure in reading Sony Labou Tansi's *La vie et demie*. What I propose to do in this chapter is to set into productive collaboration the reinvented "ontology" of contemporary African philosophical thinking and Derrida's "hauntology" (*hantologie*), a thinking of the phenomenological and ontological dimension of Marxism that gives due recognition to the ghosts that Marx wanted to exorcise or conjure away, and whose insistent effects Derrida so painstakingly traces. The elusive phantom I am after is the notion of a "spectrographic subject," a term informed by Derrida's reading of Marx in *Specters of Marx*. In so doing I will be rearticulating the question of the relevance of "deconstruction" for African philosophy and literature, which was broached in chapter 1 in discussing the theoretical operations of Mudimbe's project, and in chapter 5 when invoking Gayatri Spivak's intertwining of deconstruction and postcolonial theory. I am aware of Sony's legendary suspicion of intellectuals. Indeed, as I proceed I will be keeping in mind his own remarks in *La vie et demie* on the "Martial phenomenon": "Nous connaissons tous la manie des intellectuels: ils théorisent sur les pratiques de la vie sans oser la pratiquer, et la grande majorité de leurs théories restent impraticables. A l'institut national des affaires du guide, on continuait donc à théoriser sur le phénomène Martial et ses conséquences sociopsychologiques . . . " [We all know how obsessed intellectuals are: they theorize about the practical side of life without daring to practice it themselves, and the great majority of their theories remain impracticable. At the National Institute of the Guide's Affairs, then, they continued to theorize about the Martial phenomenon and its sociopsychological consequences . . .] (87).

The Hauntological Subject of Africa

Ancestor worship and reverence for the deceased is an indissociable part of traditional African cultures and mythologies, so the appearance of ghosts in contemporary works of fiction should not be in the least surprising and should even be expected. A whole spectrum of shades, shadows, spirits, and phantoms figure prominently in oral legends and tales and are indeed an integral dimension of most African belief systems and cosmologies. It is furthermore true that witchcraft, sorcery, and spirit mediumship continue to play an active role even in urbanized, Westernized African society. It is tempting, therefore, to take Martial's ghost simply as a figure for the contemporary condition of Africa, as an anguished wandering soul who expresses the tragic failures of the postcolonial African world. In this world, living often amounts to little more than survival, and the survivors can apparently do little except cast mournful glances back toward a way of life that has vanished or been transformed beyond recognition. One is reminded here of the Ghost Dances that sprang up among the Native American Indians in the West toward the end of the nineteenth century, which were a desperate last self-affirmation in the face of cultural annihilation.

Frantz Fanon refers to similar manifestations of cultural despair in colonial Africa in *The Wretched of the Earth:*

> After centuries of unreality, after having wallowed in the most outlandish phantoms, at long last the native, gun in hand, stands face to face with the only forces which contend for his life—the forces of colonialism. And the youth of a colonized country, growing up in an atmosphere of shot and fire, may well make a mock of, and does not hesitate to pour scorn upon the zombies of his ancestors, the horses with two heads, the dead who rise again, and the djinns who rush into your body while you yawn.[3]

Fanon consigns these specters to the traditional past as it was lived during the period of slavery and colonization, and sees continued obsession with such phantoms as inimical to emancipatory action. As Fanon describes them, these ghostly simulacra of the authentic past of Africa are essentially products of the colonial period, born out of a defensive reaction to the violence of the colonialist project, and thus they remain tethered to Western historicity, within which they can only be figured as temporally static or ahistorical. In a dialectic that echoes Mudimbe's prognosis for a reaffirmed African *pour-soi* to counter the *en-soi* of colonial objectification, in all its forms, Fanon urges a revolutionary counterviolence on the part of the colonized in order to wrest subjectivity and historical agency from this subjugated, lifeless condition.[4]

As we saw in chapter 1, Mudimbe's writings in his early "insurrectionist" phase (*L'autre face du royaume* and *L'odeur du père*) were overtly influenced by Fanon. Since Fanon offered a means of reconciling discursive liberation and political emancipation, he was for Mudimbe an important theorist of African subjectivity. It will be recalled that, in order to strategically dismantle the various modes of discursive objectification to which Africans had been subjected, Mudimbe conceived of subjectivity in fundamentally concrete, existential terms as "le cri et le témoin de ce lieu singulier" [the cry of and witness to this singular place]. Mudimbe continues in the preface to *L'odeur du père:* "So for us it is a matter of promoting this important norm: coming to rest upon ourselves, or more exactly, turning back to ourselves, with a particular fervor and attention, which are attuned to our archaeological environment."[5]

The Eritrean philosopher Tsenay Serequeberhan has given a more hermeneutical orientation to this insistence on an existential present, drawing heavily on the political writings of Fanon in support of his argument. Serequeberhan is essentially seeking a way for African thinking to move beyond the either/or dichotomy that continues to set the advocates of ethnophilosophy (Senghor, Tempels, and their successors) in opposition to such "professional" philosophers as Nyerere or Nkrumah, who propose modern political solutions to the problems of postcolonial African society. For Serequeberhan, applying "scientific socialism" to an African political context has led to impasse and failure, since Marxist-Leninist inspired revolutionary programs such as those articulated by Nkrumah were grounded in an ideology that is the legacy of the European Enlightenment and bourgeois liberal democratic revolutions. As

Serequeberhan puts its, "It is clear that for Marx and the European Left as a whole the class war of the proletariat is waged on the terrain of a homogenized historicalness constituted by the worldwide hegemonic power of the West."[6] Fanon occupies a crucial position in the recovery of historical agency and the articulation of truly emancipatory political action. According to Fanon, this could be achieved only by the urban political activists and intellectuals—whose theories were modeled on the European Left—coming together with the indigenous and uneducated rural population. Serequeberhan summarizes the "central idea" of *The Wretched of the Earth* as "the radical self-transformation of decolonized society such that the Westernized and non-Westernized native overcome their mutual self-estrangement and in their cultural-historical fusion institute and actualize the possibility of African self-emancipation."[7] Yet how is it possible to "historicize," to take the risk of articulating an African hermeneutics, without subscribing to a form of Hegelian dialectical philosophy or Marxist historical materialism?

The most celebrated example of both a philosophical and a political appropriation of the African situation by the European Left is Sartre's essay "Orphée noir," which has been critiqued on precisely these grounds, although Mudimbe performs his own particular resurrection and reinvention of Sartrean existentialism, as we saw earlier. Can a reaffirmed African subjectivity grounded in the ontology of its own lived historical present truly guard against the incursion of what Serequeberhan terms "the seductive 'universalist' rhetoric of the European Left"?[8] How could it do so without at the very least bearing the ghostly traces of this legacy? This question takes on added resonance in the work of Sony Labou Tansi, since everything about his novels, plays, and poetry confounds the dialectical model proposed by Fanon. Sony's writing vigorously rejects any claim to social realism or political commitment, yet it in fact testifies to a profound political passion, perhaps most manifest in his theatrical activity and his little-known involvement with two anticolonial messianic movements, which I will discuss later on. His texts push the French language and literary conventions to extremes of innovation and are nonetheless profoundly rooted in Kongo mythology and cosmogony, in the past glories of its empire before colonization, and in Kikongo language oral traditions.[9] Sony is perhaps the most sensual or visceral of all African writers, yet his texts are haunted by countless phantom presences that are not so easily recuperable in cultural or mythological terms and are quite different from Fanon's lifeless remnants of the past. I will pursue the notion of "ghostwriting" in Sony Labou Tansi as a way of understanding these apparently irreconcilable tensions.

The preface to *La vie et demie* reads both as an affirmation of subjectivity ("This book takes place entirely within me," 10) and as a series of rather disconnected instructions to the reader about how best to handle the text. It could also be read as the product of a sort of "spectral subject" that sets up an analogy between Sony "himself" as a writer and the "Martial phenomenon," an analogy I'll go on to explain more fully. Although Sony's works are firmly anchored in the worldly, the sensual, or carnal, the preface talks of an "out-of-body" experience. He "spooks himself" ("I write so that it will scare me inside . . . I invent an outpost of fear . . . ") and at the same time spirits himself away ("where do you expect me to talk from if not from the outside? [. . .] I have cruelly chosen to appear as a second version of the human," 9). This takes the form of a strange prophetic or proleptic vision ("this *fable* which sees tomorrow with the eyes of today," 10), which I will also come back to a little later.

Such a departure from realism is to some extent consistent with a general trend away from the imperatives of social realism or politically engaged writing in African fiction, and is thus certainly not intended to project an idealized, utopian world, a fantasy of the future to supplant the unbearable present. As we have seen in the course of this study, postcolonial African writers have asserted their freedom and right to literary experimentation on its own terms, which is no longer seen as a prerogative of the more "mature" Western literary tradition. Sony's fables are not intended to be transcendental, in any dialectical or idealistic sense, but are fundamentally ontological; the writing is paradoxically anchored firmly in lived experience, it is a real flesh and blood simulacrum of life: "I speak [. . .] in flesh passwords [*en chair-mots-de-passe*]"; "*La vie et demie* leaves those marks made by life alone" (9, 10). These "marks made by life alone" are figured in the novel by the black stains of Martial's blood, which the successive guides are unable to erase from their walls or their bodies (in exasperation, one of them, Jean-Coeur-de-Pierre, finally resorts to a grandiose public self-immolation). But what of this nonpresent "life"? It could not be called "ghostly" in the traditional sense (although it does resemble African myths or legends of reincarnation, or of dead bodies wandering to their resting place prior to the separation of body and soul), since Sony's self, like the "Martial phenomenon," is somewhere in between reincarnation, resurrection, and haunting.

One way of circumscribing this "life and a half" might be to think of it as a "living on" (as opposed to survival), what Derrida calls "le survivre" or "la survivance" in his reading of Blanchot's *L'arrêt de mort*.[10] He articulates this concept far more expansively in *Specters of Marx,* where he develops a "phantasmatology," as he calls it, the effect of which would be to open up "a dimension of *sur-vival* or *surviving* that is irreducible both to being and to any opposition between living and dying."[11] Although I would be unable within the space of this chapter to do justice to the complexity and rigor of Derrida's reading of Marx, I would like to focus on one crucial moment in his concluding maneuvers. Derrida is drawn to Marx's obsessive references to specters and in particular to his concern to make, as a precondition of his theory of dialectical materialism, the conjuration or exorcism of the "ghosts," the simulacra, of German idealist philosophy (that is, the "ontology" of Marx's theory is founded upon on a prior hunting down and clearing away of the "hauntological"; just as, perhaps, much African writing wants to start out by exorcising the colonial specters still haunting its own discursive theories and practices). The specters Marx attempts to get rid of keep reappearing, of course, sometimes in the unlikeliest places, and this leads Derrida to the following elegant formulation: "To haunt does not mean to be present, and it is necessary to introduce haunting into the very construction of a concept. Of every concept, beginning with the concepts of being and time. That is what we would call here a hauntology. Ontology opposes it only in a movement of exorcism. Ontology is a conjuration."[12]

Sony Labou Tansi, in contrast to Marx and Fanon (but like Derrida), affirms an ontology that does not deny the effects of simulacra or spectrality but even makes them a condition of possibility of ontology (Martial stubbornly resists the guide's pleadings to "die your death," to die a "proper death"). At one level, then, the prevalence of the spectral in Sony Labou Tansi represents a break both with traditional cultural values and with the early politically committed literary tradition of Francophone Africa, and could be read instead, at the ironic remove that its biting humor invites, as a political satire or allegory ("fable"). Martial's insistent survival beyond death could be taken as an affirmation of an African subjectivity beyond or outside of the various forms of its political, historical, or ethnological discursive subjection (despite everything he is subjected to, however absurd in its excess, he refuses to die). The suggestion of "martyr" in the name Martial likewise seems to define the parameters of this allegory, which is how the novel is often read, as representing the undying democratic aspirations of the people when confronted by a brutal and randomly oppressive neocolonial dictatorship. As the novel unfolds, however, Martial's martyrdom itself turns into a vindictive campaign of revenge that does not spare his own daughter (during one of his spectral reincarnations he in fact rapes her). The characters are then continuously recycled as different versions of themselves; Chaïdana's children from Martial's rape of his daughter are the "second" Martial and Chaïdana, and the latter's children from her relationship with one of the guide's successors, Henri-au-Coeur-Tendre [Henry the Tender Hearted], form a splinter movement that becomes infinitely more destructive than any of the various guides' tyrannical regimes. This confounds any attempt to order or rationalize the narrative logic of the novel, since the more or less stable relationship required of allegory is relentlessly eroded, and the possibility of any kind of coherent allegorical identification is undone.

This could be seen as a rhetorical strategy similar to Dadié's in his travel writings; the European reader's inability to make sense of the text might from this perspective be the consequence of a reversal of the poles of African and Western, the European reader by virtue of this reversal being repositioned as the objectified and therefore alienated Other of Sony's African subject, that is, "the others, who would never be my others," to quote from the preface again. Yet this does not fully account for the disruptive effect of the text, since there is also a deliberate *self-defamiliarization* at work (and this is perhaps the *unheimlichkeit* of Sony's "spooking himself").[13] The pressure of the language of Sony's writing constantly tests the very limits of invention. There are comprehensible neologisms such as "tropicalité" and "excellentiel"; expressions that are calques of African idioms and syntactical constructions, which is fairly typical of much recent Francophone African writing; distortions of meaning as words pass through several translations; arbitrarily imposed catachreses that neither the reader nor the characters understand and that mirror the random exercise of tyrannical power; and finally words that take on a life of their own (for example, *enfer* [hell] starts out as a misunderstood term among several characters, then comes to be one of the many censored words that provokes an outrageous series of repressive measures by the providential guide, and then seems itself to trigger off the apocalyptic ending to the novel).

It is *time,* however, which is perhaps the most unstable of all the elements of the narrative. This disruption of time is not uncommon in contemporary Francophone African novels, which should hardly be surprising, since these texts often take the form of a rewriting of a precolonial and colonial past, which necessarily involves a rethinking of the historical legacy and the temporal frames of reference that have structured it. We are often presented with two kinds of time, as in the novels of Ahmadou Kourouma or Boubacar Boris Diop, for example: Western linear time and African mythical time, with a whole range of complex interferences between the two. Sony Labou Tansi's novels likewise have little respect for the conventional measurement of time, although in another sense this is a sign of Sony's far deeper respect for time itself.[14] *La vie et demie* opens as if it were going to be a realist historical narrative ("It was the year Chaïdana had turned fifteen," 11), but then it is immediately brought back to the "present" with a jolt: "But time. Time is all over the place. The sky, the earth, everything. All over the place." Then, it begins "again": "It was in a time when the earth was still round, when the sea was the sea . . . " (11). But we know from the preface that "The earth is no longer round." The earth is not the earth, time is not time, nothing "is" anymore.[15] From the outset we are denied even the possibility of two distinct temporal planes (say, a kind of prelapsarian past time of order and a present time of chaos), since the past is only narratable in terms of the chaotic (non-) time of the (non-) present.

The most dizzyingly unsettling instance of this disruption of time and history comes at the end of the novel. From his town Granita, Jean Calcium has unleashed wave after wave of "vibrations meurtrières" [deadly vibrations] on the enemy town of Félix-Ville, the destruction being of such magnitude that it forms a crater 750 meters deep full of molten lava. This lasts for two months, after which time "the Nile, the pharaohs, Victoria, the lake region" come into existence. So this allegory of postcolonial devastation itself predates precolonial Africa; posthistory collapses into prehistory. Jean Calcium, who falls asleep during this nuclear apocalypse, then "wakes up" to an alternative "reality," and it is impossible to tell whether it is in a rebuilt replica, a simulacrum of Granita, from which all collective memory of the period of war has been erased, or whether the war never in fact took place. Jean Calcium wanders around in a daze: "I wonder whether we're still alive, whether this is still Granita, whether I'm not dreaming forever [. . .] Am I still in this world [. . .] I'm a corpse, a burial. I am my corpse" (189).

Ghosts are, as Derrida says in *Specters of Marx,* untimely, "intempestifs," they have no time, or are in a sense outside of time: "It is a proper characteristic of the specter, if there is any, that no one can be sure if by returning it testifies to a past living being or to a future living being, for the *revenant* may already mark the return of the specter of a promised living being. Once again, untimeliness and disadjustment of the contemporary."[16] Time in Sony Labou Tansi is indeed "out of joint," "*dis-joint,*" "deranged, both unruly and mad," some of the terms Derrida uses in referring to Hamlet's temporal predicament. This disjunctiveness of time is, he argues, one of the most deconstructive of spectral effects: "To maintain together that which does not hold together [. . .] can be thought (we will come back to this incessantly as well as to the spectrality of the specter) only in a dis-located time of the present, at the joining of a radically dis-jointed time, without certain conjunction."[17] If this is indeed the case, how is it then possible to read *La vie et demie* in terms of effective subjective or historical agency?

A helpful detour might be provided by Homi Bhabha's discussion, in his chapter "The Postcolonial and the Postmodern: The Question of Agency" in *The Location of Culture,* of the "enunciatory present." Bhabha outlines possible postcolonial narrative strategies of emancipation and empowerment and says that it is not enough simply to *represent* differently if we do not fundamentally alter the time frame of representation: "It requires a radical revision of the social temporalities in which emergent histories may be written, the rearticulation of the sign in which cultural identities may be inscribed." He goes on to claim that, because of the experiences of colonialism, cultural translation is an unavoidable necessity: "The natural(ized), unifying discourse of 'nation,' 'peoples,' or authentic 'folk' tradition, those embedded myths of culture's particularity, cannot be readily referenced."[18] Bhabha argues for a postcolonial agency in terms of a "shift from the cultural as an epistemological object to culture as an enactive, enunciatory site." The confluence of Bhabha's discussion and the work of contemporary African philosophers such as Serequeberhan or Mudimbe should be evident, since it is this gesture of performative enunciation that "provides a process whereby objectified

others may be turned into subjects of their own history and experience."[19] The process of reaffirming subjectivity and recovering historical agency in a postcolonial African context has to account for both the
past ("the cultural as an epistemological object") *and* the present ("culture as an enactive, enunciatory site"). As Bhabha describes it: "The indi-
viduation of the agent occurs in a moment of displacement. It is a pul-
sional incident, the split-second movement when the process of the
subject's designation—its fixity—opens up beside it, uncannily *abseits,*
a supplementary space of contingency."[20] This uncanny space that opens
up "beside" the subject is spectral through and through. It is "a second
version of the human," to quote from Sony's preface—what we might
rephrase as an individuated postcolonial subjective agency "shadowing"
or haunting colonial, Westernized "Man."

The radically disjunctive effects of spectrality thus haunt the ordered
logic of time and history, disrupting both the self-presence of the present and the anamnesic "return of the past" in present recollection. It
opens up a breach in time that then has a decisive effect on the relationship to the future. Bhabha in his conclusion to *The Location of Culture* talks of a "form of cultural reinscription that moves *back to the
future.*" "I shall call it," he says, "a 'projective past,' a form of the future
anterior." He elaborates on this "time-lagged" futurity a little later on:
"The time-lag of postcolonial modernity moves *forward,* erasing the
compliant past tethered to the myth of progress, ordered in the binarisms of its cultural logic: past/present, inside/outside [. . .] This slow-
ing down, or lagging, *impels* the 'past,' *projects* it, gives its 'dead' symbols
the circulatory life of the 'sign' of the present, of *passage.*"[21] I see a parallel articulation in Derrida's discussion of the relationship of spectrality
to the openness of a future that, because it is no longer calculable in
terms of a dialectical or linear movement of time, Derrida describes as
"unanticipatable." As he says: "Given that a *revenant* is always called
upon to come and to come back, the thinking of the specter, contrary
to what good sense leads us to believe, signals towards the future. It is a
thinking of the past, a legacy that can come only from that which has
not yet arrived—from the *arrivant* itself."[22]

To return to Sony Labou Tansi, one cannot overemphasize the proleptic, prophetic quality of his writing. He writes in the preface to *La
vie et demie,* "J'ose renvoyer le monde entier à l'espoir [. . .] cette *fable*
qui voit demain avec des yeux d'aujourd'hui" [I dare to send the whole

world towards hope [. . .] this *fable* which sees tomorrow with today's eyes]. And as he says in the preface to *L'état honteux*: "J'écris, ou je crie, un peu pour forcer le monde à venir au monde" [I write, or I scream, partly to force the world to come into the world].[23] His novels contain countless quasi-messianic figures such as Martial or Chaïdana or Ignacio Banda in *Les yeux du Volcan,* and in interviews he has affirmed over and over his strong belief in a "world to come." How is one to understand this messianism in relation to Sony's political convictions? Phyllis Clark has written a compelling account of Sony's involvement in Congolese nationalist politics and his passionate regional activism on behalf of the BaKongo. This commitment was greatly influenced by two important messianic anticolonial movements that arose during the 1920s in the Belgian Congo, around the figures of André Matswa, the founder of the "Amicale" movement (which had thousands of followers in French Equatorial Africa), and Simon Kimbangu, the charismatic prophet and founder of the "Eglise de Jésus-Christ sur terre par le prophète Simon Kimbangu," a syncretic religion that combined social and political activism with customary folk beliefs. Both men became martyrs for the anticolonial cause following their deaths, and both Amicalism and Kimbanguism spread rapidly among the Kongo-Lari community in response to the brutally repressive nature of colonial Belgian politics. Sony Labou Tansi's own political convictions were formed within the context of this complex mixture of an overt, highly public anticolonialism and a covert, secretive devotion to BaKongo spiritual folk practices. This accounts for what Clark defines as Sony's "double discourse," manifestations of which we noted earlier in the chapter. As she puts it, "From the outrage at injustice expressed in his first novel *La Vie et demie* through the last lamentation of irreconcilable offense and irreparable social division in *Le Commencement des douleurs* (1995), Sony Lanou Tansi's exploration of the conditions necessary for the realization of his ideal of human justice operates on two levels, but remains anchored in Kongo worldview."[24]

Sony's messianism is thus not to be understood solely in political or social terms, as we have seen, and it would also be wrong to see him simply as a "prophet" or "visionary" in the sense that he has a "vision" of the future (revealed to him through supernatural or extrasensory divinatory powers). As Nicolas Martin-Granel says, "He distrusts the grand eschatological narratives that presage man's emancipation."[25] Indeed, rather than reflecting messianism, Sony's proleptic statements might be closer to what Derrida describes in *Specters of Marx* as *messianicity*. In responding to various Marxist critiques of his reading of Marx, Derrida elaborates on this nonutopian quality of messianicity as follows:

> *Anything but Utopian,* messianicity mandates that we interrupt the ordinary course of things, time and history *here-now;* it is inseparable from an affirmation of otherness and justice. As this unconditional messianicity *must* therefore negotiate its conditions in one or another singular, practical situation, we have to do here with the locus of an analysis and evaluation, and, therefore, of a responsibility. But that that re-examination has to be carried out, and carried out without delay— this is an ineluctability whose imperative, always here-now, in singular fashion, can in no case yield to the allure of Utopia, at least not to what the word literally signifies or is ordinarily taken to mean.[26]

Sony's novels are in this sense not utopian but consistent with the spectral logic of his writing; he affirms "life" "now," but it is a "now" that comes from the future, that reappears in the death of the present, the nonpresence of present life. According to the logic of his writing, there "is" no "now" for him. Nor is this "openness to what is to come" a form of fatalism, since in Sony's novels the laws of logic, of physics, of nature, and of *fate,* or predictable destiny, are radically suspended and put into question, including the efficacy of divination, of spectral visitations in dreams, of sacrifices to ancestors, and so on. If this *revenance* is at the same time an *avènement* (advent), it is a coming of a future that no longer belongs to European history—it's time frame, its past—but it is a *revenance* that is marked by *invention.* Although in *La vie et demie* this is manifest in the characters' ingenuity in coming up with ever more outlandish methods of destruction, some of the characters in Sony's other novels are far more appealing inventors, for example, Hoscar Hana and Hoscar Hana Junior in *Le commencement des douleurs:* they build islands, attempt to recast whole continents (as if they were molten metal), and make remote-control storms, flying bicycles, a machine for extracting memory from water, and a time machine ("une machine à trouer le temps").[27] How original, though, can these inventions claim to be?

Specters of Márquez

We are, after all, perhaps reading too much into Sony Labou Tansi's novels, giving him too much credit. Ought we not to see them instead, more soberly, as examples of a timeworn genre, that is, *magical realism*? It is certainly true that Sony owes a great deal to the Latin American tradition, and to Gabriel García Márquez in particular. The specter of García Márquez, especially of his great satirical political novels *One Hundred Years of Solitude* and *The Autumn of the Patriarch,* is everywhere present in Sony: there are the figures of despotic patriarchs, bodies of political opponents served up at banquets and their ghosts coming back to haunt their murderers, the precision of the absurd excesses, the indelible blood stains, and even the Hispanic ring of the names of the characters. Should it not be García Márquez who ultimately gets the credit? Is Sony in a metaphorical sense employing him as his "ghostwriter"? The very gesture of defining Sony's novels by genre would seem, however, to be inadequate and rather ill conceived. In the first instance, this categorization by genre is a means ultimately of domesticating their effects (exorcising their specters, those disturbing, unaccountable elements of the text); and second, "magical realism" always seems in the final analysis to fall down on the side of "realism" (the argument is often made that what Europeans take to be fantastic and supernatural is for Africans or Latin Americans every bit as "real" as actual phenomena). It seems to me more interesting to read Sony Labou Tansi in terms of the effects of reinscription which are built into the very logic of spectrality.[28] In a sense the ghost of García Márquez does haunt him, but it sets up a very problematic relationship, not so much between the two writers as between "ghostwriting" and plagiarism, which both have the effect of apparently *undermining* the force and effectiveness of Sony's inventiveness, of his "originality."

Accusations of plagiarism in fact keep coming back to haunt Francophone African writing. Yambo Ouologuem's 1968 novel *Le devoir de violence* [*Bound to Violence*] was found to contain large sections of loosely reworded text from works by Graham Greene and Simone Schwartz-Bart.[29] A more recent cause célèbre has been the Cameroonian writer Calixthe Beyala, who was awarded the Prix de l'Académie Française for her novel *Honneurs perdus,* which was discovered by Pierre Assouline, the editor of the Parisian literary magazine *Lire,* to have borrowed rather freely from Ben Okri's *The Famished Road*. Ouologuem was consciously playing with Western literary conventions and standards, but Beyala's motives are more questionable (she had already been found guilty of "partial copying" in a previous novel). In her self-defense in a newspaper article she refers to the legacy of the oral tradition, in which rules of individual authorship are far more fluid, and the notion of intellectual property is something of an irrelevance.[30] I am not interested in arguing for or against the ethics of Beyala's gesture, but I do see the concepts of plagiarism and "ghostwriting" as complementing each other in intriguing ways that can be directly related to Marxism and its spectral others.

The term for a ghostwriter in French is *un nègre*. The historical and ideological sources of the term can easily be deduced, since "ghostwriting" figures a relationship of enslavement (in fact, *un nègre* originally meant "slave" before becoming a term of racist abuse). As a literary "copy" of African slavery, ghostwriting involves a writing subject who is simultaneously denied the recognition of authorship and occulted as a subject. Since the early days of European exploration and colonization of Africa, and philosophically sanctioned by Hegel, Africa has stood for the occult, the night from which civilization emerges, and so on. Following Fanon's Sartrean psychoanalytical existentialist analysis of the black man's "being" in *White Skin, Black Masks,* the black man's existence, or being, is constituted by virtue of its occultation and exclusion, its nonexistence. It comes into being, in other words, *as* nonbeing. Fanon's famous analysis of the black man's lived experience of his blackness in "The Fact of Blackness" is a crucial moment in the attempt to understand the ontology of colonized Africans (an understanding that for Fanon itself occurs as a painful lived subjective experience). As Fanon says, there is no individuality in the term *nègre;* it is a term that exists only at the level of objectified stereotype, there is no ontological experience of the *nègre:* "Ontology [. . .] does not allow us to understand a Black man's being."[31] To *return* so emphatically to the body, as Sony Labou Tansi does, is not to fall back into the binaristic discourse of colonialist representations of the "sensual African" and the "rational European," which are myths that operate at the level of discursive subjection. Sony's carnal ghosts could ultimately be read as a powerful act of resisting the disembodiment of objectification.

To extend this analysis to the figure of the *nègre* as ghostwriter, this exclusion and occultation enable the establishment and perpetuation of the myth of the colonialist/capitalist as "inventor" or "discoverer." "Invention," from a Marxist perspective, is determined according to the economy of bourgeois capitalism and imperialism, in which "workers" (writers) are alienated from the products of their labor (their texts). Thus the concept of "invention," and also the concept of a subject as a self-sufficient agent of Western liberal democracies, are closely bound up with the objectification from which the African subject seeks to emancipate itself. For Ouologuem, "plagiarism" becomes a strategic disruption of this economy of literary production. From this perspective, the Paris-based denunciation of Beyala as a charlatan, a fake, is a defense of the values of purity and literary originality, and by extension a form of intellectual apartheid, an attempt to exorcise the specter of Western literature's own past as occulted plagiarism (understood as a form of massive cultural plundering).[32]

Another well-known compatriot of Sony Labou Tansi's, Henri Lopès, in his novel *Le pleurer-rire* [*The Laughing Cry*] interrupts his narrative at one point in order to reply, with heavy irony, to an accusation that the previous chapter has been plagiarized from a certain Benoist-Meschin (this "accusation" being part of the narrator's intradiegetic fiction). Lopès contrasts the cold Cartesian logic that underpins the legal definition of plagiarism with an African view of the phenomenon, which is more relaxed and which makes allowance for "the marvellous world of our mysteries."[33] For him there is no incompatibility between invention and plagiarism, and he has no qualms about stating boldly, "I have done nothing [. . .] but relate one of my own adventures. If from there I have [. . .] borrowed certain words from another, that is a phenomenon both possible and well-known." He is, he says, in no way detracting from Benoist-Meschin, but through this convergence of minds, "I offer him my homage." Plagiarism, like ghostwriting, is thus strategically reappropriated and positively valorized as a way of honoring the "original" author.

This gesture of ironic reinscription, however, at the same time casts doubts on the untainted purity of the original. It is surely no accident that one of the dedications of *La vie et demie* is to Henri Lopès: "A Henri Lopès aussi, puisque en fin de compte je n'ai écrit que son livre" [To Henri Lopès as well, since I really have only written his book]. The debt to Lopès is at one level quite apparent: both novels satirize neocolonial dictatorships, and the absurd excesses of Lopès's dictator are very similar to those of Sony's guide. However, the logic of praise and indebtedness is not as straightforward as it at first seems. One could read it as say-ing something like: "He got there before me, I can only hope to emu-late him, but all credit to him. He's the real writer of this text, he ghost-wrote my book, so in a sense this is really his book." Alternatively, it could also mean: "I wrote his book before him, I am *his* ghostwriter." There is in fact a radical undecidability about who is haunting whom, which of the two celebrated self-proclaimed plagiarists is the other's ghostwriter. This aporetic doubleness is indeed, to return to Derrida, something that is predetermined by the structure of spectrality as such: "But one has to realize that the ghost is there, be it in the opening of the promise or the expectation, *before its first apparition:* the latter had an-nounced itself, from the first it will have come second. *Two times at the same time* [emphasis added], originary iterability, irreducible virtuality of this space and this time."[34] We could thus say that what Sony does is to reinvent the concept itself of originality, of invention, by making it an effect of *revenance,* a coming in to the world that is always a coming back.

To read Sony Labou Tansi in terms of ghostwriting is to uncover nar-ratives of genealogical indebtedness (Sony to García Márquez and Lopès) that hark back to scenes of debt visited in earlier chapters. I am think-ing of the debt that Mudimbe owes Foucault, for example, both in a broad theoretical sense and also in a specific one, when he borrows Fou-cault's words from *L'ordre du discours,* substituting "the West" where Fou-cault had originally written "Hegel." Can Mudimbe exorcise Foucault's ghost, any more than Foucault can Hegel's, in their efforts to free them-selves from their respective debts? And what of Dadié's debts, not only to the pan-Africanism of his predecessors but also to Montesquieu and to later ethnographers whom he ironizes so convincingly? Likewise, I have accrued my own (multiple) debts along the way, and I am left won-dering to what extent these are the same kinds of debts. What is my debt to Bhabha or to Derrida, for example? Do I owe more to Derrida than to the Francophone African writers who have provided for me the occa-sions and contexts within which to pursue a number of sometimes rather intricate and complex arguments? As I have accumulated my own bur-den of debt, have I assisted, or hindered, Mudimbe in his project of releasing African subjects from their discursive burdens, from the bur-den *of* discursive dependency?

Derrida's *Specters of Marx* sheds some light on these questions, since it is fundamentally a text about structures of indebtedness: Marx's (in-escapable) debt to German idealist philosophy, Hamlet's to his father, and the place that we, as Marx's inheritors, currently occupy at the end of the line of his political and philosophical genealogy. It is also a text that aims to question, or deconstruct, the very principle of (paternal, phallocratic) genealogical filiation. Derrida proposes a different under-standing of debt which he describes as "the radical and necessary het-erogeneity of an inheritance." This legacy involves an irreducibly ambiva-lent and contradictory movement, which carries with it the responsibility of an equally contradictory *reading:* "If the readability of a legacy were given, natural, transparent, univocal, if it did not call for and at the same time defy interpretation, one would never have anything to inherit [*on n'aurait jamais à en hériter*]."[35] Perhaps it this kind of reading, one that disarticulates the apparently straightforward logic of debt, that can best perform the discursive decolonization that Mudimbe envisages.

What does this have to do, given that I have invoked Marx's legacy throughout this chapter, with real monetary debt, now that the West is finally acknowledging (though not yet acting upon) the need to reduce (though not yet cancel) the debt repayments that have crippled the econ-omies of so many African nations and the lives of their citizens? I'd like to answer this final question, and by implication the previous ones as well, by incurring one more debt, to Bruce Janz, who has written elo-quently of the relationship between African philosophy and Western philosophy in terms of structures of indebtedness. In his article "Debt and Duty: Kant, Derrida and African Philosophy," Janz refers to two of Derrida's essays ("Mochlos, or the Conflict of Faculties" and "Of the Humanities and the Philosophical Discipline") that have as their theme the institutional place of philosophy in the West. In these texts, Derrida argues against the notion of philosophy as a monolithic discipline that can be traced back to a single origin. As he says, "It has always been bas-tard, hybrid, grafted, multilinear and polyglot."[36] How, Janz asks, does African philosophy define itself in relation to the Western philosophical tradition, from which it has been historically excluded or at the very least marginalized? The important question is not, he argues, what Afri-can philosophy *is,* its essence, but *where* it is. While it has first of all to take into account the place to which it has been assigned by the West, the history of its exclusion, at the same time it has to utilize the resources particular to Africa in order to engage, counterdiscursively, with the

West's "answers" to Africa's "problems." Although the particular frame of reference here is African philosophy, the "resources" are very much those exploited by the literary texts I have been reading:

> Philosophising in Africa means attending to language in the face of essentially technocratic disciplines. In "Mochlos" Derrida suggests that philosophy always attends to truth, and in this way the golem moves. In Africa, this may mean that philosophy can attend to showing the particular limitations of disciplinary answers to Africa's problems. Specifically, the language that is pressed into service to account for African lives often needs deconstruction [. . .] Economists interpret the problems of Africa as economic problems, with economic solutions, and when these do not work, it is not the method which is the problem but the "uncivilized" and "uncooperative" Africans. Even versions of interdisciplinarity do not help, because they simply try to add methodologies together to address a problem which is itself never really interrogated properly. Instead of the problems of Africa being economic, then, they take the interdisciplinary label "development," and ironically become more intractable because the specific methodologies involved in answering the problem of development become harder to discern.[37]

In this respect there is a direct line of descendance connecting present-day economic aid with universalist or colonialist ideologies and their various means of "assisting" Africa. Sembene's *Guelwaar*, in fact, argues along similar lines for Africa's need to break free from a syndrome of dependency. Since Western philosophy conveniently hides its own debts in arguing from a position of universality, Janz makes the point that the West is ultimately, perhaps, more in need of African philosophy than the other way around, precisely because "Africa is able to question its place in a unique way, a way that at least the West has forgotten."[38] Which is not simply to reverse the positions, and the directionality of indebtedness, celebrating Africa at the expense of the West. Mudimbe has demonstrated decisively the dangers of such rhetorical strategies, which ultimately consolidate, all the more surreptitiously, the prevailing hierarchies of power/knowledge. As Janz concludes: "African thought is not worth pursuing only because it can give a window on Western thought, but that is a useful by-product."[39] The distinction here is subtle, but crucial. Disavowing debts altogether is clearly illusory, and reversing debts leaves structures of dependency—whether philosophical, discursive, economic, or otherwise—in place. To challenge the structure of indebtedness itself is to posit a very different kind of starting point on the road to political and philosophical autonomy, one that is consonant with Mudimbe's emphasis on existential place in his rewriting of the *cogito,* or what I term his performative reinscription of subjectivity. And this may, in fact, be very close to the spectral subject of Sony Labou Tansi's "reinvention" of invention itself.

Conclusion

Reprising Francophone African Subjectivity

I am conscious of having chosen one of many possible paths through the question of what it means to think about subjectivity in Francophone Africa in terms of narrative agency, and in relation to various modes of discursive decolonization, although I hope the reasons for my particular focus are now clear. In fact, my project could have taken any number of turns. I might, for example, have spent longer situating the various subjects, integrating each of their texts in its specific cultural and historical context. There is a growing body of literature, too, on questions of agency and personhood in traditional African philosophies or cosmologies which could have been usefully invoked at relevant points.[1] Then again, I might have addressed the question of how the subject's agency sits with larger collective or communalist enterprises, both traditional and contemporary. Furthermore, since my own historical borders are left deliberately open, this could have led me to an exploration of the underappreciated but subversive and subtly effective agency in texts of African writers from the "high" colonial era, as Christopher Miller does in his book *Nationalists and Nomads.* I could also have given due recognition to Fanon the political theorist, stressing in him the *pedagogical* rather than the *performative,* to use Bhabha's terms, rather than enlisting him principally as a theorist of subjectivity, as Bhabha and Mudimbe do, thereby leaning more toward the early Fanon of *Black Skin, White Masks.*[2]

It has certainly not been my intention to deny the dialectics of history, or the importance of historical and cultural contextualization. My point has been, rather, that *reading* the subject as it is inscribed in a number of narratives *necessarily* involves a rethinking of history and time, as evidenced most clearly in Sony Labou Tansi among the writers I have studied. Since the process of writing and rewriting the subject is a performative act, each textual enunciation of the subject also stages a different performance of history, as we saw with Aoua Kéita, Bernard Dadié, V. Y. Mudimbe, Tierno Monénembo, Ousmane Sembene, and Werewere Liking. These texts often resist or rework Manichaean, oppositional accounts of African history (colonial vs. postcolonial, European vs. African, national vs. precolonial, traditional vs. modern), one crucial form of this being the destabilizing of gender oppositions. Reading these texts requires us to remain constantly vigilant about the recuperative mechanisms of essentialist thinking, which is often articulated as discourses of ethnicity, of authenticity, of purity of origins, and so forth.[3] One has to be wary, too, of falling into the opposite trap of an equally uncritical antiessentialism. The example of Sony Labou Tansi is here again quite instructive, since Sony's subject is at once strangely outside time and sociohistorically situated, both spectral and carnal, derivative and innovative, singular and reduplicative. It is indissociable either from its Kongo origins or from its political engagement with French colonialism (and Congolese neocolonialism), and thus one cannot reduce it either to an ethnophilosophical subject or to a politically or historically determined agent. Neither should we see this as a creative failing that could potentially be overcome, since the reaffirmed subject is precisely what binds together these apparently irreconcilable positions.

My own focus throughout this study has been to explore the performative effects of inscription and reinscription, since the conflicting tensions and competing energies of the texts so often coalesce around the writing subject. Attending to the performative dimension of this subjective reinscription allows us to move beyond the various binarisms or dichotomies that structure, and often seem to entrap, these narratives. For the subject, this takes its most apparent form in the competing claims of agency and determinism, and I would align my own emphasis on performative effects with Appiah's proposal, in his essay "Tolerable Falsehoods," that we consider these tensions less as a competition for causal space than as "contingently complementary" modes of narrative agency. Mudimbe's novels, indeed his entire critical project, are read most productively in this light, since this is how we can understand the purpose of his subjective investment in his extraordinarily wide-ranging archival labor and his engagement with contemporary intellectual debates. This investment corresponds, indeed, to the third sense in which he uses the word *reprendre* in discussing contemporary African art—a sense one could equally apply to the philosophical and literary narratives, Mudimbe's as well as others', that I have explored:

> The word *reprendre*—strangely difficult to translate—I intend as an image of the contemporary activity of African art. I mean it first in the sense of taking up an interrupted tradition, not out of a desire for purity, which would testify only to the imaginations of dead ancestors, but in a way that reflects the conditions of today. Secondly, *reprendre* suggests a methodical assessment, the artist's labor beginning, in effect, with an evaluation of the tools, means, and projects of art within a social context transformed by colonialism and by later currents, influences, and fashions from abroad. Finally, *reprendre* implies a pause, a meditation, a query on the meaning of the two preceding exercises.[4]

Mudimbe's own *reprise* of the "colonial library"—as well as of the contemporary theoretical library, with which he is equally familiar—works at this third level. On the one hand he promotes an African deep knowledge, or gnosis, and on the other, he approaches this gnosis, in a very similar mode to Kwasi Wiredu's, as a question of conceptual decolonization. The continuous performative reinscription of his own subjectivity, though, makes it impossible to reduce him to either one or the other of these positions.

Ioan Davies has described the continued dependency binding the African subject to predetermined systems of expression—in artistic, political, and social practices in Africa—as a form of fetishism, in both the Marxist and the Freudian senses of the term. He explores different sociopolitical strategies employed by Africans to renegotiate their positions within such constrictive double binds, and argues for the importance of what he terms "decolonizing the fetish" of African culture—or as he says, "reinventing the art object for those who want the authentic." In particular, he points to the analyses of two political theorists, David

Hecht and Maliqalim Simone, who discuss the inventive forms of theatricality and simulacrum that one finds on a micropolitical level in everyday situations in Africa. For Davies, the eclectic and playful use to which Mudimbe subjects the "colonial library," and the constant performative staging of his own subjectivity, can be seen as exemplary instances of such strategies. Mudimbe's subjective "stories" are best read, in other words, as a kind of "decolonization of the fetish," a process of reappropriation of a colonially fetishized Africa that one might term, inversely, a defetishizing of colonial Africa.

I began this study with Sony Labou Tansi's phrase "j'écris, ou je crie" as an immediate indication of the ambivalence that the subject of Francophone Africa has to contend with in writing itself into history while simultaneously rewriting that history. I would like to end by reprising Mudimbe's sentence from *L'odeur du père* which I partly quoted earlier, and which echoes Sony's: "Je pars du fait que ma conscience et mon effort sont d'un lieu, d'un espace et d'un moment donnés; et je ne vois ni comment ni pourquoi ma parole, quelle que puisse être son envol, ne devrait pas, avant toute autre chose, être le cri et le témoin de *ce lieu singulier*" (emphasis added) [I start out from the fact that my consciousness and my effort are of a given place, space and moment; and I see neither how nor why what I have to say, whichever direction it takes, should not be, before anything else, the cry of and witness to *this singular place*].[5] If Sony's writing forces one above all to rethink the relationship between the African subject and its history, its *time,* Mudimbe's stresses the importance of *place,* or more precisely the *singularity* of *this* subject's place. This is how I understand the significance of his methodological disagreement with Kwasi Wiredu about their "respective subjective choices," and his wish that "Wiredu would speak more explicitly from his own existential locus as subject."[6] Wiredu and Mudimbe are equally committed to the conceptual decolonization of Africa by returning in some way to local resources. According to Mudimbe, however, even a project as "close" to the Akan people as Wiredu's takes them out of their particular subjective place, abstracts them from the manifold complexities of each singular enunciative situation, and transforms them into a generalized universal. The "locality" of Mudimbe's existential place is not to be understood as one pole of an opposition between, say, the local and the global, or the particular and the universal, but as the condition of possibility—"avant toute autre chose"—which subtends such oppositions. Mudimbe's divergence from Wiredu might ultimately be read as the gap (*écart*) which is the very locus of this possibility or power; a power that is both a "prise d'écriture," as d'Almeida terms it, as well as a performatively (re-)inventive *reprise*.

Notes

Introduction

1. Sony Labou Tansi, *L'état honteux,* 5, my translation.
2. Miller, *Theories of Africans,* 4.
3. Mudimbe, *The Invention of Africa,* 183.
4. Mudimbe, *L'odeur du père,* 57, my translation.
5. Ngate, *Francophone African Fiction.*
6. Mudimbe, *Parables and Fables.* An earlier version of this argument was published as "I as an other."
7. Mudimbe, *Parables and Fables,* xv.
8. Mudimbe, *Parables and Fables,* xix.
9. Eze, ed., *Postcolonial African Philosophy,* 7.
10. Eze, ed., *Postcolonial African Philosophy,* 9.
11. Butler, *The Psychic Life of Power,* 15.
12. Butler, *The Psychic Life of Power,* 18.
13. Bhabha, "The Other Question," in *The Location of Culture,* 76.
14. For a fuller discussion of the ways in which postcolonial theory has often been reductively applied, see the introduction to the special issue of *Paragraph* edited by Britton and Syrotinski.
15. See, for example, Spivak's interview entitled "The Problem of Cultural Self-Representation" (1986), in *The Post-colonial Critic.*

1. V. Y. Mudimbe, African Philosophy, and the Return of the Subject

1. Mudimbe, *Le corps glorieux des mots et des êtres.*
2. Mudimbe, *Parables and Fables,* x. Subsequent references, to *Parables,* will be given in parentheses in the text.

3. Mudimbe, *The Invention of Africa*, 28. Subsequent references, to *Invention*, will be given in parentheses in the text.

4. Masolo, *African Philosophy in Search of Identity*, 181.

5. See, for example, the chapter "Discourse of Power and Knowledge of Otherness," in *The Invention of Africa*, 1–23.

6. Tempels, *Bantu Philosophy*, 35.

7. Mudimbe, *The Idea of Africa*, xiii. Subsequent references, to *Idea*, will be in the text.

8. Mudimbe, "Anthropology and Marxist Discourse," in *Parables and Fables*, 166–91, on 184. Subsequent references, to "Marxist Discourse," will be in the text.

9. Mudimbe, *L'autre face du royaume*, 101, my translation.

10. Mudimbe, *L'odeur du père*, 48, my translation. Subsequent references will be in the text.

11. Sartre, "Orphée noir," xxxix.

12. The best account in Mudimbe's work of this generation of philosophers, and the theological roots of their thinking, is this chapter in *Parables and Fables*, 32–68.

13. This particular example, and the complex relationship between myth and history it suggests, are reworked by Tierno Monénembo in his novel *Cinéma* (1997), which I look at more closely in chapter 4.

14. Hountondji, *African Philosophy*, 33.

15. These qualifications are spelled out more fully in Hountondji's preface to the second English edition of *African Philosophy* (1996).

16. English translation of Foucault, which I have followed in my translation of Mudimbe, by Ian McLeod, 74.

17. Harrow, "Mudimbe and the Power of the Word," 97.

18. Diawara, "Reading Africa through Foucault," 87.

19. Masolo, *African Philosophy in Search of Identity*, 186, 188, 179, 190.

20. I will return more fully to this articulation between deconstruction and the specter(s) of Marxism in my final chapter, on the spectral subject and the notion of "ghostwriting."

21. Wiredu, *Cultural Universals and Particulars*, 146.

22. See in particular the chapter "Formulating Modern Thought in African Languages," in *Cultural Universals and Particulars*.

23. Wiredu, *Cultural Universals and Particulars*, 144.

24. Andrew Apter, in his article "*Que faire?* Reconsidering Inventions of Africa," proceeds along similar lines in his analysis of Yoruba cosmology, which he sees as having the critical self-reflexivity demanded by Hountondji as well as the "deep knowledge" implied by Mudimbe in his choice of the term *gnosis*.

25. Masolo, *African Philosophy*, 182.

26. Masolo, *African Philosophy*, 189.

27. Derrida, "Deconstruction in America," 15, 19.

28. Derrida, *Of Grammatology*, 80, quoted by Spivak in her *A Critique of Postcolo-*

nial Reason, 281 (Spivak's emphasis). In chapter 5 I will return more fully to Spivak's invocation of deconstruction in her postcolonial critique.

29. Derrida, "Cogito et histoire de la folie."
30. Hobson, *Jacques Derrida,* 34.
31. Appiah, "The Postcolonial and the Postmodern," in *In My Father's House,* 155.
32. Appiah, "Tolerable Falsehoods," 70, 74.
33. Appiah, "Tolerable Falsehoods," 84.
34. Appiah, "The Postcolonial," 155.
35. *L'écart,* 27; English translation by Marjolijn de Jager, *The Rift,* 13. Subsequent references, to both the French and the English versions, will be in the text.
36. This reverse ethnography is a strategy used to great effect by Bernard Dadié in his ironic subversion of the tradition of travel writing—the subject of chapter 3.
37. Denis Ekpo, in an insightful reading of *L'écart* to which I shall return ("Schizophrénie et écriture avant-gardiste chez Mudimbe"), has described the self-conscious textuality of the novel both as a kind of schizophrenic writing (in which the referential order is systematically refused) and as an application of a phenomenological reduction of time and space to the text itself.
38. Mouralis, *V. Y. Mudimbe,* 120–32.
39. Diawara, "Reading Africa through Foucault," 89.
40. Diawara, "Reading Africa through Foucault," 90.
41. Ekpo, "Schizophrénie et écriture," 115.
42. Cailler, "The Impossible Ecstasy." Cailler criticizes what she sees as Mouralis's insistence on a necessary coherence between Mudimbe the novelist or poet and Mudimbe the scholar: "Whatever respect I may feel for Mouralis's knowledge and scholarship, and I do, I must say that my own reaction to Mudimbe's work is almost reverse. Not only do I not look a priori for some reassuring 'coherence' in one text or another, or even, for instance, for smooth links between the essayist, the poet and the novelist; even more, I think that the upsetting, dissonant, unresolved aspects of Mudimbe's work may very well constitute the burning core of his creativity" (25).
43. "It could well be that *L'écart* continues or reworks the same theme (that is, the 'pathological use of language') via his fiction. However, even if this seems highly likely, we cannot base our analysis on such an extratextual supposition, since the text itself provides all the elements necessary to an understanding of its function" (Ekpo, "Schizophrénie et écriture," 105, my translation).
44. Spivak, *A Critique of Postcolonial Reason,* 199.

2. The Autobiographical Subject as History-Teller

1. James Olney, in his classic work *Tell Me Africa: An Approach to African Literature,* was the first critic to address the specificity of African autobiography. The volumes to which I refer are Mouralis, ed., *Autobiographies et récits de vie en*

Afrique; Riesz and Schild, eds., *Genres autobiographiques en Afrique;* and Geesey, ed., "Autobiography and African Literature."

2. There are exceptions, of course, in the French tradition. Several French surrealist writers (Michel Leiris, André Breton, Roger Caillois, for instance) published autobiographies while still in their early twenties. Denis Hollier has referred to these texts, because of their deliberately provocative and rebellious quality, as works of an "insolent immaturity" ("Fear and Trembling," preface to Caillois, *The Necessity of the Mind*).

3. Even when their works are not strictly autobiographical, many Francophone African authors use a great deal of autobiographical material in such fictional narratives as Sembene's *Le docker noir,* Dadié's travel narratives, Mariama Bâ's *Une si longue lettre,* or Henri Lopès's early fiction, to name only a few examples. One might think of fictional narratives that are structured as a "hypodiegetic" embedding of a fictional narrative within an autobiographical one, such as Ferdinand Oyono's *Une vie de boy* or Mudimbe's *L'écart.* This chapter of course intersects significantly with the previous one on Mudimbe's writing generally, and I should mention in particular his account of his tour of the United States in the 1970s, *Carnets d'Amérique.* There might be further subdivisions of the genre into, for example, prison writings or retrospective memoirs written by more senior figures such as Birago Diop.

4. Miller, *Theories of Africans,* 161.

5. Included in the Présence Africaine edition of *Climbié.* Subsequent references to *Climbié,* both to the original and to Karen Chapman's English translation, will be in parentheses in the text.

6. Dadié, "Le rôle de la légende dans la culture populaire des Noirs d'Afrique," 165, my translation.

7. In her reading of Nafissatou Diallo's *De Tilène au Plateau,* Julia Watson—picking up on Christopher Miller's argument (*Theories of Africans,* 127) that *L'enfant noir* "performs education" for Westerners as well as for Africans—has termed such "performative" writing "autoethnography" ("Unruly Bodies," 35). Dadié's reappropriation of the discourse of ethnography is quite complex and is discussed more fully in the next chapter, on his travel writings.

8. A more detailed sociolinguistic analysis of this "creolized French" is of course called for (is it linguistic *métissage,* africanized French, frenchified African?), although my main interest is Dadié's literary exploitation of a linguistic drama. There has been a growing body of critical literature on the polyvocality of many Francophone African texts, often using the Bakhtinian concepts of dialogism and heteroglossia to describe the cultural hybridity out of which they emerge. Dadié's text could usefully be contextualized within this critical paradigm.

9. This is a considerably simplified conceptualization of the narrative structure of the text and the place of the narrator as subject within in. In Gérard Genette's terms, this moment of fusion of autobiographical narrator and autobiographical hero is in fact asymptotic. Indeed, it is more accurate to say that the autobiographical subject in *Climbié* emerges within the space of the text and could

be more productively discussed in terms of what Watson calls, in talking of *De Tilène au Plateau*, the "subject-in-process" ("Unruly Bodies," 35).

10. Dadié, *Légendes africaines*, 54, my translation.

11. See, for example, Gates, *The Signifying Monkey*.

12. Recent examples of critics who are attentive to their literary qualities include d'Almeida, in her *Francophone African Women Writers*, and Larrier, in the section on Aoua Kéita in her *Francophone Women Writers of Africa and the Caribbean*, 106–10.

13. Borgomano, *Voix et visages de femmes*, 32, my translation.

14. Turrittin, "Aoua Kéita and the Nascent Women's Movement in the French Soudan."

15. Hitchcott, "African 'Herstory,'" 27.

16. I am indebted to Christopher Miller for drawing my attention to the etymology of the term *nation*, which is particularly germane to my reading of Kéita's text. Miller performs a reading of Ferdinand Oyono's *Une vie de boy* [*Houseboy*] in a similar critical vein in the chapter "Nationalism as Resistance and Resistance to Nationalism," in *Nationalists and Nomads*.

17. Gellner, *Nations and Nationalism*, 48.

18. Gellner, *Nations and Nationalism*, 124.

19. Anderson, *Imagined Communities*, 15.

20. Anderson, *Imagined Communities*, 30.

21. Kéita, *Femme d'Afrique*, 154. Subsequent page references will be given in parentheses in the text. All translations are my own.

22. Miller correctly points out that silence is valorized in Mande oral culture, but that this is then used to justify the desired imposition of silence upon Kéita (*Theories of Africans*, 267). I agree with this interpretation of manipulative, self-serving male control of Mande restrictions on speech and silence, but see the issue as more complex and nuanced once the question of gender, and the performative dimension of Aoua Kéita's text, are factored in.

23. See chapter 1 of Larrier's *Francophone African Women Writers*, "Women and Orality," for a discussion of women's traditional oral roles—as singers, poets, storytellers, and transmitters of knowledge—in West and Central Africa and in the Caribbean.

24. Lee, *Camara Laye*, 83.

25. The most famous of these versions—considered as either transcriptions or re-tellings—are Camara Laye's *Le maître de la parole;* Djibril Tamsir Niane's *Soundjata ou l'épopée mandingue;* Massa Makan Diabaté's *L'aigle et l'épervier ou la geste de Sunjata, poème populaire;* and in English, Gordon Ines's *Sunjata, Three Mandinka Versions*.

26. Watson sees a similar "third position" in Diallo's autobiography, which she calls Diallo's "subject-in-process" and which undercuts the two obvious "competing" discursive strategies of her narrative, that of oral culture and that of ethnography ("Unruly Bodies," 43).

27. Bhabha, "DissemiNation," in *The Location of Culture*, 147.

28. Bhabha, "DissemiNation," 160.
29. Bhabha, "DissemiNation," 38–39.
30. D'Almeida, *Destroying the Emptiness of Silence,* 18.

3. The Ironic Subject in Bernard Dadié's Travel Writing

1. All three texts have been translated into English (see bibliography). References, usually to both the French original and the published translation, will be in the text. On occasion, translations will be modified where I wish to draw particular attention to the original text, since my focus is very specifically on the linguistic playfulness and rhetorical features of Dadié's French.

   The question of generic categorization is an interesting one and is addressed by Janis Mayes, who refers to these texts as *chroniques,* in "Bernard Dadié: Politics, Literature and the Aesthetics of the *Chronique,*" the introduction to her translation of *La ville où nul ne meurt,* 1–34.

2. See, for example, Chevrier, "Lecture d'*Un Nègre à Paris*"; Mudimbe-Boyi, "Travel, Representation and Difference"; Lambert, "Bernard Dadié"; and Vinceleoni, *Comprendre l'oeuvre de Bernard Dadié.*

3. Mayes has a useful discussion of Dadié's ironic narrative technique in his travel writing in the introduction to her translation of *La ville où nul ne meurt,* 20–22.

4. Mudimbe, *The Invention of Africa,* 16.

5. Mudimbe-Boyi, "Travel, Representation and Difference," 31.

6. Pratt, *Imperial Eyes,* 6.

7. Bhabha, *The Location of Culture,* 87.

8. Todorov, *Nous et les autres,* 433, my translation.

9. Vinceleoni, *Comprendre l'oeuvre de Dadié,* 165–66. A *mot pastille* is a particularly dense and suggestive word, the kind Dadié is often drawn to for its connotative power.

10. He intermittently mentions the plight of Native American Indians, but his main focus is clearly the status of blacks in the United States at this period of history.

11. As Vinceleoni states, this "redondance" is characteristic of Agni oral narration, as are many of the rhetorical flourishes of Dadié's language generally. Dadié points out early on in *Un nègre à Paris* that a certain repetitiveness in his narrative is in a sense determined by the "sameness" he finds everywhere in the Western world (to be understood, of course, in light of his mock ethnographic project): "Je n'ai pas peur des redites car avec cette ville, on semble tourner en rond, être toujours dans le même quartier, voir les mêmes personnes, les mêmes têtes blanches" (27) [I'll never be afraid of going over the same ground twice here, for in this city you always have the feeling you're going in circles. You always seem to end up in the same district, with the same people, the same white faces] (17). In the case of *Patron de New York,* this continual repetition and elaboration make it a text that is impossible to "fit" into any interpretive framework, any literary model or *patron.*

12. Appiah, *In My Father's House,* 26.

13. Appiah, *In My Father's House,* 98. Appiah in fact argues that there is a future for a more critical form of pan-Africanism, and that it has the potential to be an important progressive political force. As he says in his conclusion: "If there is, as I have suggested, hope, too, for the Pan-Africanism of an African Diaspora, once it, too, is released from bondage to racial ideologies (alongside the many bases of alliance available to Africa's people in their political and cultural struggles), it is crucial that we recognize the independence, once 'Negro' nationalism is gone, of the Pan-Africanism of the Diaspora and the Pan-Africanism of the continent. It is, I believe, in the exploration of these issues, these possibilities, that the future of an intellectually reinvigorated Pan-Africanism lies" (292).

14. Toward the end of "Illusions of Race" Appiah discusses Du Bois's "second" autobiography, *The Dusk of Dawn,* written in 1940, in which he has moved beyond theories of biological racialism, but in which he substitutes sociohistorical bonds for genetic ones. In this revised pan-Africanism, what unites Africans of Africa and of the diaspora is a "common history" of "discrimination and insult." However, as Appiah points out, this displaces rather than resolves the problem of a collective identity, since one would still not be in a position to delineate all victims of racism as a single group, or to say that they share a common experience of discrimination.

4. Subjectivity, History, and the Cinematic

1. The other instances in Sembene's oeuvre of a text following and adapting a film are *Taaw* (a 1970 short film followed by the 1988 novella) and *Niiwam* (published simultaneously with *Taaw,* but with its origins probably in a scene from his first film, *Borom Sarret*). *Xala* was also originally conceived as a film but first appeared as a book. See Murphy, *Sembene,* 65 n. 56, and 66.

2. Sembene, *Guelwaar,* 9. Subsequent references to the novel will be in parentheses in the text. All translations are my own.

3. See, for example, Harrow's article "Sembène Ousmane's *Xala,*" and Cham's chapter, "Official History, Popular Memory: Reconfigurations of the African Past in the Films of Sembène Ousmane," in Gadjigo et al., eds., *Ousmane Sembène.*

4. Niang, "Orality in the Films of Ousmane Sembene," 59–60.

5. It is important to remember that as a Christian community, the Catholic elders, the *Guelwaar-yi,* are very much a minority in an overwhelmingly Islamic Senegal. David Murphy notes that, unusually among African nations, Senegal has in fact enjoyed a good record of interreligious tolerance (*Sembene,* 205).

6. Rosen, "Nation, Inter-nation and Narration in Ousmane Sembene's films."

7. Rosen, "Nation, Inter-nation and Narration," 39.

8. Sembene uses the same narrative technique in the novel version of *Xala* in order to give us greater insight into the psychology of the main character, El Hadj. See Murphy, "Alternative Media/Alternative Genres in Sembene's Novel and Film *Xala,*" 94.

9. Rosen, "Nation, Inter-nation and Narration," 48.

10. Rosen, "Nation, Inter-nation and Narration," 38.

11. Rosen, "Nation, Inter-nation and Narration," 42.

12. Murphy makes a similar comparison in relation to Sembene's role as a socially oppositional filmmaker, and his twenty-year struggle against great financial odds to produce his epic film about Samory Touré (*Sembene,* 215 n. 54).

13. Monénembo has called the novel a "false autobiography." Private conversation with the author, November 1998, University of Aberdeen.

14. Monénembo, *Cinéma,* 38. Subsequent references to the novel will be in parentheses in the text. All translations are my own.

15. At this level, *Cinéma* offers a valuable insight into the history of European and American cinema in colonial Africa. During the 1950s Hollywood controlled most of the distribution and exhibition of films. See Diawara's *African Cinema,* especially chapter 7, "Film Distribution and Exhibition in Francophone Africa." Under Sékou Touré the cinema became essentially a state organism that functioned to disseminate government ideology, defying the French distribution companies and banning the "escapist fiction" films that were so popular during the pre-Independence period. This replacement of one propaganda vehicle with another is thematized in Monénembo's novel, as the latter part of my reading will show.

16. See McClintock, *Imperial Leather,* for a related reading of the ahistoricism of much postcolonial theory.

17. Bhabha, "The Other Question: Stereotype, Discrimination and the Discourse of Colonialism," in *The Location of Culture,* 76.

18. See, for example, Laura Mulvey's classic text, "Visual Pleasure and Narrative Cinema," 201.

19. The explicitly voyeuristic episodes range from Binguel's sly glances at his friend's sister ("I pretended not to see her," 61), to hiding in a tree and watching his mother, Mère-Griefs ("I chose to sit up on the forked branch of the tallest mango tree so that I could watch her face," 51), to watching his headteacher, M. Camille, watching out for children arriving late ("Seeing him between the mango trees and the beds of citronella, on the lookout for children swearing and arriving late," 90), to the more classically primal scene when Massadou (a Frenchman) watches the French schoolteacher Mlle Saval with her African lover, Cellou-le-Poète, a scene that Binguel himself cannot have witnessed but must have fantasized, making it a more typically cinematic form of voyeurism.

20. See Mulvey, "Visual Pleasure."

5. The Gendered Subject of Africa

1. Spivak, "Can the Subaltern Speak?" 287.

2. Spivak, "Can the Subaltern Speak?" 295.

3. Spivak, "Can the Subaltern Speak?" 295.

4. See Sylviane Agacinski's discussion of Kant's "disembodied" philosophical subject in "Another Experience of the Question," 17.

5. Fuss, *Essentially Speaking*, 72.

6. Fuss, *Essentially Speaking*, 5.

7. See in particular the chapter "Reading Like a Feminist," in *Essentially Speaking*, 23–37.

8. Butler, *Gender Trouble*, 146.

9. Butler, *Gender Trouble*, 147.

10. Spivak, interview with Walter Adamson, 1986, in *The Post-colonial Critic*, 51.

11. Spivak, interview with Sarah Harasym, October 31/November 1, 1987, in *The Post-colonial Critic*, 104.

12. Fuss writes, "This, to me, signals an exciting new way to rethink the problem of essentialism; it represents an approach which evaluates the motivations *behind* the deployment of essentialism rather than prematurely dismissing it as an unfortunate vestige of patriarchy (itself an essentialist category)" (*Essentially Speaking*, 32).

13. See Mudimbe's interview with Faith Smith, "A Conversation with V. Y. Mudimbe," *Callaloo* 14, no. 4 (1990): "MUDIMBE: [. . .] That is the history of a subjectivity. I tried to write it from an African woman's viewpoint; I don't know if I succeeded, but that's just it, a fantasy of the agnostic I am now. SMITH: Is it a feminist novel? MUDIMBE: I don't know. Does it matter, really? SMITH: What does that label mean to you? MUDIMBE: You know labels reduce the complexity of a human being and the human experience, and I would tend to think that it's very dangerous to use labels. Every year at the beginning of my undergraduate philosophy class on existentialism, I try to make sure that all my students understand the following paradoxical statement: 'I am what I am not, and I am not what I am.' That is the point, a critical position against all essentialisms. That I have learned from Jean-Paul Sartre. Thus, I can't say that this is feminist or not feminist. My own perception of what I have done in *Shaba deux* is that the narrative speaks from what I believe to be a credible subjectivity of an African woman. I am not a woman, and that is fine with me. The reactions of a number of women who read the novel have been so far very positive" (978).

14. Mudimbe, *The Invention of Africa*, 5.

15. Mudimbe, *Le bel immonde*, 162; English translation, *Before the Birth of the Moon*, by Marjolijn de Jager, 194. Subsequent page references, to both the French and the English versions, will be in parentheses in the text.

16. The reversibility of the oxymoronic structure of the title is described by André Nzunguta Siamundele as a chiasmus in which power and passion cross over. "The whole text works by the juxtaposition of opposites, the attraction of extremes, and coexistence within dissent [. . .] This novel by Mudimbe illustrates how closely linked love and power are on the one hand, and passion and power on the other" ("De *l'écart* à la *palilalie*," 55, 58).

17. Butler, *Gender Trouble*, 132–33.

18. Butler, *Gender Trouble*, 134; Kristeva, *Pouvoirs de l'horreur*.

19. Toward the end of *Gender Trouble,* Butler explores the performative disrup-
tiveness, and radical political potential, of cross-dressing. This is by no means
alien to *Le bel immonde,* since in the bar there are a number of people in drag.
Indeed the bar itself, which is ultimately the "world" that Ya inhabits, represents a fluidity of gender roles and performances.

20. Butler, *Gender Trouble,* 135.

21. Mudimbe, *Tales of Faith,* 50–56.

22. Mudimbe, *Tales of Faith,* 55.

23. Quoted in Smith, "Conversation with V. Y. Mudimbe," 977.

24. Mudimbe, *Parables and Fables,* 4. In *The Idea of Africa,* in the chapter "Domes-
tication and the Conflict of Memories," Mudimbe gives a detailed history of
the conversion of Central Africa by Christian missionaries, especially in the
Belgian Congo. He explains how the Congo was divided into ten ecclesiastical
regions—"Its geography had been turned into a kind of spiritual checkerboard
on which each unit or square was occupied by a definite religious style" (110)—
a complex configuration we see reflected in the tensions and disagreements
between the Franciscans and the other orders in the novel.

25. Semujanga, "De l'absurde comme style de vie et procès esthétique," 17.

26. Mudimbe, *Shaba deux,* 24. Subsequent page references will be in parentheses in
the text. All translations are my own.

27. Mudimbe, *Le corps glorieux des mots et des êtres,* 107–21. Subsequent page references will be in parentheses in the text. All translations are my own.

6. Reinscribing the Female African Subject

1. Irène Assiba d'Almeida describes the process as one of "destroying the empti-
ness of silence," and of a necessarily militant "prise d'écriture" [taking of writ-
ing], in her *Francophone African Women Writers,* 6.

2. See, for example, Davies and Graves, eds., *Ngambika;* "Nouvelles écritures fémi-
nines," a special issue of *Notre librairie;* Stratton, *Contemporary African Literature and the Politics of Gender;* Cazenave, *Femmes rebelles;* Nfah-Abbenyi, *Gender in African Women's Writing;* d'Almeida, *Francophone African Women Writers;*
Lionnet, *Postcolonial Representations: Women, Literature, Identity;* Green et al.,
eds., *Postcolonial Subjects;* a special issue of *Research in African Literatures,* 28
(Summer 1997); Larrier, *Francophone Women Writers of Africa and the Caribbean.*

3. For a discussion of this "early feminism," see d'Almeida, *Francophone African
Women Writers,* 12. Eileen Julien, in *African Novels and the Question of Orality,*
notes the correspondence between the hierarchic epic oral forms and patriarchal nationalist agendas (47).

4. Stratton, *Contemporary African Literature,* 51.

5. Collins, "Mammies, Matriarchs, and Other Controlling Images," 348.

6. Suleri, "Woman Skin Deep," 339. Suleri takes issue with bell hooks on similar
grounds. For other important interventions in this debate included in the vol-
ume edited by Mongia, see also Barbara Christian's "The Race for Theory," and

Chandra Mohanty's "Under Western Eyes: Feminist Scholarship and Colonial Discourses."

7. Carole Davies, *Black Women, Writing and Identity*, 8.

8. Davies, *Black Women, Writing and Identity*, 37.

9. Smith, *Subjectivity, Identity and the Body*, 123.

10. Lionnet, *Postcolonial Representations*, 18.

11. Lionnet, *Postcolonial Representations*, 8.

12. Rice-Maximin, "'Nouvelle écriture' from the Ivory Coast." Rice-Maximin claims Tadjo's text is more radical than those of the first generation of Francophone African women writers, such as Mariama Bâ, Ken Bugul, Aminata Sow Fall, and Werewere Liking. I would agree with this general assessment but disagree on the specific comparison with Liking, for reasons I hope will become clearer in the course of this chapter.

13. Tadjo, *A vol d'oiseau*, 2; English translation, *As the Crow Flies*, by Wangui Wa Goro. Subsequent references, to both the original and the English translation, will be in parentheses in the text.

14. Tadjo exploits this metaphor of love as a battlefield at greater length in her recent novel *Champs de bataille et d'amour*.

15. Rice-Maximin, "'Nouvelle écriture,'" 165, 168.

16. D'Almeida aptly refers to Tadjo's writing as directed toward a "loftier ideal" (*Francophone African Women Writers*, 154).

17. For more information on Liking and the Ki-Yi community projects, see d'Almeida's introduction to Marjolijn de Jager's English translation of *Elle sera de jaspe et de corail* and *L'amour-cent-vies*.

18. D'Almeida, "The Intertext."

19. Liking, *Elle sera de jaspe et de corail*, 149. Subsequent references, to both the original and de Jager's English translation, will be in parentheses in the text.

20. See d'Almeida, "The Intertext," 267.

21. D'Almeida, "The Intertext," 274. As d'Almeida explains in her introduction to the English translation of *Jaspe et corail*, *misovire* is more accurately translated as "a woman who cannot find an admirable man" (xix).

22. Two of the most insightful theoretical discussions of nativism are Parry's "Resistance Theory/Theorizing Resistance or Two Cheers for Nativism," and Appiah's "Out of Africa."

23. D'Almeida, "The Intertext," 270.

24. Nfah-Abbenyi, *Gender in African Womens' Writing*, 33.

7. Ghostwriting

1. Sony Labou Tansi, *La vie et demie*, 13. Subsequent references to the novel will be in parentheses in the text. All translations are my own.

2. The most visually (and aurally) striking example elsewhere in Sony's writing is the ghost of Julius Caïd Kaesaire in *Moi, veuve de l'empire*, who appears behind the wheel of a red Toyota, loudly hooting its horn. In *Le commencement des*

douleurs the ghost of Lekas Mondio Atondi, one of the admirers of Bano Maya's daughters, comes back toward the end of the novel. In addition to such literal spectral presences, the events of many of the novels (such as *L'anté-peuple*) take the characters into a world that is in every respect "other worldly."

3. Fanon, *The Wretched of the Earth,* 58.

4. Neil Lazarus, in his article "Disavowing Decolonization" (82–86), corrects Miller's misreading, in *Theories of Africans,* of Fanon's understanding of the role of African culture in the process of decolonization and national liberation. As Lazarus rightly points out, it is the ahistoricism of African native culture, as a product of colonialism, that is the target of Fanon's critique, and not precolonial or traditional culture.

5. Mudimbe, *L'odeur du père,* 13 and 14, my translation.

6. Serequeberhan, *The Hermeneutics of African Philosophy,* 36.

7. Serequeberhan, *The Hermeneutics of African Philosophy,* 50 n. 21.

8. Serequeberhan, *The Hermeneutics of African Philosophy,* 38.

9. See, for example, Miabeto, "Sony Labou Tansi et la poésie koongo," and Devesa, "Le Kongo mental de Sony Labou Tansi" (subsequently rewritten as the conclusion to his study *Sony Labou Tansi*), in Kounziliat and Malanda, eds., *Colloque Sony Labou Tansi et Sylvain Ntari Bemba.*

10. Derrida, "Survivre."

11. Derrida, *Specters of Marx,* 147 [236], trans. slightly modified. Since in several places I choose to modify slightly Peggy Kamuf's English translation, I've provided page numbers of the French original in brackets.

12. Derrida, *Specters,* 161 [255].

13. The experience of the ghostly is one of the principal manifestations of the Uncanny (*das Unheimliche*) in Freud.

14. Sony states as much explicitly on many occasions. See, for example, the following passage from *Notre douce douleur d'être différents:* "In my books time is the main thing. It is the No. 1 character. I'm telling you, in all my books, whatever the book, the No. 1 character is time. It's the hero, the main character. And the other characters have to reconcile themselves with time, or come to some compromise, they have to make a kind of transaction with time" (quoted by Martin-Granel, in "Sony *in Progress,*" my translation).

15. There is a corresponding expression of temporal disjunctiveness in *Le commencement des douleurs:* "Even time had gone awry" (12).

16. Derrida, *Specters,* 99 [162], trans. slightly modified.

17. Derrida, *Specters,* 17 [41–42].

18. Bhabha, *The Location of Culture,* 171, 172.

19. Bhabha, *The Location of Culture,* 172.

20. Bhabha, *The Location of Culture,* 185.

21. Bhabha, *The Location of Culture,* 252, 253–54.

22. Derrida, *Specters,* 196 n. 39 [276 n. 1].

23. Sony Labou Tansi, *L'état honteux.* The "cri" here recalls Mudimbe's "le cri et le témoin de ce lieu singulier," a connection I discuss further in the conclusion.

24. Clark, "Passionate Engagements," 51.
25. Martin-Granel, "Sony *in Progress,*" 215.
26. Derrida, "Marx and Sons," 249.
27. Clark sees these far-fetched inventions as symptoms of the generalized apocalyptic tone of Sony's last novel: "Science looms overhead as a means of curing maladies both social and biological, but the time has not yet come; scientific knowledge appears to be hopelessly invested in building castles in the sky" ("Passionate Engagements," 61).
28. At the end of her article, Clark reaches a similar conclusion in describing the way in which Sony's ambivalence with regard to the political effectiveness of messianic discourse is translated into the narrative of his final novel: "In an apocalyptic version of the usual attempts to reverse the colonial dialectic, Sony envisions the complete erasure of the effects of colonial history. But this desire to liberate one's people from the weight of a tortured historical past proves as impossible as escaping from the deadly consequences of sexual promiscuity in *Le Commencement des douleurs.* Just as Sony seeks to escape history by retreating to the realm of ethical absolutes, the pattern of repetition reasserts itself" ("Passionate Engagements," 62). In this respect, Sony's spectrality could be seen as a kind of intertextual self-haunting.
29. Christopher Miller performs a reading of Ouologuem's novel, along with his *Lettre à la France nègre,* in *Blank Darkness.* My own comments are indebted to his linking of *nègre* as ghostwriter to the question of plagiarism as an important element of Ouologuem's strategy. See also Riesz, "'Audible Gasps from the Audience,'" for a discussion of the Ouologuem case in the wider historical context of contested African authorship.
30. Beyala, in *Le Figaro littéraire,* 25–26 January 1997, 23.
31. Fanon, "The Fact of Blackness" ["L'expérience vécue du Noir"], 110.
32. Sony expresses a profound, visceral disgust at the concept of literature as an "objet de consommation," a consumer product, and the entire academic apparatus that supports it. In this sense, *La vie et demie* could be read as an allegory of the Western literary establishment's cannibalistic devouring of African culture, art, aesthetics, and thus life.
33. Lopès, *Le pleurer-rire;* quotation from the English translation by Gerald Moore, *The Laughing Cry,* 20.
34. Derrida, *Specters,* 163 [259].
35. Derrida, *Specters,* 16 [40].
36. Derrida, "Of the Humanities and the Philosophical Discipline," quoted in Janz, "Debt and Duty," 117.
37. Janz, "Debt and Duty," 124.
38. Janz, "Debt and Duty," 124.
39. Janz, "Debt and Duty," 124.

Conclusion

1. See, for example, Karp and Masolo, *African Philosophy as Cultural Inquiry,* and Eze, ed., *Postcolonial African Philosophy.*
2. Several critics have recently redressed this imbalance in Fanon studies by reengaging with his political texts, often via a critique of Bhabha's version of Fanon. See Gates, "Critical Fanonism"; Lazarus, *Nationalism and Cultural Practice in the Postcolonial World;* JanMohamed, "The Economy of Manichean Allegory"; and Coundouriotis, *Claiming History.*
3. Miller's *Theories of Africans,* in its emphasis on ethnicity, has been subjected to a number of critiques along these lines. See in particular Lazarus, "Disavowing Decolonization," and Murphy, *Sembene,* 20–23.
4. Mudimbe, "Reprendre," 276.
5. Mudimbe, *L'odeur du père,* 13–14.
6. Mudimbe, *The Idea of Africa,* 200–201.

Bibliography

Adams, Anne. "To W/rite in a New Language: Werewere Liking's Adaptation of Ritual to the Novel." *Callaloo* 16, no. 1 (1993): 153–68.

Adotévi, Stanislav. *Négritude et négrologues*. Paris: Plon, 1972.

Agacinski, Sylviane. "Another Experience of the Question, or Experiencing the Question Other-Wise." Translated by Christine Laennec and Michael Syrotinski. In *Who Comes after the Subject?* ed. Edouardo Cadava, Peter Connor, and Jean-Luc Nancy. New York: Routledge, 1991.

Amselle, Jean-Loup. *Logiques métisses: Anthropologie de l'identité en Afrique et ailleurs*. Paris: Payot, 1990.

Anderson, Benedict. *Imagined Communities: Reflections on the Origin and Spread of Nationalism*. London: Verso, 1983.

Appiah, Kwame Anthony. *In My Father's House: Africa in the Philosophy of Culture*. New York: Oxford University Press, 1992.

———. "Out of Africa: Topologies of Nativism." *Yale Journal of Criticism* 1, no. 2 (1988): 153–78.

———. "Tolerable Falsehoods: Agency and the Interests of Theory." In *Some Consequences of Theory*, ed. Barbara Johnson and Jonathan Arac. Baltimore: Johns Hopkins University Press, 1990.

Apter, Andrew. "*Que faire?* Reconsidering Inventions of Africa." *Critical Inquiry* 19 (Autumn 1992): 87–104.

Bal, Mieke. "Three-Way Misreading." *Diacritics* 30 (Spring 2000): 2–24.

Barlet, Olivier. *Les cinémas d'Afrique noire: Le regard en question*. Paris: L'Harmattan, 1996. Translated by Chris Turner as *African Cinemas: Decolonizing the Gaze* (London: Zed Books, 2000).

Bates, Robert H., V. Y. Mudimbe, and Jean O'Barr, eds. *Africa and the Disciplines:*

The Contributions of Research in Africa to the Social Sciences and Humanities. Chicago: University of Chicago Press, 1993.

Beyala, Calixthe. *C'est le soleil qui m'a brûlée.* Paris: Editions J'ai Lu, 1987. Translated by Marjolijn de Jager as *The Sun Hath Looked upon Me* (London: Heinemann, 1996).

Bhabha, Homi K. *The Location of Culture.* London: Routledge, 1994.

―――. "Remembering Fanon: Self, Psyche and the Colonial Condition." In *Remaking History,* ed. Barbara Kruger and Phil Mariani, 131–48. Seattle: Bay Press, 1989.

Bisanswa, Justin Kalulu. "Life Is Not a Book. Creuse: Literature and Representation in Sony Labou Tansi's Work." *Research in African Literatures* 31 (Fall 2000): 129–46.

Blachère, Jean-Claude. *Négritures: Les écrivains d'Afrique noire et la langue française.* Paris: L'Harmattan, 1993.

Bobika, André-Patient. *Ecriture et identité dans la littérature africaine.* Paris: L'Harmattan, 1998.

Borgomano, Madeleine. *Voix et visages de femmes.* Condé-sur-Noireau: CEDA, 1989.

Bowao, Charles Z. "'Désethnologiser': Réouverture du débat Hountondji-Diagne." *Bulletin du CODESRIA* 1 (1995): 15–19.

Britton, Celia. *Edouard Glissant and Postcolonial Theory: Strategies of Language and Resistance.* Charlottesville: University Press of Virginia, 1999.

Britton, Celia, and Michael Syrotinski, eds. "Francophone Texts and Postcolonial Theory." Special issue, *Paragraph* 24 (Nov. 2001).

Bugul, Ken. *Le baobab fou.* Dakar: NEF, 1982.

Butler, Judith. *Gender Trouble: Feminism and the Subversion of Identity.* New York: Routledge, 1990.

―――. *The Psychic Life of Power: Theories of Subjection.* Stanford: Stanford University Press, 1997.

Cailler, Bernadette. "The Impossible Ecstasy: An Analysis of V. Y. Mudimbe's *Déchirures.*" *Research in African Literatures* 24 (Winter 1993): 15–28.

Caillois, Roger. *The Necessity of the Mind.* Translated by Michael Syrotinski, with a preface by Denis Hollier. Venice, Calif.: Lapis Press, 1990.

Camara Laye. *Dramouss.* Paris: Plon, 1966.

―――. *L'enfant noir.* Paris: Plon, 1953.

―――. *Le maître de la parole.* Paris: Plon, 1978.

Cazenave, Odile. *Femmes rebelles: Naissance d'un nouveau roman africain au féminin.* Paris: L'Harmattan, 1996. Translated by the author as *Rebellious Women: The New Generation of Female African Novelists* (Boulder, Colo.: Lynne Rienner, 2000).

Cham, Mbye Boubacar. "Ousmane Sembene and the Aesthetics of African Oral Traditions." *Africana Journal* 13, nos. 1–4 (1982): 24–40.

Chevrier, Jacques. "Lecture d'*Un Nègre à Paris;* où il est prouvé qu'on peut être parisien et raisonner comme un Agni." *L'Afrique littéraire et artistique* 85 (1989): 42–50.

Christian, Barbara. "The Race for Theory." In Mongia, ed., *Contemporary Postcolonial Theory*, 148–57.

Clark, Phyllis. "Passionate Engagements: A Reading of Sony Labou Tansi's Private Ancestral Shrine." *Research in African Literatures* 31 (Fall 2000): 39–68.

Clifford, James. *The Predicament of Culture: Twentieth-Century Ethnography, Literature and Art*. Cambridge, Mass.: Harvard University Press, 1988.

————. *Routes: Travel and Translation in the Late Twentieth Century*. Cambridge, Mass.: Harvard University Press, 1997.

Clifford, James, and George Marcus, eds. *Writing Culture: The Poetics and Politics of Ethnography*. Berkeley: University of California Press, 1986.

Collins, Patricia Hill. "Mammies, Matriarchs, and Other Controlling Images." In Eze, ed., *African Philosophy*, 346–54.

Coundouriotis, Eleni. *Claiming History: Colonialism, Ethnography, and the Novel*. New York: Columbia University Press, 1999.

Dadié, Bernard. *Climbié*. Paris: Présence Africaine, 1956. Translated by Karen C. Chapman as *Climbié* (London: Heinemann, 1971).

————. *Légendes africaines*. 1954. Paris: Presses Pocket, 1982.

————. *Un nègre à Paris*. Paris: Présence Africaine, 1959. Translated by Karen Hatch as *An African in Paris* (Urbana: University of Illinois Press, 1994).

————. *Patron de New York*. Paris: Présence Africaine, 1969. Translated by Jo Patterson as *One Way: Bernard Dadié Observes America* (Urbana: University of Illinois Press, 1994).

————. "Le rôle de la légende dans la culture populaire des Noirs d'Afrique." *Présence africaine*, special no. 14–15 (June–September 1957).

————. *La ville où nul ne meurt*. Paris: Présence Africaine, 1968. Translated by Janis A. Mayes as *The City Where No One Dies*. Washington, D.C.: Three Continents Press, 1986.

d'Almeida, Irène Assiba. *Francophone African Women Writers: Destroying the Emptiness of Silence*. Gainesville: University Press of Florida, 1994.

————. "The Intertext: Werewere Liking's Tool for Transformation and Renewal." In Green, ed., *Postcolonial Subjects*, 265–84.

Davies, Carole Boyce. *Black Women, Writing and Identity: Migrations of the Subject*. London: Routledge, 1994.

Davies, Carole Boyce, and Anne Adams Graves, eds. *Ngambika: Studies of Women in African Literature*. Trenton, N.J.: Africa World Press, 1986.

Davies, Ioan. "Negotiating African Culture: Towards a Decolonization of the Fetish." In Jameson and Miyoshi, eds., *The Cultures of Globalization*, 125–45.

Derrida, Jacques. "Cogito et histoire de la folie." In *L'écriture et la différence*. Paris: Seuil Points, 1967. Translated by Alan Bass as *Writing and Difference* (Chicago: University of Chicago Press, 1978).

————. "Deconstruction in America." Interview with James Creech, Peggy Kamuf, and Jane Todd. *Critical Exchange*, no. 17 (1985): 15–19.

————. "Marx and Sons." In Sprinker, ed., *Ghostly Demarcations,* 213–69.

————. "Mochlos, or, the Conflict of the Faculties." In *Logomachia: The Conflict of the Faculties,* ed. Richard Rand, 1–34. Lincoln: University of Nebraska Press, 1992.

————. *Of Grammatology.* Translated by Gayatri Chakravorty Spivak. Baltimore: Johns Hopkins University Press, 1976. Originally published as *De la grammatologie* (Paris: Minuit, 1967).

————. "Of the Humanities and the Philosophical Discipline: The Right to Philosophy from the Cosmopolitical Point of View (the Example of an International Institution)." *Surfaces* (online journal, Montreal), vol. 4, no. 310 (1994).

————. *Specters of Marx.* Translated by Peggy Kamuf. London: Routledge, 1994. Originally published as *Spectres de Marx* (Paris: Galilée, 1993).

————. "Survivre." In *Parages,* 117–218. Paris: Galilée, 1986.

Devesa, Jean-Michel. *Sony Labou Tansi: Ecrivain de la honte et des rives magiques.* Paris: L'Harmattan, 1996.

Diabaté, Massa Makan. *L'aigle et l'épervier ou la geste de Sunjata, poème populaire.* Paris: Pierre-Jean Oswald, 1975.

Diallo, Nafissatou. *De Tilène au Plateau: Une enfance dakaroise.* Dakar: NEF, 1975.

Diawara, Manthia. *African Cinema: Politics and Culture.* Bloomington: Indiana University Press, 1992.

————, ed. *Callaloo,* special issue on V. Y. Mudimbe, 14, no. 4 (1991).

————. "Reading Africa through Foucault: V. Y. Mudimbe's Reaffirmation of the Subject." *October* 55 (Winter 1990): 79–92.

Downing, John D. H. "Post-tricolor African Cinema." In Sherzer, ed., *Cinema, Colonialism, Postcolonialism,* 188–228.

Eboussi-Boulaga, Fabien. "La bantoue problématique." *Présence africaine,* no. 66 (1968): 4–40.

Ekpo, Denis. "Schizophrénie et écriture avant-gardiste chez Mudimbe—une phénoménologie structurale de *L'Ecart.*" *Neohelicon: Acta Comparationis Litterarum Universarum Amsterdam* 18, no. 1 (1991): 99–116.

Eze, Emmanuel Chukwudi, ed. *African Philosophy: An Anthology.* Oxford: Blackwell, 1998.

————, ed. *Postcolonial African Philosophy: A Critical Reader.* Cambridge, Mass.: Blackwell, 1997.

Fanon, Frantz. *Black Skin, White Masks.* Translated by Charles Lam Markmann. London: MacGibbon and Kee, 1968. Originally published as *Peau noire, masques blancs* (Paris: Seuil, 1952).

————. *The Wretched of the Earth.* Translated by Constance Farrington. New York: Grove Press, 1968. Originally published as *Les damnés de la terre* (Paris: Maspéro, 1961).

Foucault, Michel. *L'ordre du discours.* Paris: Gallimard, 1971. Translated by Ian McLeod as *The Order of Discourse,* in *Untying the Text,* ed. Robert Young, 48–78. Boston: Routledge and Kegan Paul, 1981.

Freud, Sigmund. "The Uncanny." In *The Standard Edition of the Complete Psycho-*

logical Works of Sigmund Freud, ed. James Strachey, 17:217–52. London: Hogarth, 1953–74. Originally published as "Das Unheimliche," in *Gesammelte Schriften von Sigmund Freud,* 10:369–408 (Leipzig: Internationaler Psychoanalytischer, 1924–34).

Fuss, Diana. *Essentially Speaking: Feminism, Nature and Difference.* New York: Routledge, 1989.

Gadjigo, Samba, Ralph Faulkingham, Thomas Cassirer, and Reinhard Sander, eds. *Ousmane Sembène: Dialogues with Critics and Writers.* Amherst: University of Massachusetts Press, 1993.

Gates, Henry Louis, Jr. "Critical Fanonism." *Critical Inquiry* 17, no. 3 (1991): 457–70.

———. *The Signifying Monkey: A Theory of African-American Literary Criticism.* New York: Oxford University Press, 1988.

Geertz, Clifford. *The Interpretation of Cultures.* New York: Basic Books, 1973.

Geesey, Patricia, ed. "Autobiography and African Literature." *Research in African Literatures* 28 (Summer 1997): 1–44.

Gellner, Ernest. *Nations and Nationalism.* Oxford: Blackwell, 1983.

Green, Mary Jean, et al., eds. *Postcolonial Subjects: Francophone Women Writers.* Minneapolis: University of Minnesota Press, 1996.

Hallen, Barry. "Some Observations about Philosophy, Postmodernism and Art in Contemporary African Studies." *African Studies Review* 38 (Apr. 1995): 69–80.

Harrow, Kenneth, ed. *African Cinema: Postcolonial and Feminist Readings.* Trenton, N.J.: Africa World Press, 1999.

———. "*Le bel immonde:* African Literature at the Crossing." *Callaloo* 14, no. 4 (1991): 987–97.

———. *The Marabout and the Muse: New Approaches to Islam in African Literature.* Portsmouth, N.H.: Heinemann, 1996.

———. "Mudimbe and the Power of the Word." In *African Literary Studies: The Present State,* ed. Stephen Arnold et al., 91–100. Washington, D.C.: Three Continents Press, 1985.

———, ed. *Research in African Literatures,* special issue on African cinema, 26 (Autumn 1995).

———. "Sembene Ousmane's *Xala:* The Use of Film and Novel as Revolutionary Weapon." *Studies in Twentieth Century Literature* 4 (Spring 1980): 177–88.

Hecht, David, and Maliqalim Simone. *Invisible Governance: The Art of African Micropolitics.* Brooklyn, N.Y.: Autonomedia, 1994.

Hitchcott, Nicki. "African 'Herstory': The Feminist Reader and the African Autobiographical Voice." *Research in African Literatures* 28 (Summer 1997): 16–33.

Hobson, Marian. *Jacques Derrida: Opening Lines.* London: Routledge, 1998.

Hountondji, Paulin. *African Philosophy: Myth and Reality.* Translated by Henri Evans and Jonathan Rée. 1983. 2nd ed., Bloomington: Indiana University Press, 1996. Originally published as *Sur la philosophie africaine* (Paris: Maspéro, 1977).

Ines, Gordon. *Sunjata, Three Mandinka Versions.* London: School of Oriental and African Studies, University of London, 1974.

Jameson, Fredric. "Third-World Literature in the Era of Multinational Capitalism." *Social Text* 15 (Autumn 1986): 65–88.

Jameson, Fredric, and Masao Miyoshi, eds. *The Cultures of Globalization.* Durham, N.C.: Duke University Press, 1998.

JanMohamed, Abdul. "The Economy of Manichean Allegory: The Function of Racial Difference in Colonialist Literature." In *"Race," Writing and Difference,* ed. Henry Louis Gates, 78–106. Chicago: Chicago University Press, 1986.

Janz, Bruce. "Debt and Duty: Kant, Derrida, and African Philosophy." *Janus Head,* supplement (Winter 2001): 109–24.

Jules-Rosette, Bennetta. *Black Paris: The African Writers' Landscape.* Chicago: University of Chicago Press, 1998.

Julien, Eileen. *African Novels and the Question of Orality.* Bloomington: Indiana University Press, 1992.

———. "Dominance and Discourse in *La Vie et demie,* or How to Do Things with Words." *Research in African Literatures* 20 (1989): 371–84.

Kadima-Nzvji, Mukala, Abel Kouvouama, and Paul Kibangou, eds. *Sony Labou Tansi ou la quête permanente du sens.* Paris: L'Harmattan, 1997.

Kagamé, Alexis. *La philosophie bantu comparée.* Paris: Présence Africaine, 1976.

Kane, Cheikh Hamidou. *L'aventure ambiguë.* Paris: 10/18, 1975.

Karp, Ivan, and D. A. Masolo. *African Philosophy as Cultural Inquiry.* Bloomington: Indiana University Press, 2000.

Kéita, Aoua. *Femme d'Afrique: La vie d'Aoua Kéita racontée par elle-même.* Paris: Présence Africaine, 1975.

Ki-Zerbo, Joseph. *Histoire de l'Afrique d'hier à demain.* Paris: Hatier, 1972.

Kounzilat, Alain, and Ange-Séverin Malanda, eds. *Colloque Sony Labou Tansi et Sylvain Ntari Bemba.* Corbeil-Essonnes: Editions ICES, 1996.

Kourouma, Ahmadou. *Les soleils des indépendances.* Paris: Seuil, 1970. Translated by Adrian Adams as *The Suns of Independence* (London: Heinemann, 1981).

Kristeva, Julia. *Pouvoirs de l'horreur.* Paris: Seuil, 1980. Translated by Leon Roudiez as *Powers of Horror* (New York: Columbia University Press, 1982).

Lambert, Fernando. "Bernard Dadié: L'écriture et le voyage." *L'Afrique littéraire et artistique* 85 (1989): 35–41.

Larrier, René. *Francophone Women Writers of Africa and the Caribbean.* Gainesville: University Press of Florida, 2000.

Lazarus, Neil. "Disavowing Decolonization: Fanon, Nationalism, and the Problematic of Representation in Current Theories of Colonial Discourse." *Research in African Literatures* 24, no. 2 (1993): 69–98.

———. *Nationalism and Cultural Practice in the Postcolonial World.* Cambridge: Cambridge University Press, 1999.

———. *Resistance in Postcolonial African Fiction.* New Haven: Yale University Press, 1990.

Lee, Sonia. *Camara Laye.* Boston: Twayne Publishers, 1984.

Liking, Werewere. *Elle sera de jaspe et de corail (journal d'une misovire).* Paris: L'Harmattan, 1983. Translated by Marjolijn de Jager as *It Shall Be of Jasper and Coral;*

and, *Love-across-a-Hundred-Lives: Two Novels,* with an introduction by Irène Assiba d'Almeida (Charlottesville: University Press of Virginia, 2000).

Lionnet, Françoise. *Postcolonial Representations: Women, Literature, Identity.* Ithaca, N.Y.: Cornell University Press, 1995.

Loba, Aké. *Koucoumba, l'étudiant noir.* Paris: Flammarion, 1960.

Lopès, Henri. *Le pleurer-rire.* Paris and Dakar: Présence Africaine, 1982. Translated by Gerald Moore as *The Laughing Cry: An African Cock and Bull Story* (London: Reader's International, 1987).

————. *Tribaliqes.* 1971. Paris: Presses Pocket, 1995.

Martin-Granel, Nicolas. "*Le quatrième côté du triangle,* or Squaring the Sex: A Genetic Approach to the 'Black Continent' in Sony Labou Tansi's Fiction." *Research in African Literatures* 31 (Fall 2000): 69–99.

————. "Sony in Progress." In Kadima-Nzvji et al., eds., *Sony Labou Tansi ou la quête permanente du sens,* 219–20.

Masolo, D. A. *African Philosophy in Search of Identity.* Bloomington: Indiana University Press, 1994.

Mbiti, John. *African Religions and Philosophy.* London: Heinemann, 1969.

McClintock, Anne. *Imperial Leather: Race, Gender and Sexuality in a Colonial Context.* New York: Routledge, 1995.

Miabeto, Auguste. "Sony Labou Tansi et la poésie koongo." In Kadima-Nzvji et al., eds., *Sony Labou Tansi ou la quête permanente du sens,* 135–49.

Miller, Christopher L. *Blank Darkness: Africanist Discourse in French.* Chicago: University of Chicago Press, 1985.

————. *Nationalists and Nomads: Essays on Francophone African Literature and Culture.* Chicago: University of Chicago Press, 1998.

————. *Theories of Africans: Francophone Literature and Anthropology in Africa.* Chicago: University of Chicago Press, 1990.

Mohanty, Chandra. "Under Western Eyes: Feminist Scholarship and Colonial Discourses." In Mongia, ed., *Contemporary Postcolonial Theory,* 172–97.

Monénembo, Tierno. *Cinéma.* Paris: Editions du Seuil, 1997.

Mongia, Padmini, ed. *Contemporary Postcolonial Theory: A Reader.* London: Arnold, 1996.

Moura, Jean-Marc. *Littératures francophones et théorie postcoloniale.* Paris: PUF, 1999.

Mouralis, Bernard, ed. *Autobiographies et récits de vie en Afrique.* Paris: L'Harmattan, 1991.

————. *V. Y. Mudimbe: Le discours, l'écart et l'écriture.* Paris: Présence Africaine, 1988.

————. "V. Y. Mudimbe et l'odeur du pouvoir." *Politique africaine* 13 (Mar. 1984): 21–32.

Mudimbe, V. Y. *L'autre face du royaume: Une introduction à la critique des langages en folie.* Lausanne: L'Age d'Homme, 1973.

————. *Le bel immonde.* Paris: Présence Africaine, 1976. Translated by Marjolijn de Jager as *Before the Birth of the Moon* (New York: Simon and Schuster, 1989).

————. *Carnets d'Amérique.* Paris: Editions Saint-Germain-des Prés, 1976.

————. *Le corps glorieux des mots et des êtres: Esquisse d'un jardin à la bénédictine.* Montreal: Humanitas; Paris: Présence Africaine, 1994.

————. *Déchirures, poèmes.* Kinshasa: Editions du Mont Noir, 1971.

————. *L'écart.* Paris: Présence Africaine, 1979. Translated by Marjolijn de Jager as *The Rift* (Minneapolis: University of Minnesota Press, 1993).

————. *Entre les eaux.* Paris: Présence Africaine, 1973.

————. *Entretailles.* Paris: Editions Saint-Germain-des-Prés, 1973.

————. "I as an other: Sartre and Lévi-Strauss or an (Im)possible Dialogue on the Cogito." *American Journal of Semiotics* 6, no. 1 (1988–89): 57–68.

————. *The Idea of Africa.* Bloomington: Indiana University Press, 1994.

————. *The Invention of Africa: Gnosis, Philosophy and the Order of Knowledge.* Bloomington: Indiana University Press, 1989.

————, ed. "Nations, Identities, Cultures." Special issue, *South Atlantic Quarterly* 94 (Fall 1995).

————. *L'odeur du père: Essai sur les limites de la science et de la vie en Afrique noire.* Paris: Présence Africaine, 1982.

————. *Parables and Fables: Exegesis, Textuality, and Politics in Central Africa.* Madison: University of Wisconsin Press, 1991.

————. *Réflexions sur la vie quotidienne.* Kinshasa: Editions du Mont Noir, 1972.

————. "Reprendre." In Vogel and Ebong, eds., *Africa Explores,* 276–87.

————. *Shaba deux: Les carnets de Mère Marie-Gertrude.* Paris: Présence Africaine, 1989.

————, ed. *The Surreptitious Speech: Présence Africaine and the Politics of Otherness, 1947–1987.* Chicago: University of Chicago Press, 1992.

————. *Tales of Faith.* London: Athlone Press, 1997.

Mudimbe, V. Y., and B. Jewsiewicki, eds. *History Making in Africa.* Middletown, Conn.: Wesleyan University Press, 1993.

Mudimbe-Boyi, Elisabeth. "Travel, Representation and Difference: Or, How Can One Be a Parisian?" *Research in African Literatures* 23 (Fall 1992): 25–39.

Mulago, Vincent. *Un visage africain de christianisme.* Paris: Présence Africaine, 1965.

Mulvey, Laura. "Visual Pleasure and Narrative Cinema." In *Narrative, Apparatus, Ideology: A Film Theory Reader,* ed. Philip Rosen. New York: Columbia University Press, 1986.

Murphy, David. "Alternative Media/Alternative Genres in Sembene's Novel and Film *Xala.*" *ASCALF Yearbook 4,* 2000, 89–99.

————. *Sembene: Imagining Alternatives in Film and Fiction.* Oxford: James Currey, 2000.

N'da, Pierre. "*Un Nègre à Paris* et l'art romanesque chez Bernard Dadié." *Présence francophone* 21 (1980): 79–94.

Nfah-Abbenyi, Juliana Makuchi. *Gender in African Women's Writing: Identity, Sexuality and Difference.* Bloomington: Indiana University Press, 1997.

Ngate, Jonathan. *Francophone African Fiction: Reading a Literary Tradition.* Trenton, N.J.: Africa World Press, 1988.

Niane, Djibril Tamsir. *Soundjata ou l'épopée mandingue*. Paris: Présence Africaine, 1960.

Niang, Sada, ed. *Littérature et cinéma en Afrique francophone: Ousmane Sembene et Assia Djebar*. Paris: L'Harmattan, 1996.

———. "Orality in the Films of Ousmane Sembene." In Petty, ed., *A Call to Action*, 56–66.

Obenga, Théophile. *Pour une nouvelle histoire*. Paris: Présence Africaine, 1980.

Olney, James. *Tell Me Africa: An Approach to African Literature*. Princeton, N.J.: Princeton University Press, 1973.

Ongoum, Louis-Marie. "Satire et humanisme de Bernard Dadié dans *Un Nègre à Paris*." *Etudes littéraires* 7 (1974): 405–19.

Oyono, Ferdinand. *Une vie de boy*. Paris: René Julliard, 1956. Translated by John Reed as *Houseboy* (London: Heinemann, 1966).

Parry, Benita. "Resistance Theory/Theorising Resistance or Two Cheers for Nativism." In Mongia, ed., *Contemporary Postcolonial Theory*, 85–109.

Petty, Sheila, ed. *A Call to Action: The Films of Ousmane Sembene*. Trowbridge: Flick Books, 1996.

Pfaff, Françoise. "The Uniqueness of Ousmane Sembene's Cinema." In Gadjigo et al., eds., *Ousmane Sembène*, 14–21.

Pratt, Mary Louise. *Imperial Eyes: Travel Writing and Transculturation*. London: Routledge, 1992.

Research in African Literatures 28 (Summer 1997).

Rice-Maximin, Micheline. "'Nouvelle écriture' from the Ivory Coast: A Reading of Véronique Tadjo's *A vol d'oiseau*." In Green et al., eds., *Postcolonial Subjects*, 157–72.

Riesz, Janos. "'Audible Gasps from the Audience': Accusations of Plagiarism against Several African Authors and Their Historical Context." *Yearbook of Comparative and General Literature* 43 (1995): 84–97.

Riesz, Janos, and Ulla Schild, eds. *Genres autobiographiques en Afrique*. Berlin: Dietrich Reimer, 1996.

Rigby, Peter. *Persistent Pastoralists: Nomadic Societies in Transition*. London: Zed Books, 1985.

Rosen, Philip. "Nation, Inter-nation and Narration in Ousmane Sembene's Films." In Petty, ed., *A Call to Action*, 27–55.

Sartre, Jean-Paul. "Orphée noir." Preface to *Anthologie de la nouvelle poésie nègre et malgache de langue française*. 1949. Paris: PUF, 1969.

Sembene, Ousmane. *Le docker noir*. Paris: Nouvelles Editions Debresse, 1956.

———. *Guelwaar*. Filmi Doomireew/Galatée Films, 1992.

———. *Guelwaar*. Paris: Présence Africaine, 1994.

Semujanga, Josias. "De l'absurde comme style de vie et procès esthétique: *Shaba deux* de V. Y. Mudimbe." *Etudes francophones* 11 (Spring 1996): 5–20.

Serequeberhan, Tsenay. *The Hermeneutics of African Philosophy*. New York: Routledge, 1994.

Sherzer, Dina, ed. *Cinema, Colonialism, Postcolonialism: Perspectives from the French and Francophone Worlds.* Austin: University of Texas Press, 1996.

Shetty, Sandhya, and Elizabeth Jane Bellamy. "Postcolonialism's Archive Fever." *Diacritics* 30 (Spring 2000): 25–48.

Siamundele, André Nzunguta. "De *l'écart* à la *palilalie,* ou le croisement de deux regards: V. Y. Mudimbe et Sony Labou Tansi." Ph.D. dissertation, Yale University, 1999.

Smith, Sidonie. *Subjectivity, Identity and the Body: Women's Autobiographical Practices in the Twentieth Century.* Bloomington: Indiana University Press, 1993.

Sony Labou Tansi. *L'anté-peuple.* Paris: Editions du Seuil, 1983.

———. *L'autre monde: Ecrits inédits.* Edited by Nicolas Martin-Granel. Paris: Editions Revue Noire, 1997.

———. *Le commencement des douleurs.* Paris: Editions du Seuil, 1995.

———. *L'état honteux.* Paris: Editions du Seuil, 1981.

———. *Moi, veuve de l'empire.* In *L'avant-scène théâtre,* no. 815 (October 1987).

———. *La vie et demie.* Paris: Seuil Points, 1979.

Sow, Ibrahim. *Psychiatrie dynamique africaine.* Paris: Payot, 1977.

———. *Les structures anthropologiques de la folie en Afrique Noire.* Paris: Payot, 1978.

Spivak, Gayatri Chakravorty. "Can the Subaltern Speak?" In *Marxism and the Interpretation of Culture,* ed. C. Nelson and L. Grossberg, 277–313. London: Macmillan, 1988.

———. *A Critique of Postcolonial Reason: Towards a History of the Vanishing Present.* Cambridge, Mass.: Harvard University Press, 1999.

———. *The Post-colonial Critic: Interviews, Strategies and Dialogues.* Edited by Sarah Harasym. New York: Routledge, 1990.

Sprinker, Michael, ed. *Ghostly Demarcations: A Symposium on Jacques Derrida's "Specters of Marx."* London: Verso, 1999.

Spurr, David. *The Rhetoric of Empire: Colonial Discourse in Journalism, Travel Writing and Imperial Administration.* Durham, N.C.: Duke University Press, 1993.

Stratton, Florence. *Contemporary African Literature and the Politics of Gender.* New York: Routledge, 1994.

Suleri, Sara. "Woman Skin Deep: Feminism and the Postcolonial Condition." In Mongia, ed., *Contemporary Postcolonial Theory.* First published in *Critical Inquiry* 18 (Summer 1992): 756–69.

Tadjo, Véronique. *A vol d'oiseau.* Paris: L'Harmattan, 1992. Translated by Wangui Wa Goro as *As the Crow Flies* (Oxford: Heinemann, 2001).

———. *Champs de bataille et d'amour.* Abidjan: Nouvelles Editions Ivoiriennes; Paris: Présence Africaine, 1999.

Tchak, Sami, and Boniface Mongo-Mboussa, eds. "Dossier masculin-féminin." *Africultures,* no. 35 (Feb. 2001): 5–64.

Têko-Agbo, Ambroise. "Werewere Liking and Calixthe Beyala: Le discours féministe et la fiction." *Cahiers d'études africaines* 37, part 1 (1997): 39–58.

Tempels, Placide. *Bantu Philosophy.* Translated by the Rev. Colin King. Paris: Présence Africaine, 1959. Originally published as *La philosophie bantoue* (Paris: Présence Africaine, 1945).

Todorov, Tzvetan. *Nous et les autres: La réflexion française sur la diversité humaine.* Paris: Seuil Points, 1992.

Towa, Marcien. *Essai sur la problématique philosophique dans l'Afrique actuelle.* Yaoundé: Clé, 1971.

——. *L'idée d'une philosophie africaine.* Yaoundé: Clé, 1979.

Turrittin, Jane. "Aoua Kéita and the Nascent Women's Movement in the French Soudan." *African Studies Review* 36 (Apr. 1993): 59–89.

Ukadike, Nwachukwu Frank. *Black African Cinema.* Berkeley: University of California Press, 1994.

Vinceleoni, Nicole. *Comprendre l'oeuvre de Bernard Dadié.* Issy-les-Moulineaux: Les Classiques Africains, 1986.

Vogel, Susan, and Ima Ebong, eds. *Africa Explores: 20th Century African Art.* New York: The Center for African Art, 1991.

Watson, Julia. "Unruly Bodies: Autoethnography and Authorization in Nafissatou Diallo's *De Tilène au Plateau.*" *Research in African Literatures* 28 (Summer 1997): 34–56.

Wiredu, Kwasi. *Cultural Universals and Particulars: An African Perspective.* Bloomington: Indiana University Press, 1996.

Wright, Katherine. "Werewere Liking: From Chaos to Cosmos." *World Literature Today: A Literary Quarterly of the University of Oklahoma* 69 (Winter 1995): 56–62.

Yewah, Emmanuel. "The Nation as a Contested Construct." *Research in African Literatures* 32 (Summer 2000): 45–56.

Young, Robert. "Deconstruction and the Postcolonial." In *Deconstructions: A User's Guide,* ed. Nicholas Royle. Basingstoke: Palgrave, 2000.

——. *Postcolonialism: An Historical Introduction.* Oxford: Blackwell, 2001.

——, ed. *Untying the Text: A Post-structuralist Reader.* Boston: Routledge, 1981.

Index